W9-AMT-074

KITH AND KIN

Canada, Britain and the United States from the Revolution to the Cold War

KITH AND KIN

Canada, Britain and the United States
from the Revolution to the Cold War

Edited by

C. C. ELDRIDGE

UNIVERSITY OF WALES PRESS • CARDIFF • 1997

British Library Cataloguing in Publication Data

A catalogue record for this book is available from the British Library.

ISBN 0–7083–1360–4

Typeset by the Midlands Book Typesetting Company
Printed in Wales by Dinefwr Press, Llandybïe

Contents

The Editor and Contributors

Colin Eldridge is Reader in History at the University of Wales, Lampeter, and past Chairman of the History Group, British Association of Canadian Studies.

Gill Bennett is Head of Historians, The Library and Records Department at the Foreign and Commonwealth Office.

Phillip Buckner is Professor in the Department of History at the University of New Brunswick, and past President of the Canadian Historical Association.

Muriel Chamberlain is Professor in the Department of History at University of Wales, Swansea, and President of the University of Wales Canadian Studies Group.

Peter Marshall is Professor Emeritus in the Department of American Studies, University of Manchester.

Ged Martin is Professor in Canadian Studies and Director of the Centre of Canadian Studies at the University of Edinburgh, past President of the British Association of Canadian Studies and present Chairman of the History Group.

Ritchie Ovendale was formerly Professor in the Department of International Politics at the University of Wales, Aberystwyth.

Keith Robbins is Vice-Chancellor of the University of Wales, Lampeter, and past President of the Historical Association.

Tim Rooth is a Principal Lecturer in the Department of Economics, University of Portsmouth.

James Sturgis is a Lecturer in the Department of History, Birkbeck College, London, Co-Director of the Centre for Canadian Studies, University of London, and past President of the British Association of Canadian Studies.

Martin Thornton is a Lecturer in International History in the Department of History, and Deputy Director of the Centre of Canadian Studies, University of Leeds.

Harold Wright was formerly Senior Lecturer in Economics at McGill University.

Foreword

The chapters in this volume, including others not published here, began life as papers delivered at two conferences at the University of Wales Lampeter, sponsored jointly by the Canadian Studies in Wales Group and the History Group of the British Association of Canadian Studies, with the assistance of the Academic Relations Department of the Canadian High Commission. The object was to take a fresh look at aspects of the history of Anglo-American-Canadian relations since the late eighteenth century and to assess the condition of the relationship today. To this end, representatives from the British Foreign and Commonwealth Office, the United States Embassy and the Canadian High Commission were present, and the survey of contemporary relations given by the Foreign and Commonwealth Office representative, Mrs Gill Bennett, is printed at the end of the editor's introduction.

Since these papers were delivered, interest in the history of the 'North Atlantic Triangle', the term used by J. B. Brebner in a celebrated book published in 1945, has increased considerably. The most recent addition to the literature has been B. J. C. McKercher and L. Aronsen (eds.), *The North Atlantic Triangle in a Changing World: Anglo-American-Canadian Relations, 1902–1956* (Toronto, 1996). While there is some chronological overlap with the present volume, the contents are of an entirely complementary character and the conclusions proffered this side of the Atlantic do not differ markedly from those offered in the Canadian collection of papers. It is to be hoped that American historians will now see fit to respond with a series of essays giving an American perspective on the tripartite relationship.

In overseeing the publication of the present volume, the editor has incurred a number of debts: to the University of Wales Press for agreeing to endorse the publication after protracted negotiations with the University; to the contributors for their forbearance and patience; to the University of Wales Canadian Studies Group for a generous grant towards the costs of publication; and for the much appreciated and continuing support from Michael Hellyer and Vivien Hughes in the Academic Relations Department of the Canadian High Commission. Without their help, the financial support of the Canadian government, and the way successive Canadian High Commissioners have placed academic initiatives at the top of their agenda, this volume would not have seen the light of day. That Canadian Studies continue to flourish in a climate of financial cutbacks and contraction is a tribute to the foresight and generosity of all those who seek to foster the study of our transatlantic partners, not only in the creation of Canadian Studies centres, but in the transformation of American Studies in British universities into *North* American Studies.

Finally, the editor would like to thank Ceinwen Jones, Susan Jenkins, and the director, Ned Thomas, at the University of Wales Press, for their efficient and prompt handling of the manuscript, once the decision was taken to go ahead, to ensure that publication coincided with the annual conference of the British Association of Canadian Studies held at the University of Wales Swansea, 24–7 March 1997.

C. C. Eldridge

Introduction: The North Atlantic Triangle Revisited

C. C. ELDRIDGE

In 1927 William Lyon Mackenzie King confided to a friend: 'As Canadians we can only seek to do all that lies in our power to fulfil our role as friendly interpreters of Britishers and Americans alike in a manner which may substitute good-will for ill-will.' The Canadian prime minister was certainly well aware that the existing and future well-being of his country was inextricably linked, economically, strategically and culturally, with its increasingly isolationist (but undeniably powerful) neighbour to the south, and the fading (but still only truly global) power across the Atlantic with which Canada had such close familial ties. While all three countries shared the same language, the same liberal political beliefs and the same capitalist economic philosophy, they did not share the same world-view. Besides having different external interests, they frequently followed separate economic and financial objectives. This was certainly true of the late 1920s when Mackenzie King recognized that the continuing good will and co-operation of Great Britain and the United States of America were the surest guarantees for continuing Canadian peace and prosperity.

It comes as no surprise, then, that the concept of a 'North Atlantic Triangle' is largely Canadian in origin. While Theodore Roosevelt occasionally spoke of an 'English-speaking accord', and Winston Churchill frequently referred to a wider group of 'English-speaking peoples', most British and American commentators have usually chosen to concentrate on the so-called 'special relationship' between Britain and the USA, seeing the *ménage à trois* simply as an extension of the Anglo-American axis through entirely separate bilateral relationships between the USA and Canada, Canada and Britain. For, despite the shared history and ties of kinship and culture, the dissimilarities between this triplice of English-speaking nations have been as important as the similarities. Consequently, the three countries have not always worked harmoniously together. Indeed, at various times they have been deeply suspicious of, and occasionally mutually antagonistic towards, each other. Canada's position in this relationship, until quite recent times as the most junior partner, was particularly difficult. According to one Canadian historian: 'In endeavouring to be the linchpin between the two great powers, the dominion tended to find itself squeezed as though in a vice, ineluctably bending towards the stronger jaw.' The position was a delicate one as Canada first sought to create a national identity, to establish its credentials as an independent country, and then to find a distinctive role as a 'middle power' in world affairs.

It is probably no coincidence that the most celebrated account of the triangular relationship, J. B. Brebner's *North Atlantic Triangle: The Interplay of Canada, the United States and Great Britain*, was published in Toronto in 1945 after a period of intense, and successful, wartime collaboration. Franklin D. Roosevelt, Winston Churchill and Mackenzie King developed a mutual understanding and respect for each other, even if their personal relations were never close. The three powers continued to co-operate in the late 1940s in the founding of the United Nations and the establishment of the North Atlantic Treaty Organization. It was one of the high points in Anglo-American-Canadian harmony in external relations and communality of purpose. After this their national interests began to diverge. Canada's gradually closer association with the newly emerging American superpower was more a product of circumstance and military and economic necessity than of a shared attitude towards the problems confronting the world.

The fragile nature of the relationship, and the new American dominance within it, was clearly revealed during the Suez crisis in 1956 when the USA publicly opposed Great Britain in the international arena. To British discomfort, it was the Canadian minister of External Affairs, Lester B. Pearson, who instigated the proceedings that secured the authorization of a United Nations peacekeeping force, with a Canadian commander and a large contingent of Canadian troops, before the British and French troops had even landed in Egypt (Pearson later received the Nobel Peace Prize for his endeavours). The British prime minister, Sir Anthony Eden, was even more furious at what he saw as the American betrayal:

the implementation of an embargo on oil exports from the Gulf of Mexico and the withholding of loans from the International Monetary Fund and the American Export–Import Bank. His successor, Harold Macmillan, later ruefully mused, 'We are the Greeks of the Hellenistic age: the power has passed from us to Rome's equivalent, the United States of America, and we can at most aspire to civilise and occasionally to influence them.' For their part, the Canadians, as they became increasingly tied economically and politically to the American continent (a process culminating in the signing of the North American Free Trade Agreement with the USA and Mexico in 1993), sought to retain some independence by establishing for themselves a role in the world as a middle power working through the United Nations Security Council and its peacekeeping forces – as an 'honest broker' in international disputes. Little wonder, then, that as the Anglo-American 'special relationship' has increasingly been dubbed a myth, as Canada has turned away from Britain, and Britain has somewhat hesitantly turned to Europe, there have been few attempts, and little encouragement, to follow in the footsteps of Brebner's path-breaking study.

However, there are signs of change. It is, of course, easy to cite occasions when Britain and Canada have differed since the late 1940s – especially during the Suez crisis in 1956, over the expulsion of South Africa from the Commonwealth in 1961, and in numerous Commonwealth matters since – and also appeared to be going their separate ways as Canada completed the nation-building process: the replacement of the Judicial Committee of the British Privy Council by the Supreme Court of Canada as the final court of appeal in 1949, the departure of the last British governor-general in 1952, the substitution of the red and white Maple Leaf flag for the Red Ensign and Union Jack as the flag of Canada in 1965, the replacement of 'God Save the Queen' by 'O Canada' as the national anthem in 1967, and the final patriation of the Canadian constitution in 1982. Also, as early as 1957, Canada's trading patterns had made it quite clear that Canada was a North American country whose trade and financial connections would henceforth be with the USA.

But, alternatively, the emotional bonds – the ties of kith and kin – between Canada and Britain, which continued to bind them together, need to be stressed. After 1815 the British North American colonies had largely been settled by immigrants of British and Irish stock and their institutions, political, legal and social, had been modelled on those of Great Britain. Unlike the Thirteen Colonies to the south, the Canadians had achieved nationhood through a process of peaceful constitutional evolution, without a revolution or the shedding of blood. Great Britain had acted as the guarantor of Canadian security throughout the nineteenth, and into the twentieth, century, despite constant fears that Canadian interests would be sold out to the cause of harmonious Anglo-American relations. Canada had sent volunteers to serve in the South African War of 1899–1902 and entered both the First and Second World Wars as a much needed ally (a decision freely taken as an independent country in 1939), while the Americans had initially remained aloof on both occasions. The British people remembered the Canadian contribution to both wars, materially and financially, as well as the sacrifice in men. The Canadian people in response expressed a genuine affection and admiration for their British allies.

While time has no doubt diminished the sense of common purpose, and memories are fading, it should not be forgotten that nearly one million Britons emigrated to Canada in the twenty-five years following the end of the Second World War, a process that has continued on a lesser level to this day. Canadian and British governments continue to co-operate closely in the UN, NATO, GATT (General Agreement on Tariffs and Trade) and the G-7 Finance Ministers' meetings, while they agree to differ over certain Commonwealth matters and the Falklands War. They operate exchange training programmes between their armed forces and they co-operate closely in less prominent fields such as arms control, human rights, drug trafficking, AIDS and international terrorism. Britain remains Canada's second largest overseas investor and her third largest export market. Remarkably, the two countries continue to share the same head of state. But perhaps one of the most unsung areas of continuing co-operation is in cultural, educational and youth exchanges. The creation of the British Association of Canadian Studies numbering several hundred academics among its membership, the establishment of Canadian Studies centres, the expansion of American Studies programmes to include Canada at various British universities and the inclusion of Canadian literature in the syllabuses of several English departments, along with the increasing flow of students and publications on Anglo-Canadian relations, are sure signs of the enduring vitality of the connection.

The same vitality can be detected in recent studies of the USA and

Canada, no doubt a product of the increasing intimacy, economically, strategically and diplomatically, between the two countries, especially during the era of the Cold War. American historians, who for long showed little interest in their country cousins across the border, have now repeatedly turned their eyes northwards in studies of past American–Canadian rivalries, antagonisms and friendly collaboration. Closer co-operation, however, has not always led both countries to see eye to eye. Canadian reservations about Harry S. Truman's conduct of the Korean War were repeated in the 1960s and 1970s, with John F. Kennedy's fury at the refusal of the Canadian prime minister (John Diefenbaker) to put Canadian troops on alert during the Cuban missiles crisis, Lyndon Johnson's attack in 1965 on the criticism by Prime Minister Lester Pearson of American policy in Vietnam, and Richard Nixon's opposition in 1970 to Pierre Trudeau's recognition of communist China (although, on this occasion, where the Canadians led the Americans soon followed). A similarly independent line was taken in the same year when the Canadians, conscious that the circumpolar north was the route missiles would follow, and aware of the dangerous games American and Soviet submarines were playing beneath the polar ice, declared a 100-mile Arctic pollution zone and a 200-mile economic zone in these hotly disputed waters and frozen wastes. Once again, where narrow national interests were at stake, there was no more room for altruism in Canadian–American relations than there had been in the North Atlantic Triangle relationship. Just as in the nineteenth and early twentieth centuries, when Canada made great efforts to assert its independence of action and control its own destiny in relations with its dominant partner Great Britain, so in the late twentieth century Canada has shown an equal determination not to become simply the tail on the American dog.

Study of the third side of the triangle, the Anglo-American relationship, has long been a popular pastime of historians. It has all the best dramatic incidents: the decline and fall of one world power and the emergence of a new super power; the replacement of a 'weary titan', virtually bankrupt with its empire disintegrating, by a young and vigorous industrial giant armed with nuclear weapons, an event that influenced the direction of twentieth-century international history. It was but another dramatic twist in the story of antagonism, rivalry and partnership that had characterized the interaction of the two leading Anglo-Saxon nations since the Americans had fought for their independence in the late eighteenth century.

Canada could not lay claim to so glorious a past. There was no revolution, not even an Independence Day to celebrate, and the slightest shift in Anglo-American relations was sufficient to send shock waves through the Canadian political scene. Canada's development and destiny not only depended to an unprecedented degree on her relations with the United States of America and Great Britain, but on the relationship between those powers. This external factor has been used to explain not only spasmodic American antagonism towards Canada in the nineteenth century, but the transformation of Canada in the twentieth century, in little more than a generation, from leading dominion in the British Empire and Commonwealth into an apparent satellite of the USA (see, for example, J. L. Granastein, *How Britain's Weakness Forced Canada into the Arms of the United States*, Toronto, 1989). Such studies have placed the North Atlantic Triangle at the centre of historical investigation once again. As Canada's role in the United Nations as an international peacekeeper is studied (Canadian troops have served in Europe, Africa, Asia, Latin America, the Middle East and the Pacific – in Afghanistan, Bosnia, Cambodia, Croatia, Cyprus, Egypt, Germany, India, Iraq, Kashmir, Korea, Kuwait, Laos, New Guinea, Pakistan, Palestine, Rwanda, Serbia, Somalia and Vietnam to name but a few countries), and the history of Canada's external relations is written, Brebner's ideas and concepts have come under discussion once again. The outcome has been such studies as L. Aronsen and M. Kitchen, *The Origins of the Cold War in Comparative Perspective: American, British and Canadian Relations with the Soviet Union, 1941–1948* (London, 1988); Ian Drummond and Norman Hillmer, *Negotiating Freer Trade: The United Kingdom, the United States, Canada and the Trade Agreements of 1938* (Waterloo, Ont., 1989); and, most pertinently of all, B. J. C. McKercher and L. Aronsen (eds.), *The North Atlantic Triangle in a Changing World: Anglo-American-Canadian Relations, 1902–1956* (Toronto, 1996).

The present volume begins in 1763 with a survey by Peter Marshall of the events surrounding the run-up to the American Revolution, the departure of the Loyalists, and subsequent developments in British North America up to the War of 1812–14. He examines, in particular, the political structure of the new colonies and concludes that by 1815 the population, whether of British or French ancestry, was as fully American in outlook and origin as the citizens of the USA. The repeated emphasis on the conservative origins of societies, however, ensured a continuing distinctiveness so that future American and Canadian political history had little in common.

After examining the composition and the distribution of the population in 1815, Phillip Buckner, in 'Making British North America British, 1815–1860', traces the massive influx of British emigrants during these years that transformed not only the land but the economy and culture of British North America, making it truly British. (But British after their own fashion as the newcomers had no wish to re-create the political and social structure they had left behind.) As time passed these immigrants and their descendants began to think of themselves as British North Americans with English, Irish, Scottish or Welsh ancestors, a distinctive North American community distinguished by its British-ness.

One of the factors that most reinforced the necessity of the British connection was the continuing fear of American aggression. Fear of American invasion lingered on after 1814 and was revived by the border troubles of 1838–9 following the abortive Canadian rebellions of 1837. From the 1840s to the 1870s, especially after the American Civil War and the Fenian raids, Canadians remained nervous about the intentions of their southern neighbour. In the third chapter, Muriel Chamberlain recounts one filibustering incident on the north-east boundary between Maine and New Brunswick in 1839 that caused embarrassment to both the British and the American governments. The exact position of the boundary was unclear since the written description in the Treaty of Paris (1783), though detailed, did not correspond to geographical realities. In an attempt to settle outstanding issues, the new Peel administration sent Lord Ashburton to Washington and, after the 'ludicrous affair of the maps', the Ashburton–Webster Treaty was concluded in 1842. While most of Canada's interests were preserved, the New Brunswickers, who had been invited to Washington, were merely consulted informally by Ashburton and had no influence over the outcome of the negotiations. This only increased the Canadian suspicion, which surfaced regularly throughout the nineteenth century and came to especial prominence in 1903 at the time of the Alaska boundary dispute, that Canadian interests would be sacrificed by Britain in order to ensure continuing good relations with the USA. Suspicion of the British and fear of American expansionism were two of the factors that led an increasing number of colonial politicians to embrace the idea of a union of the British North American colonies.

That many of the politically aware in Great Britain came to support the idea of union was also largely due to the American presence. It was not so much interest in, or concern for, the inhabitants of British North America that led them to this conclusion, or even current fears about American intentions; it was the doubts about the future role of this growing giant that brought Canada into the equation as a valuable counterweight to American dominance of the North American continent. Ged Martin's survey of English newspapers, principally *The Times*, during the years 1841–61, reveals a distinct lack of knowledge about, and interest in, the realities of colonial life, a frequently superior and mocking tone, a great deal of misinformation, and a strong prejudice against the Americans. Yet while the British North Americans might not for long be governed by the British, it was 'highly to the interests of this country to cultivate their friendship and good-will'.

Indeed, the years following the creation of the Dominion of Canada were a particularly difficult period in Anglo-American relations, with the victorious North seething at the partisan attitude shown by some British politicians and ministers during the recent Civil War. They were particularly intent on gaining compensation for the damage wrought by the *Alabama*, a British-built Confederate warship, allowed by the British to leave port, which subsequently sank sixty-eight Union merchant ships before being destroyed in 1864 off the coast of France. The acquisition of Canada, some suggested, might be suitable compensation. Nothing so drastic happened. Even so, with the *Alabama* Award and the Treaty of Washington in 1871, which permitted American entry to the inshore fisheries of the Maritimes and the Gulf of the St Lawrence without reviving the 1854 Reciprocity Treaty agreement for reciprocal trade, the Canadians once again felt their interests had been sacrificed to the British desire for harmonious relations with the USA.

In fact, latent anti-Americanism and the acknowledged need for a British protective shield against American expansionism provided the background for the emergence of 'a territorial Canadian nationalism', imperial in sentiment, by the late 1890s. James Sturgis, in 'Learning about Oneself: The Making of Canadian Nationalism, 1867–1914', traces the development of this English Canadian nationalism. The inculcation of national sentiments through various agencies of socialization in the closing decades of the nineteenth century produced a duality of outlook in which there was no apparent contradiction in regarding oneself as being both British and a Canadian nationalist.

As usual, however, while critical of the instability and corruptness of the American political system, the Canadians were prepared to adopt and adapt those American ideas and practices that suited their purposes. The Americans were particularly good at inculcating a sense of identity in their citizens – the flamboyant celebration of national holidays being one obvious example. It is no coincidence that 'Empire Day' (24 May, Queen Victoria's birthday) was celebrated first in Canada, several years ahead of its adoption in Britain. The high-water mark of imperial loyalty, the late 1890s, also coincided with a new British search for a *rapprochement* with the USA. The growth of imperial sentiment obliged Sir Wilfrid Laurier to allow Canadian volunteers to fight in South Africa during the Anglo-Boer War and, when Britain declared war on Germany in 1914, and the Empire was at war, the Canadians fulfilled the role expected of them.

Canada's contribution to the Allied war effort, especially the role of the Canadians in holding the Ypres salient, in the battle of the Somme, at Vimy Ridge and Passchendaele – a war in which Canada suffered a quarter of a million casualties and some 60,000 dead – has been well documented. By the end of the First World War, Canada had clearly come of age, as its signature to the Treaty of Versailles, in its own right, and its role as a founder member of the League of Nations attested. Mackenzie King's subsequent drive for Canadian autonomy within the framework of the British Commonwealth of Nations has also been well told in considerable detail. In this volume, attention has been focused on less well covered aspects: Harold Wright concentrates on the role of Thomas White, the Canadian minister of finance, who had a major responsibility for Canada's contribution to the Allied war economy; and Keith Robbins, in 'Partners and Rivals: Britain, Canada and the United States and the Impact of the First World War', places the position of Canada in the wider setting of the North Atlantic Triangle. He concludes, however, that in 1919 the 'ultimate direction in which the Triangle would tilt was obscure'.

Besides the concentration on Canada's constitutional evolution, economic developments in the 1920s, especially the tensions created by the onset of depression, have received most attention. The impact of these events has been ably summed up by Gregory Johnson and David Lenarcic in 'The Decade of Transition: The North Atlantic Triangle in the 1920s' in the McKercher and Aronsen collection of essays cited earlier. Tim Rooth, who has written widely on Anglo-Canadian economic relations in the inter-war period and the role of British protectionism in the international economy, continues our story with a detailed examination of 'The Political Economy of the North Atlantic Triangle in the 1930s' – a further decade of transition, 'with the UK adopting protection and with attitudes in the USA undergoing something of a sea-change'.

The British 'revolution' in commercial policy in the winter of 1931, when protection against a wide range of imported foreign goods was embraced, provided an opportunity for the Canadians to negotiate privileged access to the British market. Tortuous and ill-tempered discussions ensued, pushed on by increasingly heavy American duties on Canadian copper and lumber, which finally resulted in agreement at a conference in Ottawa in July–August 1932. The British, no doubt, hoped that the introduction of imperial preferences would offset the loss of political influence enshrined in the Statute of Westminster, 1931. They forgot, however, that Canada was locked into a North American economy and no real recovery could occur until American markets had been reopened. They also reckoned without American determination to undermine the economic empire. This determination, fuelled by domestic considerations, led first to an agreement in November 1935 concerning reciprocal trade arrangements with the Canadian government, and then to tripartite discussions with the UK that, after several acrimonious exchanges, led to a series of commercial treaties between Britain, Canada and the USA in 1938. These arrangements were more concerned with narrow bilateral advantage than the creation of a multilateral economy. That the British agreed to the new economic arrangements at all, overcoming their economic objections and general antipathy towards the Americans, was largely dictated by anxieties about the European situation and the worsening international situation. Neville Chamberlain certainly viewed the agreements as a partial answer to the Berlin–Rome–Tokyo axis.

In 1938 Britain could not afford to forgo the good will of the United States of America. Nor could she neglect Canada and the Dominions. The interweaving of economic policy and international diplomacy in the late 1930s is explained in Ritchie Ovendale's chapter,

'Canada, Britain, the United States and the Policy of "Appeasement"'. Tracing the events from Mussolini's occupation of Abyssinia in 1935, and Hitler's reoccupation of the Rhineland in 1936, Professor Ovendale focuses on the role of the Canadian prime minister, Mackenzie King, and the Canadian high commissioner in London, Vincent Massey, in an attempt to show why, despite the USA's guarantee of Canada's security in September 1938, Canada chose, of her own free will, to declare war on Germany on 10 September 1939. He concludes that, while the British element was still strong and patriotic fervour was not lacking, the Canadian people chose to fight not for a vague concept of collective security but for the values of the Commonwealth.

In the McKercher and Aronsen collection of essays, John English in a chapter entitled 'Not an Equilateral Triangle: Canada's Strategic Relationship with the United States and Britain, 1939–1945' has shown how Mackenzie King's determination to maintain Canadian autonomy in the military and civilian spheres, and his overriding interest in domestic affairs, ensured for Canada only a tactical role during the Second World War. Canada thus became the 'passive receiver of information and direction' and never carried the diplomatic weight in the war-planning councils of the Allies that its military contribution merited. Mackenzie King, therefore, on the one hand, viewed with some dismay the dominant Roosevelt–Churchill relationship and, on the other, failed to see how much the power of the British empire had declined. The admission to the press corps in 1945 by the British ambassador in Washington, 'Boys, Britain is broke', consequently came as a tremendous shock to the Canadian people. It began their gradual reassessment of their position in the North Atlantic Triangle and, as Britain also stood in the shadow of the USA, it initiated the now inevitable closer association of Canada and the USA.

At first, however, while the three English-speaking countries were in general agreement as to what shape the new political world order should take, Canada played little part in the early discussions concerning the creation of the United Nations. Excluded from the Dumbarton Oaks conference in 1944, Canada's contribution to the final drafting of the UN charter at the San Francisco conference was more modest than most Canadian historians like to admit, being limited, in the main, to Articles 23 and 44 concerning the status of 'middle powers'. As always, the continuing co-operation of the USA, Britain and Canada depended on a particular combination of ideology, interests and personalities. As it happened, the combination of Ernest Bevin, the British foreign secretary (1945–51), George C. Marshall, the American secretary of state (1947–9), and Lester B. Pearson, the Canadian under-secretary (1946–8) and then secretary of state (1948–57) for external affairs, ensured a continuing high level of co-operation. This is traced in Martin Thornton's concluding chapter in this volume which focuses on the problem of Palestine and the establishment of the North Atlantic Treaty Organization. The three countries faced the onset of the 'Cold War' both supporting and restraining each other, a combination, in Dr Thornton's words, of 'patience, firmness and prudence'.

The history of relations between Britain, Canada and the USA since 1949 has frequently been placed under the microscope. Undoubtedly, by that date relations among the three countries had become less intimate than they had been during the Second World War. Nevertheless, despite all the subsequent disagreements concerning policy and actions, the three countries have remained closely associated and continue to confer, and attempt to remain in step, even when following different objectives. Disagreements, especially between Britain and the USA (a fairly recent example being the unexpected American intervention in the island of Grenada), are always patched over as each country recognizes the value of continuing association, whether it be in the supply of American intelligence during the Falklands War or the making available of British airbases for the American attack on Colonel Khaddhafi of Libya.

In fact, from the American Revolution (which began with the rejection by the Thirteen Colonies of the British connection along with British traditions and many British values) and the mutual antagonisms of the nineteenth and early-twentieth centuries, has emerged an informal entente of the three Atlantic countries, which reached a high point in formal alliance during the Second World War that has since dissolved into a less spectacular steady partnership. Whatever the language of domestic politics and international relations, the commonality of purpose of the three countries has survived the trials and tribulations of the twentieth century. While the countries of the North Atlantic Triangle do not always agree, the shared history and culture, the former ties of kith and kin, still count for much in the behind-the-scenes diplomacy of the 1990s, as the following personal comment made to our 1993 conference by a member of the British Foreign and Commonwealth Office indicates.

Introduction: The United Kingdom, Canada and the United States in the Early 1990s [1]

GILL BENNETT

Looking across the Atlantic in the 1990s, the triangular relationship between the UK and our traditional friends and allies, the USA and Canada, looks in many ways to have weathered a turbulent decade and a half remarkably well. Our relations, on a bilateral and trilateral level, are still close and friendly and there are no major disagreements. Looked at from another viewpoint, however, the triangular relationship looks quite different from how it looked ten to fifteen years ago. The basic elements remain: we are still closely connected by history, culture, tradition and commonality of vital interests to both the USA and Canada, albeit in rather different ways. But the world surrounding these elements, the global context, has changed. I would argue that two significant factors in this change have been globalization, and the collapse of the Soviet Union and Warsaw Pact organization.

The globalization of all aspects of our countries' interests and policies – not just trade and economics, but environmental issues and social policy, terrorism and non-proliferation, crime and peacekeeping – proceeded apace during the 1980s, driven by political and economic imperatives. An increasing realization, enforced by a global recession, that no country could survive economically in isolation has led to movements for increased economic and sometimes political integration. We act in closer concert with our neighbours, allies and fellow members of multilateral organizations on a wide range of issues, from relieving famine in Africa to combating drugs-related crime. While this co-operation is beneficial, it also increasingly means that a problem for one is a problem for all. Like it or not, we are interdependent: as President Clinton said in his first inaugural speech in 1993, there is no longer any distinction between domestic and foreign policy.

While in practical terms our governments recognize the effects and implications of globalization, the full significance is still a subject for debate. From the UK's standpoint, we know that there is scarcely an area of our national interest which is not also the subject of international interest and concern. The United States of America, with interests and influence on a world-wide scale, has a particular interest in multilateral consensus on international affairs, but if possible on its own terms. Both the USA and Canada, with Atlantic and Pacific coasts, face both east and west and recognize an increasing Asian dimension to all their policies, while Britain, partly for commercial reasons, is attaching increasing significance to the Asian market. Thus we all accept the global context, but perhaps we do not as yet allow it sufficiently to inform our planning and policy-making. Differences of approach on subjects as diverse as global warming and arms sales indicate that all governments, particularly those of the North Atlantic Triangle, need to work hard to establish the right balance between national sovereignty and global responsibility: to find a complementarity between Atlanticism and Europeanism.

Globalization was the watchword of the 1980s. On top of this major shift of perspective came at the end of the decade what is often called for convenience the end of the Cold War. The reunification of Germany, the emergence of the countries of Eastern Europe as fledgeling democracies, the break-up of the Soviet Union itself and the emergence of its constituent republics as pivotal if somewhat confused elements of the Central Asian landscape, have changed the way in which we view the present and future world.

As with globalization, however, the end of the Cold War has brought with it the need for a change of both outlook and role on the part of the rest of the world, and in particular for the USA, UK and Canada who were intimately involved partners in a long struggle against totalitarianism and repression. On one hand, there is widespread relief and gladness at the end of a destructive and draining conflict. The term 'East/West' no longer has the same connotations. We all welcome the re-establishment of the national identity of the former Soviet bloc countries, although we recognize the uphill struggle they face. On the other hand, we now face an unfamiliar and troubled European landscape. 'National identity' is not straightforward. Recent events have made clear that there are important and difficult questions to be addressed on what part the

'West' should play in the affairs of the former 'East'. It is important for us to agree, in both the trilateral and multilateral context, on the role we wish and are able to assume in the transition from a Europe locked in two armed blocs to a community with neighbours to the east and endeavouring to form new relations with it.

I would like to take a closer look at how the triangular relationship is functioning within the altered global context, looking at it more generally and then with respect to some specific issues. The UK's relationship with Canada and the United States of America can be looked at on three levels: bilateral; in the context of the United Kingdom's membership of the European Union; and multilateral. I would argue that while there are ways in which as individual nations our co-membership of regional and multinational organizations may seem increasingly important, the UK, USA and Canada still have a special solidarity, both bilateral and trilateral, which informs our relations with the rest of the world and is significant for the future.

The relationship between the UK and Canada is traditionally very close. Our links are both historical and constitutional, we share a head of state, we are fellow members of the Commonwealth. However, as the then secretary of state for foreign affairs, Douglas Hurd, said in Ottawa in 1991 when asked whether the Anglo-Canadian historical relationship was in fact becoming history: 'We don't just sit twiddling our thumbs and thinking of history'; all good relationships have to be worked at. The two major planks of the bilateral relationship are trade and investment, and defence. The UK is the second largest foreign investor in Canada, and Canada in the UK: in 1991, £9.47 billion of UK direct investment went to Canada, while Canada invested £4.89 billion in the UK. On defence, the closeness of the relationship is illustrated by the agreement of September 1991 whereby UK forces carry out extensive training programmes in Canada. Most importantly, however, the United Kingdom and Canada share a world-view. We agree on global priorities, responsibilities and on approach. As part of the global context this level of concurrence is important.

The term 'special relationship', as applied to the United Kingdom's relations with the United States, has fallen into disfavour and, in some media circles, disrepute. Personally, however, I am unwilling to dig its grave, although perhaps it may be better described as a 'natural' relationship. The USA/UK relationship is still very special, with an unparalleled level of interchange on the official, political, commercial and cultural levels which transcends policy differences. We have an important bilateral defence and intelligence relationship. The USA is our single most important commercial partner, American investment constituting 38 per cent of all foreign investment in the UK. USA interests and influence world-wide are important to the UK, from China to Latin America.

On the other side of the coin, contrary to the impression given in the press, the United Kingdom is still widely seen in the USA as being the closest and most dependable partner. If one reads President Clinton's 1992 campaign speeches dealing with foreign policy – and contrary to popular impression, there were a considerable number – one omission is notable. Nowhere is the United Kingdom mentioned. This, however, is surely evidence of the strength of the relationship rather than the contrary. The USA values the UK as a major power of the second rank and a reliable ally, and for her world-wide diplomacy, interests and contacts. That is not to say that there are not differences of emphasis and of opinion. Perhaps there is not the same identity of view as in the UK/Canada relationship. Nevertheless, we share similar political values and ideological perceptions which are often brought to bear on global and regional issues, the Falklands and Gulf crises being clear examples of this convergence of view and interest.

While it is true that the United Kingdom enjoys close bilateral relationships with both Canada and the United States of America, it is equally true that both those countries attach increasing importance to the UK as a member of the European Union. The development of the Community in the 1980s, through enlargement and movement towards greater integration, has in fact added a new dimension to the triangular relationship. In December 1992 the Canadian prime minister, Mr Mulroney, told the British prime minister, Mr Major, and the president of the European Commission, M. Delors, that he considered the EC to be the 'political and economic centre of gravity for Europe', with the UK as a gateway to the Community. After all, two-thirds of EU direct investment in Canada originates in the UK, and the UK accounts for 30 per cent of Canada/EU trade. Parallels have been drawn between the multiracial, federal structure of Canada and that of the EU.

For the USA, also, the UK plays an important role as an interface with the Union. While the USA is directly involved in European security through organizations like NATO and OSCE, there are many more facets to the transatlantic relationship, such as trade, where traditional links with the UK provide a useful bridge between the USA and the European Union. The USA wishes for a closer relationship with Europe on the basis of partnership with a large and integrated Community, but the USA is generally closer to the UK than to any other European partner on a wide range of transatlantic issues.

On a multilateral level, the close relations between Canada, the United States of America and the United Kingdom are very important to all three governments as fellow members of a wide range of organizations. Each plays a significant and individual part in the counsels and wide-ranging activities of the United Nations, which has taken on a new lease of life in the aftermath of the Cold War and with the emergence of new agenda items. Each is currently displaying close interest in the UN both institutionally and as an instrument of international action. As the instigators and founder members of NATO, all three countries are also preoccupied with the future role and membership of that organization. At present, instability and civil war in Europe are focusing attention on defence and security organizations, but there are many other multilateral fora, ranging from the GATT to the Dublin Group for co-ordinating policy towards drug-producing and trafficking countries, in which Canada, the USA and UK are working together and with others to promote common aims. Shared values, ideals and aims may seem nebulous in a world of very concrete crises, but it is still true that the 'North Atlantic Triangle' constitutes a stabilizing and influential force in multilateral counsels. With the globalization of so many issues, the need for new agreed approaches as part of a reconfigured Transatlantic Bargain will become increasingly important.

On a visit to Canada in 1926 to attend the celebrations for the sixtieth anniversary of Confederation, Prime Minister Stanley Baldwin said that Britain was overwhelmed by history, and Canada by geography. By this he meant that history prevented Britain from divorcing herself from the European context, and geography prevented Canada from divorcing herself from the USA. (I leave aside the question of whether either Britain or Canada would wish to enter into legal proceedings.) Although the world has changed even more since 1926 than it has in the last ten years, there is still

some truth in Baldwin's observations. The United Kingdom is drawing closer to the heart of Europe through participation in moves
towards greater political and economic integration within the
European Union and, with Maastricht, co-operation on foreign and
security policies. Canada, already closely linked to the USA, has
forged even closer economic links through NAFTA. These tighten-
ings of conjugal knots are not universally welcomed, nor without
strain. They are, however, a natural and inevitable development in
the new global context. They also contribute to a broadening and
deepening – to borrow the EU terms – of the triangular relationship
itself, by widening the network of countries bound together by common interest in the search for joint approaches on a wide range of
issues.

Note

[1] The opinions expressed in this paper are the author's own and should
not be taken as an expression of official government policy.

1

The Political Persistence of British North America, 1763–1815

PETER MARSHALL

If 1783 represents the earliest date from which it seems possible to entitle that aggregation of colonies, French or English by origin, places of permanent or seasonal settlement, and areas of trade, as British North America, it remains the case that events before that time have to be taken into account if subsequent political developments are to be understood. This applies particularly to the course of the political conflicts within the Thirteen American Colonies after 1763. The emergence and triumph of the independence of the United States and the consequent exodus from the new nation of the Loyalists brought division and separation not only to the territory but equally to the history of North America. Scholars, more decisively than trade, may be seen to have followed the flag, and in the last half-century those who have attempted a double allegiance have proved exceptions to the rule. But later, national, concerns should not be allowed to obscure the inability of a peace treaty, no matter how conclusive its terms, to put an end to a continental process of institutional and political activity that had occupied almost two centuries: British North America, as it became organized after 1783, owed much to its colonial pasts. These gave rise to conditions that exercised decisive significance in the next thirty years.

Any suggestion that the origins and fate of the Loyalists have not received careful scholarly attention would not only prove to be unjust but positively wrong-headed. Who they were, why they left, where they went, how they fared, have been described in detail. For the most part, however, expulsion and arrival have offered points for emphasis and dramatic episodes: the utility of a Harvard degree as protection against a Nova Scotian winter is not easily overlooked. What has, in my view, been insufficiently stressed, is the significance of the political experience, rather than the ideology, acquired by Loyalists in their participation in colonial and imperial affairs after 1763. This, I believe, holds good even of such excellent studies as those by Janice Potter and Ann Condon.[1] Why should these reservations be expressed?

The Liberty We Seek stresses the formation of Loyalist beliefs and bids farewell to the exiles as they leave Massachusetts and New York. If they sought liberty elsewhere, we do not learn whether they found it. This is not a comment that is applicable to *The Loyalist Dream*. Ann Condon bridges a national divide, but in terms of ideas rather than institutions. What more needs to be said?

The political convictions of those who engaged in the growing disputes that marked colonial affairs from 1763 were intensified by the belief that their opponents were employing every possible means to form conspiracies intended to extinguish liberty and install despotism.[2] Those who in these years voiced support for the Patriot cause did so through a cumulative emphasis upon a series of episodes that linked the Writs of Assistance case of 1761 with the Quebec Act of 1774 as tyranny sought incessantly to eliminate its foes. The crowning contrast of Parliament's determination to put an end to the established rights of Massachusetts by the passage of the Coercive Acts and to create a new province deliberately deprived of the essential guarantees of liberty – an elected Assembly, a Protestant establishment, the common law – gave rise to a situation which sharply divided American opinion. Was freedom in the New World in peril? In retrospect, the stridency of the protests might seem more evident than the gravamen of the charge. Conservative Americans located the conspiracy as proceeding against the established order and not as engaged in the destruction of civil and religious liberty. The arguments on both sides may have been removed from reality but the division was deep-seated at a time when the concept of a loyal Opposition had not yet emerged. Indeed, from the viewpoint of government, dissenters intended to be *dis*loyal: that differences in policy and principles could be expressed through common unity had not yet been acknowledged nor, so soon after the momentous consequences of the French and Indian War and of the Revolution, was such a concept likely to gain acceptance. The new governments were marked by an imposed, if necessary authority rather than by a general declaration of allegiance.

This did not mean that their rule should be arbitrary or autocratic.

Those colonists who, after 1763, had first in politics and then in arms, resisted the Patriots, did not at any time abandon beliefs in constitutional process. This was especially true of their steadfast commitment to maintenance of the part of the Assembly in government. After 1775 opportunities to demonstrate this conviction were, of course, limited by the paucity of areas that could be declared to be at, or restored to, the King's Peace. Where this was held to be so, in the Floridas, Georgia and Nova Scotia, Assemblies were continued or called. Possibly the most significant example, despite a failure to reach any effective resolution, was to be observed in New York, with the raising of the question as to what proportion of the colony's extent would need to be restored to imperial authority before an Assembly and courts could be brought into being. The intention, if not the opportunity, to take such steps remained in prospect throughout the war years. It was the use to which colonial Assemblies might be put, not acceptance of their existence, that served to distinguish conservative from Patriot Americans.

This amounted to more than a theoretical difference and was of immediate importance after 1783 in forming the political structure of British North America. This would depend, if the colonies were to enjoy more than a brief, segmented, existence while awaiting absorption by their new neighbour, on what constitutional decisions were reached in relation to the creation, in 1784, of the province of New Brunswick. Nova Scotia, an established colony, was on that account alone of lesser significance: it remained to be seen what would be the consequence of a Loyalist addition to a population whose New England, republican origins could only give rise to suspicion. New Brunswick possessed the virtues of unprecedented simplicity. For all practical purposes the Loyalists, if the imperial government would give its consent, could devise there a colony fit for conservative Americans. A separation of the St John River lands from Nova Scotia brought the new settlement into being, and the appointment of Thomas Carleton, brother of Sir Guy, as governor installed an officer whose views might seem to be firmly opposed to local dissent. While assuring the secretary of state that he had no intention of dispensing with an Assembly he stressed his anxiety to ensure that 'the spirit of American innovation should not be nursed among the Loyal refugees'. He had, with his Council, endeavoured to introduce 'the practice of the best regulated Colonies' and, by 'strengthening the executive powers of Government discountenance it's leaning too much on the popular part of the Constitution'. Carleton was thus well placed to demonstrate the integrity and continuity of imperial practices.[3]

Those prepared to assume responsibility for the politics of the new colony did not, quite evidently, intend to do so by entrusting all authority to the governor: Ann Condon has stressed that the 'Loyalist definition of the imperial role . . . provided for a substantial, indeed striking, increase in the colonial powers of self-government'. The governor would possess executive power over internal affairs but would need to consult his council on matters of policy. Taxation, conforming with the 1778 imperial proposals, would be a matter for colonial decisions. Remaining within the Empire did not involve the reduction of local powers but, on the contrary, their formal recognition.[4]

The question that requires an answer was: to whom did these local powers devolve? Ann Condon's account turns largely on the activities of some twenty Loyalist leaders whose significance is seen to be pre-eminent in the establishment of the new colony and can be followed in official and personal records. Perhaps this does not tell the full story. Other Loyalists, less evident, articulate, ambitious or influential, also contributed to events. While it would be absurd to suggest that party distinctions had come into being, it is equally unacceptable to ignore the presence of vigorous, if inchoate, political controversy. The debates and divisions traced by D. G. Bell,[5] though incapable of reduction to established or persistent groupings, demonstrate the simultaneous emergence in New Brunswick of institutional and political activities. In consequence, the hold on the colony of Loyalist leaders was never as complete and unshakeable as it may have appeared. What was the lesson to be learnt from the Revolution? Should the view of the governor and council prevail, that colonial politics always bear in mind the American menace? Or should stress be laid on the maintenance of liberties whose preservation had committed thousands to flight and suffering? These alternatives, faced by New Brunswick in common with other British North American colonies, offered a later and revised version of the questions which Carl Becker saw as determining party history in New York between 1765 and 1775. 'The first was the question of home rule; the second was the question . . . of who should rule at home.'[6] For all the bitterness and upheaval invoked by the Revolutionary

War, a change of scene had not brought about a change of political conflict.

The constitutional establishment of New Brunswick complicated rather than confirmed the colonial pattern of British North America. But the differences to be observed between its form and that of Nova Scotia, Prince Edward Island, Cape Breton and Newfoundland, pale in comparison with those immediately and widely noted in respect of Quebec. The absence, confirmed by statute in 1774, of an Assembly for thirty years, attracted particular attention, even if excessive emphasis was placed on this omission in radical and mercantile circles. Beliefs in conspiracy to extinguish liberty gained much strength from this condition. An issue of much more substantial and lasting importance was incidentally obscured through concentration on the question of the Assembly: the continuing existence under British rule of the civil and religious institutions of New France would prove of far greater significance.

With the possible exception of Ireland, then as on many future occasions not a precedent to be greeted with enthusiasm, imperial administrators had no example to which to appeal for a solution. If only the Canadians had been sufficiently few in number to invite an Acadian answer, an expulsion might have been arranged. As it was, the departure of French rulers severed the head of the Empire and left in place its colonial body. The exodus does not seem to have given any particular rise to sentiments of abandonment – the links between mother country and province did not bear much comparison, either in extent or nature, with those present in the British case – but did serve to sustain a resolve to maintain a society that, though bereft of sustained and substantial external supports, was already conscious of its distinctive identity. Initial imperial assumptions amounted to a policy that would lead, if the Canadians persisted in staying put, to absorption within a British world. In the face of the conquerors' unwillingness to take substantial advantage of their acquisition, this prospect soon disappeared. The British presence, such as it was, was comprised of military suppliers and camp followers, not of virtuous farmers. Whatever their worth, fur traders and importers could not guarantee the triumph of Anglicization. Deprived of popular political institutions, the government of the province remained entrusted to a succession of generals, advised by councillors and lawyers who sought to bridge the gap between British and French systems. Such circumstances systematically magnified a distinctiveness that made the existence of Quebec within the Empire a matter of continued surprise rather than of steady incorporation into a general pattern of government.[7]

Any assessment of the impact of British imperial influence upon Quebec society encounters difficulties. On balance, however, it would seem considerably easier to argue that it assumed conservative rather than radical guise. For different reasons neither the Quebec Act of 1774 nor the Constitutional Act of 1791, despite their introduction of English criminal law and parliamentary-style institutions, could be considered agents of changes sufficient to put an end to Canadian exceptionalism. As S. D. Clark concluded:

> The strengthening of the representation of Canadian 'gentlemen' in the legislative council, the securing through a government annuity the warm support of the Roman Catholic bishop, and the maintenance of the form of civil law and the form of land tenure of the old regime provided means of effectively offsetting any disturbing influence that might develop through conceding the right to a legislative assembly.[8]

Not until the arrival of some 6,000 Loyalists after 1783 had any substantial number of anglophones reached the province. By that time a practical accommodation had been reached between British rulers and French ruled, creating a relationship that would prove more enduring than the boundaries within which it existed. The detachment of Upper Canada in 1791 does not seem to have engendered Canadian indignation – it may have seemed a price well worth paying if it shielded the population from absorption into an English majority.

Although the most lately established, Upper Canada did not on that account differ markedly in structure or outlook from the other provinces. Its conservatism was influenced not by the past but by immigrants. There, even more evidently than elsewhere, and particularly towards the west, Loyalist founders continued to be confronted by the old enemy. By 1808 Lieutenant Governor Francis Gore could inform Sir James Craig that, after making some exceptions,

> the residue of the Inhabitants of this Colony, consist chiefly of Persons who have emigrated from the States of America, and of consequence, retain those ideas of equality and insubordination, much to the prejudice of this Government, so prevalent in that Country.[9]

This American presence, no matter that the arrival was prompted by prospects of acquiring land, not of national expansion, served to sustain and prolong Loyalist sentiment. More practically, identification of the internal threat justified a demand for loyalty in ways that distinguished from others the Tories of Upper Canada.[10] A province that had not known the events of the Revolution proved nevertheless enduring in its collective memory of the conflict.

And what, in terms of United States policy, were Americans attempting in these years? Up to 1815 there is little hard evidence on which to draw. Failing recourse to such an all-purpose description as 'The Era of Defensive Expansion, 1775–1815'[11] attempts to locate in this period the antecedents of Manifest Destiny prove unavailing. Political Anglophobia justified armed hostility towards the continued imperial presence in North America but territorial acquisition remained a task for individuals, not for governments who had yet, in any case, still to determine where boundaries fixed by the treaty of 1783 were to be found. For the moment, the hopes, however uninformed they may have been, of the makers of the Articles of Confederation, that Quebec and, presumably, if Massachusetts ever found time to consider it, Nova Scotia, would enter the new nation, had been abandoned.[12]

This did not mean, however, that British North America could be ignored by its southern neighbour. Colonial experience still prevailed over national ambition in forming views of what might occur. Until 1761 military incursions from New France were much to be feared: thereafter, the alarms persisted, if anything in mounting measures, as the threat became British in nature. The continuity became the more evident by virtue of the British need to find a solution to the basic problem that had confronted the French: their massive numerical inferiority. In both cases, failing the provision of massive and unattainable imperial protection, only one possible resource could be employed: Indian alliances.[13]

The protraction into the nineteenth century of these positions sustained rooted prejudices and offers a more convincing interpretation of the outbreak of war in 1812 than is usually forthcoming. Satisfactory though it is to engage in superior pacifism by stressing the total futility of a war that gained nothing for either side and in which the only decisive battle was fought after a pointless peace had concluded a pointless conflict, it may be preferable to regard the conflict as constituting the last colonial campaign and not as forming an inexplicable or at least eccentric clash of nations. Such a shift of emphasis might be encouraged by a change of name – the War of 1812 in any event hardly supplies a dramatic title. A more accurate title would be the British and Indian War or possibly, if Americans found it more familiar, the Prince Regent's War. After 1815 the explosive growth of the United States observable in terms of population and inhabited territory would indicate the undeniable reduction of any imperial threat from British North America, a region that would within thirty years be vying with Texas as the next step in a process of national expansion. But such changes, at the signing of the Treaty of Ghent, would have adjudged visions, not even ambitions.

What did British North America amount to by the end of this period? It is customary to contrast the undoubted achievement of the establishment of its colonies with the presence of a sparse population strung out across a vast extent of territory. This, though true, does not convey much in the way of enlightenment. Greater significance attaches to the undertaking of the process for the most part not by new settlers but by old colonists. It was a task assumed by the inhabitants of two empires whose military and political failures had in large part cut them adrift from the rulers and lands of their upbringing. These disruptions, for those who remained in North America, did not occasion fundamental changes of culture or belief. In consequence, those who, until 1815, composed a great part of the numbers and an even greater part of the quality of the colonial population, must be considered, whether of French or British ancestry, fully as American as any citizen of the United States. Conservative Americans in a certain sense, to be sure, but it is hardly necessary to accept claims that radicalism, however that may be defined, represents an essential element of the American national character.

If this argument seems intended to confer on Canadian history after 1783 an equality of origins with that of the United States, it does not necessarily follow that the consequences of the division of North America can be seen to have assumed similar forms. Two basic conditions ensured that distinctiveness would persist. First, a constant assertion of the conservative origins of societies that, partly on this account, had rejected inclusion in the United States, stimulated not altogether accurate beliefs in a prospect of perennial separation. A less recognized but more significant consequence of this expression of conservative political doctrine was the delivery of radical rebuttals: Canadian and American political history, no matter what similar issues are addressed, do not have much in common.[14] Second, the remnants of not one but of two empires were brought together. The implications of this imposed union did not immediately become apparent. Contemporaries were so anxious to deny the existence of a permanent problem, preferring to believe it would expire of its own volition, that this was not surprising. It took time for the conservatism of the Canadians of Quebec to find public forms of self-expression. That inception could not, however, be indefinitely postponed and, once begun, would not be silenced. As good a date as any from which to note a beginning is 1807, with the publication of *Le Canadien*. This was an event that did not pass unremarked by the English, one of whom wrote from Quebec that

> it is evident that steps are taking to alienate the Minds of the Canadians from their fellow Subjects – Two Newspapers, wholly in French, which have a strong tendency that way, have lately started up. The Editors are those firebrands of Society (Lawyers) who make themselves so conspicuous in all Civil Commotions, which frequently end in subverting the Government that gives them Protection, perhaps bread to some.

The letter was passed through an intermediary to the ministry with a further comment by the recipient that 'Since the Conquest of Canada French News Papers have not been in use, why should they now appear, after an Assimilation of above 40 years, but for some bad purpose . . .'[15] If British North America might proclaim its conservative origins, it had also, by 1815, to acknowledge that they had to be observed as existing within a political system divided by institutional, religious and linguistic factors. These might, at times, establish a mutual understanding, or more often grudging recognition, but proceed no further towards a national unity. That is the record of the eighteenth, nineteenth and twentieth centuries. One wonders what will be the nature and forms of this fundamental relationship in the twenty-first century and whether its historians will be required to write yet another chapter on the French and Indian War.

Notes

[1] Janice Potter, *The Liberty We Seek: Loyalist Ideology in Colonial New York and Massachusetts* (Cambridge, Mass., 1983); Ann Gorman Condon, *The Envy of the American States: The Loyalist Dream for New Brunswick* (Fredericton, NB, 1984).

2   Gordon S. Wood, 'Conspiracy and the Paranoid Style: Causality and Deceit in the Eighteenth Century', *William and Mary Quarterly*, 3rd ser., xxxix (1982), 401–41.

3   Condon, op. cit., pp.137–8.

4   Ibid., p.65; Vincent T. Harlow, *The Founding of the Second British Empire 1763–1793* (London, 1952), I, pp.495–501; Charles R. Richeson, *British Politics and the American Revolution* (Norman, Okla., 1954), pp.260–3.

5   *Early Loyalist Saint John* (Fredericton, NB, 1983).

6   Carl Lotus Becker, *The History of Political Parties in the Province of New York 1760–1776* (Madison, Wis., 1960), p.22.

7   Peter Marshall, 'The Incorporation of Quebec in the British Empire, 1763–1774', in Virginia Bever Platt and David Curtis Skaggs (eds.), *Of Mother Country and Plantations* (Bowling Green, Ohio, 1971), pp.43–62.

8   S. D. Clark, *Movements of Political Protest in Canada 1641–1840* (Toronto, 1959), p.175.

9   Quoted ibid., p.229.

10   David Mills, *The Idea of Loyalty in Upper Canada 1784–1850* (Kingston and Montreal, 1988), pp.12–51.

11   Reginald C. Stuart, *United States Expansionism and British North America, 1775–1871* (Chapel Hill and London, 1988), p.1.

12   Murray G. Lawson, 'Canada and the Articles of Confederation', *American Historical Review*, 58 (1952), 39–54.

13   Peter Marshall, 'The Disruption of British America: Nation and Empire', *The Diaspora of the British*, University of London Institute of Commonwealth Studies Collected Seminar Papers, 31 (1982), 81–92; Colin G. Calloway, *Crown and Calumet* (Norman, Okla., and London, 1987).

14   Louis Hartz, *The Liberal Tradition in America* (New York, 1955).

15   Quoted Clark, op. cit., p.196.

2

Making British North America British, 1815–1860

P. A. BUCKNER

In 1815 the British North American colonies could aptly be described as the orphans of the first British Empire in North America. Indeed, except for a handful of islands and a vast area in the West populated by aboriginal peoples, all that remained of that empire were the territories which had been acquired by conquest from the French in the eighteenth century. The British had established their jurisdiction over peninsular Nova Scotia by the Treaty of Utrecht in 1713 and extended their power over the rest of the region during the Seven Years War from 1756 to 1763. During this prolonged transition from the French to the British Empire the region attracted few British emigrants. To secure its control, the British government established Halifax in 1749, but it remained essentially a naval and military base which attracted only a few thousand settlers, many of whom did not stay for very long. The British government also encouraged some 2,700 'Foreign Protestants', mainly of German extraction, to settle near Halifax, at Lunenburg. The failure of Nova Scotia to attract more immigrants meant that the Acadians, whose population grew steadily through natural increase, continued to form a majority of the European population in the colony until 1755, when the British government in Halifax moved to resolve what it saw as the Acadian problem. Between 1755 and 1758 nearly 9,000 of the roughly 13,000 Acadians were deported either to the Thirteen Colonies or to Europe, and the Acadian heartland along the Bay of Fundy was opened up for resettlement. More than 8,000 New Englanders were transported to Nova Scotia at British expense between 1759 and 1763, but as soon as the subsidies dried up, the flow of emigrants dwindled to a trickle. New France was conquered during the Seven Years War and ceded to Britain by the Treaty of Paris in

1763, but except for a few hundred American colonial and British merchants and the officials and military sent to govern the colony, now renamed Quebec, the population remained overwhelmingly of French origin. Between 1763 and 1775 there was substantial emigration from the British Isles to North America but only a tiny proportion – probably under 5,000 – made their way to the peripheries of the Empire in Quebec and Nova Scotia.[1]

After 1783 approximately 60,000 Loyalists flowed into the remnants of the first Empire, doubling the population of Nova Scotia and creating the nucleus of a substantial non-French minority in Quebec. The Loyalist influx contained British regular troops, often recruited in the Scottish Highlands and Ireland, and Hessian mercenaries, as well as a number of first-generation British emigrants to the Thirteen Colonies, but the vast majority of those who became permanent residents of British North America were native-born Americans, drawn heavily from the Middle Colonies of New York and Pennsylvania.[2] The arrival of the Loyalists led to the creation of New Brunswick in 1784 and to the partition of Quebec into Upper and Lower Canada in 1791, but their major contribution was to ensure that British North America was not easily absorbed into the new United States, while Britain's attention and resources were absorbed by the long wars with revolutionary France that lasted from the 1790s until 1815. Obsessed by fears of a French invasion, the British Government sought to discourage emigration during this period and, except for a steady trickle of Scots, only small numbers of British emigrants crossed the Atlantic to British North America. The Maritimes may even have had a net loss of migrants as many of the Loyalists returned to the United States and a few made their way to the Canadas. The largest group of migrants were the so-called late Loyalists from the United States who began arriving in the 1790s. In fact, few of them had been Loyalists and they were attracted to the Canadas because of the ease with which they could obtain land rather than by any desire to live under the British Crown. By 1812 perhaps as many as 50,000–60,000 had settled in Upper Canada.[3] An important minority were German-speaking immigrants from Pennsylvania, many of them members of dissenting sects such as Mennonites, who emigrated in part because they had been persecuted for their neutrality during the Revolution.[4]

In 1815 a clear majority of the population of British North America was thus still composed of the descendants of those emigrants who had settled in Acadia and New France during the French regime. In Lower Canada the population by 1815 numbered over 300,000, nearly 90 per cent of whom were francophones. The vast majority lived in the rural areas of Lower Canada, where English was seldom, if ever, heard. Only in the urban centres of Montreal and Quebec city, where barely 10 per cent of the population lived, were there small concentrations of still greatly outnumbered anglophones. 'When passing through the different States of the federal Republic, and even when crossing the boundary to Upper Canada, I could scarcely perceive the slightest difference of national character', one British visitor reported in the early 1820s, 'but the moment I entered Lower Canada, I found every thing changed, as completely indeed, as if I had passed from England to France.'[5] In the Maritimes the Acadians had been dispersed after 1755 but some Acadians had escaped deportation and others had returned after 1763. By 1815 they numbered over 10,000, scattered in largely self-contained enclaves across the region. Their settlements were quickly recognizable by a distinct style of housing and by their distinctive dress. In 1813 Lieutenant-Colonel Gubbins noted that the women wore 'the full dress of the Norman mode as it was perhaps a century before'.[6] Since the Acadians depended for a supply of priests on the Catholic Church in Quebec, they retained loose ties with their co-religionists in French Canada, but even in northern New Brunswick there was limited contact with the French Canadians, who, according to one observer, referred to the Acadians as 'Les Sauvages'.[7] Many of the Acadian settlements were so isolated that it was reported that they were 'in utter ignorance of what was going on in the world, they had not even heard of Bonaparte or the war with France'.[8] That seems doubtful but it surely does reflect how little communication there was between the Acadians and their anglophone neighbours.

Moreover, a substantial majority of the non-francophone population of British North America in 1815 had not come directly from the British Isles but was of American origin. In the Maritimes their largest settlements were clustered around the Bay of Fundy and up the St John River. Divisions between the pre-Loyalists and Loyalists persisted, in part based on the fact that the Loyalists believed (with considerable justification) that the loyalty of the pre-Loyalists during the American Revolution had been grounded in expediency rather than principle, and in part based on the fact that the majority of the pre-Loyalist Americans had come from disloyal New England while the majority of the Loyalists had not. In any event, since there was limited room for the Loyalists in areas settled by pre-Loyalists, there was limited mingling of the two groups.[9] Over time, of course, these distinctions would become blurred, particularly through intermarriage, although as late as the 1850s one New England visitor touring Nova Scotia was overjoyed when he reached the Annapolis valley to find himself among 'genuine Yankees, the true blues of Connecticut, quilted in among the Bluenoses'.[10] In Upper Canada the Loyalist migrants had been overwhelmed by the arrival of the late Loyalists. Here too there was limited mingling initially, since the Loyalists settled predominantly in eastern Upper Canada while the late Loyalists had gravitated overwhelmingly to the north and west of the capital at York and in very much smaller numbers to the sparsely populated Eastern Townships in Lower Canada, but here too intermarriage would soon begin to blur the distinction between Loyalist and non-Loyalist. Yet the distinction between pre-Loyalist, Loyalist and late Loyalist is to some extent a false one, for all three groups imported with them American cultural patterns and values. The majority built American-style housing, belonged to Nonconformist religious denominations whose roots lay in the United States, imported from the United States most of the goods they could afford to buy, including foodstuffs, and were buried beneath gravestones of American origin. The bordering American states were the source of most of the information they received from the outside world. In 1811 when Lieutenant-Colonel Gubbins toured New Brunswick, the colony with the largest proportion of Loyalist settlers, he found it 'remarkable that amongst the immediate descendants of the English, little of British manners or customs are to be found'.[11] British visitors to Upper Canada were even more struck by the completely American character of the settlements there. 'In Upper Canada,' John MacTaggart, a Scottish civil engineer, reported in the mid-1820s, 'the feeling is totally Yankee, and the inhabitants care not a fig for the institutions of Great Britain.'[12]

The Loyalist influence was undoubtedly greatest in the Maritimes but even there when most Loyalists talked of living under the British constitution it was the American colonial derivative of that constitution that they had in mind. The Loyalist élite tended to maintain close ties with neighbours and friends they had left behind, went back to the United States to find wives, and frequently sent their children there to be educated. Many of them had not wanted to leave the United States and they saw themselves as exiles.[13] It is worth stressing that most Loyalists saw the Revolution as an unnecessary event, a tragic accident that should not and would not have taken place except for the foolish policies of the British government which were exploited by a small minority of demagogues and agitators. In fact, their supposed anti-Americanism has been much exaggerated. In 1815 both the Maritimes and the areas settled by anglophones in the Canadas have been aptly described as 'borderland' communities where 'a sense of cross-border community worked against national allegiance. Family and friendship ties reinforced economic linkages to produce the borderland mentality, a product of American frontier expansion where the people from one society intermingled with the people of another.'[14] Undeniably the long struggle against France followed by the short war with America in 1812–14 strengthened the imperial loyalty of British North Americans but it did not make the majority of the non-francophone population any less receptive to American cultural influences.

There were also substantial pockets of non-francophones who were neither of American origin nor English-speaking. Between 1770 and 1815 about 15,000 Scots had emigrated to British North America, a high proportion of them from the Western Highlands and Islands, a region which was both Catholic and Gaelic-speaking. The Highlanders settled in enclaves scattered across eastern Upper Canada, eastern Nova Scotia and Prince Edward Island (PEI), and Gaelic continued to be more commonly used than English in their homes and churches. They might, John McGregor observed in 1828, 'with more propriety be called genuine counterparts of the Highlanders who fought at Culloden, than can now, from the changes which have during the last fifty years taken place, be found in any part of the Highlands'.[15] Since they had migrated to escape the results of the enforced integration of the Highlands into England, their communities remained strikingly distinctive from those of their neighbours.[16] So did the communities established by the German-speaking Protestants. In Lunenburg, Nova Scotia, the houses reflected a distinctive architectural style and German was spoken in the streets and used in the town's schools and Lutheran churches.[17] In Upper Canada groups like the Mennonites clung even more firmly to their distinctive way of life; their communities were also self-contained and they communicated among themselves in German. The Irish were too few in numbers in 1815 to establish any self-contained communities, but they had begun to drift into British North America and to many of them English was a second language. Although they formed a declining proportion of the population, the native peoples also continued to live apart and to speak their own languages; except in Upper Canada they were likely to be Catholic and in Lower Canada more likely to speak French rather than English as a second language. In fact, the first language of a substantial minority of the non-francophone population was not English and the vast majority of the rest spoke English with a distinct American accent.

Only in the small urban centres and provincial capitals, most of which were little more than country villages, were there communities with direct links with Britain. In these outposts of Empire small groups of officials and merchants, some of them Loyalists but a number of them recent immigrants from the British Isles, sought to emulate metropolitan standards and to impose those standards on the rest of the colony. In Halifax, where the large military establishment continued to strengthen imperial enthusiasm, the corner-stone was laid in 1800 for a new and extremely spacious Government House, which was designed to reflect 'the loyalty and attachment' of Nova Scotians 'to the best of Sovereigns'.[18] In 1809 the British minority in Montreal raised through private subscription £1,300 to erect a Doric column, five feet wide and seventy feet high, adorned by a statute of Lord Nelson.[19] But these efforts to promote a greater sense of an imperial identity went largely unrewarded. The scattered communities of colonists, in fact, had limited contact with each other, since roads were non-existent, and even less with the distant mother country. Most settlers lived in small, relatively homogeneous communities. A market economy was slow to develop and most of the production was for subsistence; what small surpluses there were went largely to the West Indies and the United States, although the timber trade had begun to alter this pattern. Indeed, the British North American colonies continued to resemble a patchwork quilt composed of what Jack Bumsted has aptly described as a collection of 'ethnic nodes'. Prior to 1815 settlement had consisted of a series of waves of colonists, each of which carried with them their own distinctive cultural traditions and each of which tended to occupy a separate geographical space. The British North American colonies, in Bumsted's words, were 'a collection of relatively and culturally distinctive provinces with weak colonial administrations incapable of melding their various emergent cultures into a coherent whole'.[20]

During the decades following 1815, however, British North America was transformed by the arrival of a flood of emigrants from the British Isles. Between 1815 and the early 1860s well over a million people crossed the Atlantic to arrive in ports in British North America.[21] Although there was a small minority of European – particularly German – immigrants, the overwhelming majority came from the British Isles.[22] Between 1815 and 1837 British North America received more British emigrants than the United States and more than the rest of the Empire combined. During the 1840s the proportion of British emigrants arriving in British North America dropped from a third to a quarter of the North American total and through the 1850s and 1860s remained fairly constant at about a tenth, but the numbers each year were still substantial.[23] If the British North American colonies were the orphans of the first British Empire, they grew to maturity as the children of the second. In the century and a half from 1608 until 1763 the territories of the French Crown in what became British North America had attracted no more than 30,000 emigrants, and a large majority – nearly 70 per cent – had not stayed.[24] Under British rule, Nova Scotia after 1713 and Quebec after 1763 had done marginally better. Yet even the total number of emigrants the British regime had attracted to become permanent residents prior to 1815 could not have exceeded 150,000, and most of these came, not from Europe, but from other parts of North America, either as a response to British government incentives, as in the case of the pre-Loyalists and late Loyalists, or because they had nowhere else to go, as in the case of the Loyalists, who also received generous assistance from the British government. Largely through natural increase the population of British North American colonies had grown to around 500,000 by 1815.[25] Without further emigration or a much higher rate of natural increase after 1815 (which was most unlikely since birth rates were already extremely high), the population of those colonies could not much have exceeded 1,500,000 by 1861 and nearly 1,000,000 of those would have been francophones. In fact, by 1861 the francophone population had increased to about 1,000,000 but the total population numbered well over 3,000,000. In other words the francophone population had increased about threefold, almost entirely through natural increase, but the non-francophone population had increased tenfold, largely because of the massive influx of British emigrants.

We will never know the exact number of emigrants who came to British North America in this period. British records only give a partial list of the numbers who sailed from British ports and record only the country of destination. Moreover, these records do not capture those emigrants who sailed to American ports and then decided or were persuaded to proceed to British North America, nor those who came from Europe to British North America either directly or via American ports. They also do not give any information about how many returned to Britain after a few years in the colonies, although it seems most unlikely that there were high rates of return migration before the 1870s, except perhaps during the exceptionally depressed 1840s.[26] Colonial records at the port of arrival are incomplete and inadequate, particularly since they tell us nothing about the flow-through factor and do not include those emigrants who came overland from the United States. It is also impossible to know what proportion of the emigrants became permanent residents of British North America or what proportion they and their offspring formed of the colonial population. During the years of heaviest migration in the later 1840s, British North America was suffering from a severe recession and a very high proportion of the emigrants left almost immediately, but in other periods the retention rate seems to have been extremely high, particularly during the later 1820s, the early 1830s and the 1850s. Moreover, we cannot assume that all of those who chose to leave for the United States were recent emigrants. In the aftermath of the War of 1812–14, and again following the rebellions of 1837, many of those who left the Canadas (sometimes involuntarily) were clearly drawn primarily from the pre-1815 emigrants and their children; in the Maritimes the flow of migrants to the United States contained from the beginning a substantial number of the descendants of the pre-1815 settlers (especially descendants of the pre-Loyalists);[27] and during the severe economic recession of the 1840s the out-migration from British North America included older as well as more recent settlers. There was also a small counterflow of American-born migrants about which we know even less, other than that it is unlikely to have been all that significant after 1815 except in the Canadas, where the American-born still formed only a small proportion of the population in comparison to the British-born.[28]

Unfortunately even census data provide only a rough guide to the issue of origins. We have only fragmentary and unreliable data for the earlier period. Later censuses, taken in the 1850s and 1860s, are more reliable and give some indication of the numbers of those who were born outside British North America, but we do not know what proportion of the native-born were the offspring of the British emigrants. In fact, intermarriage between the emigrants and the native-born makes this an impossible question to answer. But in 1851, by which time a majority of the non-francophone native-born must have been the children of earlier immigrants, the British-born still formed just over 20 per cent of the total population of British North America. In 1861 that percentage had dropped to just under 18 per cent, and by 1871 to just under 14 per cent, but the effective increase added by British immigration alone to the British North American population in the 1850s and 1860s (excluding any children that these immigrants contributed to the total) has been estimated at 197,000, a number almost equal to the total non-francophone population in 1815.[29] Indeed, since the emigrant population was drawn more narrowly from the childbearing ages than the host population, the children of emigrants were likely over-represented among the native-born in every decade from the 1820s until the 1860s.

What is clear is that only in a few communities in the densest areas of pre-1815 settlement could the British immigrants and their descendants have been outnumbered by the descendants of the earlier settlers. Upper Canada grew from around 80,000 in 1815 to nearly 1,400,000 in 1861. In the newer townships and the urban communities the earlier settlers were swamped.[30] Only in a very few areas just north of Toronto could the descendants of the earlier American-born immigrants have continued to constitute a majority of the population, and given the sheer volume of migration and the tendency of the pioneer settlers to sell their farms and relocate in frontier communities, it seems unlikely that they did so even there. In Lower Canada the population grew from something over 300,000 in 1815 to just over 1,100,000 in 1861 but the proportion of non-francophones increased from under 10 per cent to over 22 per cent of the population. In the densely populated townships along the St Lawrence and north of Montreal the French Canadians continued to compose the overwhelming majority, but there was a non-francophone majority in the Eastern Townships and even for a time in Montreal and Quebec city.

In the Maritime colonies population growth was smaller but still substantial, from around 130,000 in 1815 to over 660,000 in 1861.[31] Bill Acheson's study of Charlotte County gives some idea of what was happening in New Brunswick. Charlotte County was originally settled by Loyalists and contained the second largest concentration of Loyalists in the Loyalist province. By 1851 the descendants of the Loyalists formed at most a third of the population. The dominant element in the population consisted of the British-born and their children. The Loyalist County had become an immigrant county, probably with an Irish majority.[32] Indeed, so had the Loyalist city of Saint John which by mid-century had an Irish majority and very substantial Scottish and English minorities.[33] It is hardly surprising that St Patrick's Day was the occasion of more general celebration than the anniversary of the arrival of the Loyalists, which as the Saint John *Morning News* reported in 1862, 'appears to be dying out'.[34] In fact, it did not die out, largely because as a growing number of the descendants of the British-born acquired a Loyalist ancestor through intermarriage, they resurrected the Loyalists as the founders of the province and thus misled generations of historians into exaggerating the significance of the Loyalists. But a majority of the 660,000 residents of the region in 1861 must have been emigrants from the British Isles or the children and grandchildren of British emigrants. Although the proportion was probably highest in PEI, which started from the lowest population base in 1815, and lowest in Nova Scotia, which started with the highest, there were few communities even in Nova Scotia which did not receive a substantial influx of emigrants. As in the Canadas, the emigrants did not displace the earlier settlers; they absorbed them. In the United States the British became 'invisible immigrants', forced to adapt to the social, cultural and political values of the host society.[35] In British North America the immigrants came in such overwhelming numbers that the host societies had to adjust to them.

The arrival of such huge numbers of immigrants transformed the British North American colonies. In 1815, except in the older seigneurial areas in Lower Canada and around the coastline of the Bay of Fundy, the countryside consisted of a wilderness broken only by the occasional farm or cluster of farms, surrounded by impenetrable forests. By the 1860s every acre of arable land and much that was only marginally arable had been granted to settlers, and much of it was under cultivation, the forest was receding rapidly and the British North American colonies were dotted with small towns and villages, which acted as service centres for the surrounding population. Roads, telegraph lines, steamships and post offices linked all of the population centres and railways were being constructed. There remained isolated communities, but fewer and fewer lacked regular communication with the outside world and with each other. Moreover, a complex market economy had taken root, geared to the export of timber, wheat and fish to foreign (especially British) markets. Even in the agricultural sector, fewer and fewer farmers were engaged in purely subsistence production. The growth of towns and urban centres stimulated demand and encouraged market production and crop specialization, and farmers had to respond to that demand in order to purchase imported goods, most of them now coming from Britain. Emigrants also provided much of the labour supply needed in the urban centres and in the staple trades of the colonies, especially the timber trade.

Put out of your mind the classic image of the immigrants as being poor and helpless. This was, of course, part of the picture, but only a part. The majority of the emigrants paid their own passage across the Atlantic. Many of the migrants were certainly poor but only a minority were destitute. During the later 1820s and 1830s British North America may have ended up with more of the poorer immigrants than the United States, because the passage across the Atlantic was cheaper to British North America and most of the assisted emigrants travelled by this route,[36] but the number of assisted emigrants was not large and the majority of British emigrants who remained in British North America in this period appear to have come as members of a family unit with some (if usually small) reserves of capital. In the 1840s the flow of destitute emigrants, particularly from Ireland and Scotland, was probably higher, but even during the Great Famine in Ireland it was not the poorest who left but those from more affluent farming communities. In any event America (and England) absorbed the bulk of the emigrants pushed out by the Great Famine; British North America received relatively few of them, at least as permanent settlers, and by the 1850s, when Irish emigration did come from the regions of greatest poverty, the flow was overwhelmingly to the United States.[37] British North America may have received a rather higher proportion of the destitute Highlanders forced out 'in grotesque poverty and ill health' during the famines of 1836–7 and 1847–8 but by the 1840s the majority of the poorest emigrants from England and Scotland probably were given assisted passages to Australia.[38] Moreover, in every period the influx of British emigrants included a sizeable number of merchants and army officers with more than a little capital and sizeable numbers of tradesmen and professionals with valuable skills to market.

The first few years of pioneer life were hard for all emigrants. Earlier emigrants, who came out when good land was easier to acquire, undoubtedly fared better than later emigrants, particularly since the later waves did include a larger number of impoverished Irish and Scottish migrants. Many emigrants did end up in pockets of rural poverty in the backlands of the Maritimes and the Canadas. Others eked out a marginal existence as unskilled labourers in the urban centres. But a substantial proportion were able to acquire land of their own or employment that provided them with a modest but, by the standards of the day, adequate level of income. In this sense, as many contemporary observers claimed, British North America was a good poor man's country, at least for those with a strong back and blessed with good health.[39] The story of the majority of the British emigrants was similar to those elsewhere in the British colonies of settlement: a few prospered spectacularly, the majority slightly improved their lot or stayed roughly the same, and a few found themselves even poorer.

The emigrants also transformed the cultural landscape of British North America. They destroyed much of the fragmentation that had been such a pronounced feature of the colonies prior to 1815 and forged a new sense of identity among the dominant groups. Put crudely, they made British North America *British*. By the beginning of the 1860s the British emigrants and their descendants were not only proportionately represented in the colonial élites; they were disproportionately well represented, particularly in all commercial activities and in the professions.[40] British-born ministers and priests provided the leadership in the various colonial churches, and British-born lecturers staffed the majority of the positions in most of the institutions of higher education. When James Buckingham visited McGill in 1839 he found that the professors included 'one of Divinity, from Oxford; one of Moral Philosophy and the Classics, from Oxford; one of History and Civil Law, from Aberdeen; one of Mathematics and Natural History, from Oxford; and one of Medicine and Surgery, from Edinburgh'.[41] British textbooks were increasingly used in the schools, and the children of the élite, whether the children of the native-born or the immigrants, were sent to Britain to receive specialized training not available at home. Despite his impeccable pre-Loyalist credentials, the young Charles Tupper, for example, went to Edinburgh, not to New England, for medical training; so too did the three sons of the captain of the Water Police at Quebec city.[42] Indeed, when the Montreal Medical Institution (the forerunner of the Medical Faculty of McGill University) was established in 1824, all of the faculty were graduates of Edinburgh. Three of the five doctors who founded L'École de Médecine in 1843 had also studied at Edinburgh, as had all but one of the fourteen doctors practising in Halifax in 1845.[43] To be successful, the wealthiest merchants had to have access to British markets and British capital, and increasingly the real control over the largest financial empires in the colonies was in the hands of the British-born or British creditors. Literate British North Americans devoured pirated editions of British books, flocked to hear British itinerant lecturers and looked to Britain for their cultural models.

Moreover, the Atlantic had shrunk and colonial newspapers carried up-to-date reports on British events that were seldom more than a few weeks, and after the completion of the transatlantic cable seldom more than a few days, out of date. British North Americans celebrated British victories during the Crimean War and viewed with the same horror and anger as Britons at home the news of the atrocities committed during the Indian Mutiny. When travellers dined at the Victoria Hotel in Windsor, Nova Scotia, they were confronted by a panorama of British India.[44] When they crossed Lake Ontario in a steamboat, they saw hanging 'portraits of Wellington, Prince Albert, Queen Victoria, and the whole royal family'.[45] In their efforts to replicate British culture the colonials often incurred the scorn of British visitors. One British visitor to London, Canada West, in 1864 noted that 'There is an Oxford Street, a Regent Street, a Holborn (with an "H"), a Bond Street, Picadilly and Pall Mall, too', but 'it is all on such a diminutive scale that the comparison is ludicrous' and 'I could scarce restrain my laughter at the toy-like imitation'.[46] But to the colonials there was nothing ludicrous about their desire to show their 'loyalty and attachment' to the Empire.[47] Like Britons at home, they gloried in the military achievements of British troops overseas, particularly when British North Americans were involved.

Sir William Fenwick Williams, the Nova Scotian-born commander of the British troops during the unsuccessful defence of Kars during the Crimean War, became the 'Hero of Kars' and Henry J. Morgan – 'a British American by birth and feeling' – proudly noted in *The Place British Americans Have Won in History* that the recipient of the first Victoria Cross, Lieutenant-Colonel A. R. Dunn, who had taken part in the charge of the Light Brigade, was a native of Toronto and that 'In India and the Crimea the tombs of a number of our countrymen, who sacrificed their lives for England's glory, speak more eloquently than I can do'.[48] British Americans had little sympathy with those who wished to 'emancipate' the colonies; that would be, Egerton Ryerson proclaimed, 'the retracing of the policy by which Great Britain has become the greatest national power of the globe; the reduction of an empire over hundreds of millions to a kingdom including thirty millions; the shrivelling of an empire on which the sun never sets to a minor island of Europe'. Indeed, Ryerson denounced the term 'emancipation' with its implication that 'Canadians are in a state of enslavement'. They were, he proclaimed, 'not slaves, not even colonists in the old and popular sense of that term, but freemen and an *integral* part of a nation whose liberty, science, wealth and power are pre-eminent among the nations of the world'.[49]

During the middle decades of the nineteenth century the monarchy in Britain became a popular institution and Queen Victoria a figure of veneration. These attitudes too crossed the Atlantic. In 1841 the Montreal *Gazette* advertised a 'Grand Moving Diorama of the Coronation of Victoria . . . painted on nearly 2,000 square feet of canvas and featuring "1500 mechanical figures of ingenious instruction"'.[50] The Queen's Birthday on 24 May became a source of sentimental effusion in the newspapers.[51] When the Prince of Wales toured British North America in 1860 he was met everywhere by huge and enthusiastic crowds. In Halifax the ride through streets 'almost clothed in evergreen, and spanned with innumerable arches of sweet spruce-fir' was 'one continuous ovation' and the Prince was taken to a raised platform holding 4,000 school children who rose as he approached and 'sang, or *attempted* to sing, "God Save the Queen"'. When he departed Saint John, 'the whole population seemingly, – accompanied him to the water's edge.' In Quebec city he was met by 'people crowding in dense masses up from the water's edge to the heights of Cape Diamond' and the streets were 'literally wreathed with evergreens'. In Montreal two balls, one attended by 4,000 and a second by 7,000, were held in his honour in 'a circular building of wood – especially constructed at an estimated cost of 25,000 dollars'. And in Toronto, 'Thousands upon thousands lined the shore, and stretched away upwards and inwards in one large amphitheatre of human faces, interspersed with flags, arches, and decorations.' Everywhere what struck the royal party was 'the extraordinary feeling of devotion and attachment to the Queen'.[52] As the correspondent for the *New York Herald*, Kinahan Cornwallis noted, the Prince's tour was carefully stage-managed. In the dining cabin of the ship in which the Prince arrived were 'four long silver lantern-like candle holders, which were once the property of Lord Nelson and used by him on board the Victory, from which they were taken after the battle of Trafalgar' and a cabinet 'made out of the timbers of old Victory itself'. At each point of landing it was 'evident that the hand of preparation has been busy, and nothing has been left undone'. The Prince's ship even contained a library filled with books about British North America. 'Hence, to some extent', Cornwallis pointed out, 'the ready information expressed with regard to places visited, historical and otherwise, in the royal replies'. Yet even the cynical journalist admitted: 'Wherever I went there was but one sentiment distinguishing the people with respect to their royal visitor, and that was of admiration for the man, and loyalty to the throne.'[53] Indeed, it is doubtful whether there was an affluent English-speaking household in British North America after 1860 without a portrait of Queen Victoria, except for some Irish Catholic homes where the portrait was more likely to be of Daniel O'Connell.[54] In this sense the British immigrants had succeeded where the pre-1815 élites had failed in establishing metropolitan culture as the norm throughout British North America.

In fact, if British North America was an embryonic multicultural society in 1815, by 1860 the baby had died and been replaced by a thoroughly British lad. English, for example, had become the normal language of everyday use throughout the colonies. Hector McLean, a Highland Scot who served as an ensign in the 84th Regiment during the American Revolution and then settled in Pictou County, was bilingual, but his son, Donald, born in 1805, 'refused to permit his children to speak Gaelic in the house, altho he and his wife were more fluent in Gaelic than in English'.[55] By mid-century Gaelic was everywhere in retreat. In 1851 John Boyd began the Antigonish

Casket, devoting two of its four pages to material in Gaelic, but the Gaelic content was gradually reduced and by 1857 'it had virtually disappeared from the paper'.[56] In 1860 the Lutheran Church in Lunenburg changed its language of service from German to English.[57] Nearly 60 per cent of all the people of German origin in British North America were settled in and around Waterloo County in Upper Canada. German newspapers had been available there since the 1830s and most of the German population 'worshipped their God in the German language', but the sheer size of the German community could only delay assimilative pressures. Daily newspapers in English would gradually come to take the place of German weeklies in the later nineteenth century and the number of unilingual English speakers would continue to increase.[58] It has been estimated that at least one-third and as many as one-half of all the Irish emigrants to New Brunswick during the 1840s may have had Gaelic as their native tongue, but in Ireland English was already seen as the language of progress and in New Brunswick Gaelic quickly disappeared from sight.[59] Isolation might delay the decay of languages and so would religion; Catholic Highlanders, for example, retained Gaelic longer than Protestants.[60] But in the long run the only non-francophone groups who were able to resist the pressure to adopt English as the language of normal use were those who lived in cohesive communities with values different from the British majority, like the Mennonites and the native peoples. Even the large francophone minority had to accept the primacy of English. 'Most of the French [merchant] houses have adopted English as the language of business, not merely in their correspondence, but also in the counting-houses and private books, and this not only because it is more convenient in Canada, but because they consider it generally preferable for commercial purposes', J. G. Kohl reported in 1861. Even at the Seminary of Quebec English was taught in preference to all other languages.[61] The élites in both the Acadian and French Canadian communities had perforce to be fluently bilingual.

Of course, to a considerable extent the appeal of English was that it was also the language used by Americans. Indeed, it would be foolish to deny that there was much that was 'American' in the culture of British North America. The material culture of both the United States and British North America was shaped by the same imperatives and was remarkably similar on both sides of what remained a remarkably porous border.[62] British North Americans were willing to sell to American markets and buy American imports if they were cheaper than British. They borrowed capital and technology from both sources. But those who see the border as almost meaningless ignore the selectivity with which British North Americans chose which aspects of American culture to adopt. Indeed, what is sometimes seen as American culture was frequently part of a shared Anglo-American culture. Anti-slavery movements flourished on both sides of the Atlantic in the mid-nineteenth century and so did the temperance movement. In British North America these movements were usually led by British immigrants who had participated in similar movements in Britain, even if they were strengthened by a flow of lecturers and literature from the United States.[63] Moreover, historians have for too long fallen into the trap of assuming a crude dichotomy between liberal or radical influences emanating from the United States and conservative influences emanating from Great Britain. In fact, there were conservatives and radicals in both societies and, while British North Americans preferred British constitutional models, they drew eclectically upon both British and American experience for their institutions and for sources of political inspiration. No intelligent British North American denied that their society must inevitably be both American and British.[64] Indeed, the British immigrants who were drawn to British North America were drawn by the same promises of social mobility and material betterment as those who went to the United States, and they had no desire to recreate the social and political structure they had left behind. They wished to remain British, but British in their own way.

The very term 'British' is, of course, fraught with difficulties, for Britain had only come into being with the union of England and Scotland in 1707, and Ireland was not integrated into that union until 1801. British historians have themselves recently remembered that Britain was never one nation but four, each of which was in turn subdivided by regional and local peculiarities. British North America drew its emigrants from all four, although disproportionately from Ireland and Scotland.[65] One prominent Canadian historian has even argued that ethnic historians should avoid the term 'British' altogether since it is a 'semantic nest' of limited analytical value.[66] In fact, this seems akin to throwing out the baby with the bathwater. As Linda Colley has persuasively argued, the idea of being British had become increasingly common by the early decades of the nineteenth century.[67] Indeed, except in Ireland most Britons by the middle decades of the nineteenth century did not see as incompatible their allegiance to imperial Britain and their sense of a more limited ethnic identity. British emigrants carried these attitudes with them across the Atlantic and when they sang 'Rule Britannia', as they undoubtedly frequently did, it was themselves they saw as ruling the waves and never being slaves. Undeniably 'Britishness' is an elusive concept that meant different things to different people at different times, but then so do all national identities.

Canadian (and British imperial) historians have a tendency to dismiss such sentiments as representing merely the effusions of collaborationist élites. Certainly such attitudes were more strongly held by those who were the most substantial beneficiaries of the imperial tie, but they were by no means confined to them. Moreover, the very term 'collaboration' has negative connotations. It is a term which always had greater relevance in the colonies where small British élites ruled over large numbers of non-British peoples and even there it is a concept of limited analytical value. In the colonies of settlement it has virtually no value, for the British settlers did not see themselves as collaborators but as partners with Britons at home.[68] The long debate over the question of extending responsible government to the colonies destroyed the faith of a minority of British North Americans in this partnership, but only temporarily, for the British government ultimately yielded to colonial pressure and thus gave to the colonists the ability to run their own affairs.[69] This sense of partnership was also challenged by the unilateral British decision to move to free trade in the 1840s, but again only temporarily as Britain responded to colonial pressures for the abolition of the Navigation Acts and assisted British North Americans in negotiating a reciprocity agreement with the United States. In Lower Canada the fear of the British minority that they would be abandoned by the British government to the mercies of a French-dominated Assembly had conditioned their commitment to the imperial connection in the 1830s. When the Union of the Canadas seemed to deliver them into the hands of a government dominated by French Canadians, there was a serious outburst of anger against imperial authority in 1849, but that too was short-lived as it became apparent that the leaders of the dominant group in French Canada had abandoned the goal of creating a separate or at least quasi-separate state and that, indeed, many of them were as enthusiastic Anglophiles as the British themselves. In the early 1850s one visitor to Montreal noted: 'As for the "annexation" movement of a few years ago, the mention of it now excites a smile; and if universal opinion is to be trusted, those who, in a moment of temporary irritation, were most forward in it, are the last to wish to hear any allusion to the subject.'[70]

Many of the British emigrants who came to British North America did not, of course, choose British North America over the United States because they wished to remain under the British flag. As Don Akenson rightly argues,

> Probably most people who migrated before the Famine – mostly individuals with some financial resources, information on alternative opportunities, and the will to act decisively to better their chances in life – found the constitutional niceties and geopolitical boundaries to be a virtual irrelevance.[71]

Yet to argue from most to all is a dangerous habit. It may have been a historic accident that Irish Protestants formed a majority of the Irish emigrants to British North America in the period after 1815 but only around 20 per cent of the Irish who went to the United States, but it seems a most unlikely one. Moreover, the disproportionate number of Highlanders among the Scottish migrants to British North America may have simply reflected the drawing power of the Scottish communities in British North America, not any wider imperial loyalty, but given the substantial component of military men who settled in those communities and the marked loyalty the inhabitants would show during times of tension with the United States, it seems likely that the process of migration was not entirely devoid of ideological considerations. Many of the English emigrants who came to British North America following the Napoleonic Wars had also served in British regiments. It is true that they were induced to settle in British North America by the favourable terms upon which land was granted to veterans, but that so many accepted these inducements probably reflects some desire to remain within the Empire. Indeed, it was a desire to return to live under the British flag which at least in part motivated Peter Brown and his son George (a future Father of Confederation) to abandon New York, where they had lived for several years, and to move to Upper Canada in 1843.[72] By the 1850s those British emigrants who chose Canada over the United States were, in fact, frequently making a very clear choice. This was particularly true of the second (and smaller) wave of half-pay officers who migrated to British North America in the aftermath of the

Crimean War.[73] But it was also probably true of a substantial number of those who had a choice between joining relatives and friends in the United States or in British North America.

Indeed, the border by the 1840s had taken on a much harder meaning. In his recent study of American–Canadian relations Reginald Stuart argues that Canadian historians have exaggerated the hostility of the United States to the existence of British North America. Until the end of the War of 1812–14 the central theme of American foreign policy, he postulates, was 'defensive expansionism'. In other words a defensive strategy dictated the offensives that the Americans launched against Canada in 1812–14 rather than a desire for territorial expansion *per se*. After 1814, the Americans no longer feared the British nor did they pursue an aggressively expansionist policy towards British North America. 'Continentalism', Stuart declares, 'took the form of confidence in the flow of history. It was a fancy, rather than a policy to be pursued.'[74] Stuart's arguments are impressively marshalled but at best his case for a revisionist interpretation of American objectives merits the Scottish verdict of 'not proven'. Indeed, to the British government and to British North Americans who lived in fear of American expansionism such arguments would have appeared ludicrous. The British certainly did not accept American intentions as either defensive or benign, which is why they expended vast sums of money on the defence of British North America and ultimately why they so strongly pushed for colonial union.[75] To Canadians, particularly Upper Canadians, memories of the War of 1812–14 and fears of another invasion lingered on after 1814.[76] The conflict along the border which followed the abortive rebellions of 1837 hardened the latent fears of American aggression. Indeed, as one perceptive British visitor noted, the border troubles of 1838–9 were 'useful, in preventing, far more effectively than any political reasoning or even abstract feelings of patriotism could do, all undue "sympathy" between the Canadians and Americans, a sympathy which might otherwise have become dangerous to British connexion'.[77] The Maritimes were less directly affected by these events but the Maine–New Brunswick boundary dispute led to violence and Maritimers were aware that if the Canadas were lost to the Empire, their chances of survival were slim. Moreover, all British North Americans shared anxiety over American intentions during the last stages of the American Civil War and both regions suffered from the Fenian raids. In retrospect, Canadian historians, most of whom have never lived in a society whose soil has been invaded, are inclined to dismiss all these incidents as amusing rather than threatening. After all, few lives were lost and the enthusiasm and anger displayed by those British North American volunteers who sprang to meet a non-existent threat now seem more comic than heroic. But hindsight is a luxury reserved for historians. From the 1830s until the 1870s British North Americans felt threatened, and not without justification. In turn, the American threat seemed to make the British connection all the more necessary and desirable. However, it did not create that sentiment; it merely reinforced it.

What was gradually being eroded among the British-born and their native-born descendants was not their sense of being British but their sense of being English, Irish, Scottish and Welsh. It is ironic that historians who are aware of the problematical meaning of Britishness and are reluctant to use the term do not see similar difficulties with describing people as English, Irish, Scottish or Welsh, even though those terms are equally vague and problematical; they too meant different things to different people at different times, and they too have undergone a process of continual reinterpretation. Undeniably the British emigrants who came out to British North America would have defined themselves as English, Irish, Scottish or Welsh. Also undeniable is the fact that most of them moved as part of a chain migration that linked them to friends and family at home and friends and family in the place to which they migrated. For the emigrants the bonds created by ethnicity were a critical part of what has accurately been described as their 'human capital', for it was relatives and friends of the same ethnic origin who assisted them in the process of migration and adjustment to a new environment. But because migrants naturally gravitate towards settlements of friends and family, it does not follow that they necessarily have a strong sense of belonging to a distinctive national culture which they are determined to preserve. Moreover, migration is a homogenizing experience. Even during the transatlantic crossing emigrants frequently were mixed together with emigrants from other parts of the British Isles, and upon their arrival they rarely settled in self-contained ethnic communities and rarely worked or traded or even worshipped solely with members of the same ethnic group. In fact, most British emigrants settled among emigrants from other parts of the British Isles.[78] The first generation of most British emigrants came out as families or married people of the same ethnic origin, but over time there would be considerable intermarriage between these groups and the descendants of the pre-1815 emigrants, and ethnic loyalties would be confused and blended. This was particularly true among Protestants, since religion was a greater barrier to intermarriage than ethnicity. Even among the first generation the sense of ethnic identity was frequently fluid. As memories of the ancestral home faded, increasing numbers of the emigrants and their descendants identified themselves as British North Americans (or after 1867 as British Canadians) with English, Irish, Scottish or Welsh ancestors.

For some groups the erosion came more quickly than among others. For the English-born and their children the transition was easiest because as the predominant partner in the forging of the British nation the English did not draw the distinction between being British and being English.

> It was instinctive for the English to regard the terms English and British as virtually synonymous; and the author who wrote in the early edition of the Encyclopaedia Britannica 'for Wales: see England' was only expressing an attitude of the English that they applied to other parts of the Celtic fringe.[79]

But this very attitude meant that the English emigrants rarely had a clear sense of a separate English identity that had to be nurtured and preserved. The Irish emigrants might celebrate St Patrick's Day and the Scots establish St Andrew's societies but there is relatively little evidence of the English celebrating their Englishness with the same determination in the British North American colonies. The Scots and the Irish might feel the need to proclaim the contribution they had made to the settlement of the colonies; the English rarely felt the need.[80] English emigrants rarely formed compact settlements, and they soon began to abandon even the regional variations that had so marked their cultural patterns at home. Indeed, a significant proportion of those counted as English in the census data were not descended directly from English emigrants but from the descendants of the earlier American emigrants who had begun to redefine their origins – quite enthusiastically – as English, and over time they were joined by a growing number of descendants of emigrants who had at least one parent from another part of the British Isles. But those who declared themselves to be English in this sense really did mean British.

Among those absorbed into the English core were the Welsh, who came in such comparatively small numbers that their communities quickly disappeared from sight, leaving few traces. For many Protestant Irish, who composed a majority of the Irish immigrants, the erosion of their Irishness also came fairly painlessly. For many of them Ireland was a place of unhappy memories. In describing her voyage across the Atlantic, one Irish Protestant noted that

> The hold was full of people, mighty smug and decent, with money in their pockets, going out to make their fortunes: and most of them Protestants, that found home growing too hot on them; and they had better save their poor bones, and their little earnings before it was too late.[81]

The Revd Thomas W. Magrath reported back to the Revd Thomas Radcliff, in January 1832, that

> When we contrast our peaceful and tranquil state here, with the turbulence of Ireland, our hearts overflow with gratitude to the Being who has cast our lot, where neither bars nor bolts are necessary, where neither Indian nor settler will molest; where we can leave our property lying carelessly around us, even in the solitude of the night, and where capital punishment has occurred only in three or four instances during many years.[82]

Not all Irish Protestants would have agreed with the Duke of Wellington, himself of Anglo-Irish origin, who is said to have dismissed his Irish ancestry 'with a telling analogy: being born in a stable does not make one a horse'.[83] But particularly for those Irish Protestants who had emigrated *en masse* from areas of Ireland which were predominantly Catholic and who had few relatives or friends left at home, Ireland was a place that had less and less relevance to their lives. Indeed, as tensions in Ireland mounted as Irish nationalists began to seek a repeal of the Union, peacefully if possible but by violent means if necessary, Irish Protestant settlers in British North America began to downplay their Irishness. In the 1820s and even the 1830s Irish Protestants and Irish Catholics frequently belonged to the same ethnic-based organizations, but by the 1840s Catholic Emancipation, the repeal movement and the tendency to define the Irish nation in Catholic terms had driven a wedge between Catholics and Protestants. Irish Protestants withdrew from the earlier ethnic-based organizations and participated with the other British groups in the formation of Orange Lodges to defend Protestantism and the British connection.[84] Whatever its ancestry, the Orange Lodge by mid-century had outgrown its ethnic roots in British North America: it was a British Canadian, not an Irish organization.[85] In his study of *Irish Migrants to the Canadas* Bruce Elliott concludes with the story of an exchange between the first- and second-generation members of two Irish Protestant families in western Ontario. John Atkinson, who had emigrated in 1837, published a poem expressing nostalgia for the land of his childhood, even though admitting that 'who is THERE left to greet me with one welcome smile?' In response Leonard Stanley, who was native-born, 'questioned how Atkinson could retain any affection for a land "tortured for ages/ With dynamite fiends spreading terror and woe . . . Away with you, Erin, I love you no more"'. As Elliott notes, both men viewed Ireland as British, but both accepted that their country was now Canada, which was in their minds also British. Even Atkinson's attachment 'was not to Ireland as a nation but to a fondly remembered boyhood home' and for Stanley not even nostalgia was left.[86]

For many Scottish migrants memories were less painful but over time they too began to think of British North America as home. 'We are now, of course, all Canadians', wrote a Scottish emigrant in 1845. 'I should fondly yet wish to see my old fatherland and friends there, although I could not make my home there.'[87] Indeed, for many of those who did return, the visit was disappointing. In 1856 an old Scots woman who had come from Glasgow twenty-one years earlier gave to a British visitor her opinion of 'the relative merits of *Glaskie* and *Cannady* – she infinitely preferring the latter'. She informed him that 'Two years ago she went to Scotland, but "didna just like it:" old friends were dead, their children did not care about her; when she rose in the morning felt cold and damp – could not breathe, and got the asthma'.[88] Current research suggests that the 'self-conscious awareness of belonging to a Scottish community seldom extended beyond a generation' and for many a process of fragmentation and dilution began 'much sooner than that'.[89] Highlanders undoubtedly clung to their roots more tenaciously than Lowlanders, particularly in heavily Scottish communities like those in Glengarry County and Cape Breton, but it should be remembered that much of what passes for traditional Highland culture today is part of an 'invented tradition'. When Frederic Cozzens went to Cape Breton in the late 1850s, he expected to see the 'bold Highwayman of romance', but he was disappointed.

It is true here were the Celts in their wild settlements, but without bagpipes or pistols, sporrans or philabegs . . . I have a reasonable amount of respect for a Highlandman in full costume: but for a carrot-headed, freckled, high-cheeked animal, in a round hat and breeches that cannot utter a word of English I have no sympathy.[90]

In fact, Highland traditions were rediscovered by Lowlanders in the nineteenth century, reintroduced into the Highlands and then exported to Scottish communities overseas, and the British military played a large part in spreading their popularity. The pipebands found throughout various parts of Canada today, the tartans so proudly worn by many Canadians who have never seen Scotland, even the famed Highland regiments were not necessarily part of an indigenous Highland culture in British North America.

Irish Catholics were undoubtedly to some extent a group apart. In the most detailed study yet done of marriage patterns in the pre-Confederation period, Peter Toner has shown that in New Brunswick in 1851 92 per cent of Irish Catholic men married women of their own ethnic group, compared to only 75 per cent of Irish Protestant males.[91] These conclusions are confirmed by a broader study of the Canadian population in 1871. Except for French Catholics (who chose their spouses almost exclusively from their own community), Irish Roman Catholics had the highest rates of endogamous marriages. Over 90 per cent of Irish-born Catholics had Irish wives, compared to 82·9 per cent for the Irish-born in general, 72·9 for the English-born and 76·2 for the Scottish-born. Second-generation Irish Catholic males still showed a strong propensity to marry wives of the same ethnic origin, although the proportion who did so had dropped to 79·3 per cent.[92] As Peter Toner argues, it is this high rate of endogamy, nurtured by religion and by a substantial degree of residential clustering, particularly in Saint John, which helps to explain why so many Irish Catholics preserved for longer than the other British groups in New Brunswick a sense of their distinctiveness. But New Brunswick was not, as Toner admits, necessarily typical of the Irish experience in British North America. Saint John did contain an unusually high concentration of Irish Catholics, and an unusually high proportion of them were refugees from the Great Famine. Even among New Brunswick Irish Catholics there were defections. Some simply changed their religion and became Protestants. A growing number married outside their own ethnic group, even though their rates of endogamy remained high compared to the children of other British emigrants. Outside New Brunswick the Irish sense of a separate identity seems to have been considerably weaker. The sheer scale of the Irish emigration to British North America, the fact that the bulk of the Irish emigrants came before – not after – the Great Famine, and the diffusion of the Irish geographically, socially and occupationally meant that ethnic fusion took place, even if delayed by the bitter religious disputes of the period. The Irish Catholic experience in British North America was, in fact, closer to that of Irish Catholics in the other colonies of British settlement, like Australia, than it was to that of the Irish in the United States.[93] For many Irish Catholics in British North America their Irishness became more and more peripheral and a growing number were prepared to identify themselves with the British majority. Canadian censuses after 1871 distorted this reality by insisting that Canadians define their ethnicity by reference to the first male ancestor who had set foot on Canadian soil. But for the grandchild of an Irish (or an English, Scottish or Welsh) emigrant whose parents had both been native-born and whose mother might have been from a different part of the British Isles or even the descendent of a pre-1815 American immigrant this probably meant remarkably little.

It may seem contradictory to argue that the British emigrants and their native-born offspring were becoming more British and yet more Canadian at the same time. Yet it is not. Allan Smith has persuasively argued that 'as early as the 1820s Upper Canadians had begun to think of their province, and the larger British North American society of which it was a part, as potentially a great nation within the Empire'. This conviction – that Upper Canada 'was to be understood not simply as an extension of British civilization in imperial province but as a community with a character and experience of its own' – was, he maintains, 'within forty years, matured into a belief that the territory Upper Canadians inhabited might function as the centre of a British North American civilization ripe for union within one political framework'.[94] As Smith rightly points out, critical in the formulation of a national identity was not only a sense of being a New World community but the sense of being a distinctive one, and what made their community distinctive, most British North Americans agreed, was not its North American-ness, but its British-ness. Indeed, British North American union was supported by most of the population of Canada West in the 1860s precisely because it seemed to offer the only means to secure a Canadian future within the Empire

– in other words to preserve Canada's Britishness.[95] My only argument with Smith is that, like so many Canadian historians, he accepts as a given that 'the national idea after 1867 was largely Ontario-created'.[96] This Ontario myopia blinds him to the fact that the process he is describing was common to all the British North American colonies. The fact that Confederation took place in the 1860s was undoubtedly due to a number of immediate political and economic factors, not the least of which was the American Civil War and the formation of the Great Coalition. But that it took place at all was because the majority of Maritimers shared with anglophone Canadians a common sense of being British North Americans and a desire to work out their national destiny within the framework of the second British Empire. Many Maritimers did not like the terms of union that the Canadians imposed upon them, but in the end they accepted that to remain British they must become Canadian.[97] This shared sense of being British was not simply, as Smith implies, an intellectual construct developed by Canadians to justify their national existence. It reflected a reality, a reality that had been created by those British emigrants who flooded into British North America after 1815 and made British North America *British* in fact as well as in name.

Notes

[1] The best overview of this period is J. M. Bumsted, 'The Cultural Landscape of Early Canada', in Bernard Bailyn and Philip D. Morgan (eds.), *Strangers within the Realm: Cultural Margins of the First British Empire* (Chapel Hill, 1991). For a detailed study of British emigration between 1763 and 1775, see Bernard Bailyn, *Voyagers to the West: Emigration from Britain to America on the Eve of the Revolution* (London, 1987).

[2] As Esther Clark Wright points out in her detailed study of *The Loyalists of New Brunswick* (Moncton, 1972), pp.151–67 about 90 per cent of the Loyalists who settled in New Brunswick were American-born and most of them belonged to families with deep roots in the Thirteen Colonies. Most of the Scots went to the areas of Nova Scotia which had already attracted Highland emigrants.

[3] For the difficulties of estimating their numbers, see Donald Harmen Akenson, *The Irish in Ontario: A Study in Rural History* (Kingston and Montreal, 1984), pp.110–12.

[4] K. M. McLaughlin, *The Germans in Canada* (Ottawa, 1985), p.7.

[5] W. N. Blane, *An Excursion Through the United States and Canada during the Years 1822–23* (London, 1824), p.441.

6   Howard Temperley (ed.), *Gubbins' New Brunswick Journals 1811 & 1813* (Fredericton, 1980), p.67.

7   J. McGregor, *Historical and Descriptive Sketches of the Maritime Colonies of British America* (London, 1828), p.198.

8   Temperley (ed.), *Gubbins' Journals*, p.78.

9   Graeme Wynn, 'A Region of Scattered Settlements and Bounded Possibilities: Northeastern America 1775–1800', *Canadian Geographer*, 31, 4 (1987), 323.

10 Frederic S. Cozzens, *Acadia: or, A Month with the Blue Noses* (New York, 1859), p.199.

11 Temperley (ed.), *Gubbins' Journals*, p.22.

12 John MacTaggart, *Three Years in Canada: An Actual Account of the Country in 1826–7–8* (London, 1829), I, pp.207–8.

13 This was true even of a prominent Loyalist like Jonathan Odell. See Cynthia Dubin Edelberg, *Jonathan Odell: Loyalist Poet of the American Revolution* (Durham, NC, 1987), p.155.

14 Reginald C. Stuart, *United States Expansionism and British North America, 1775–1871* (Chapel Hill and London, 1988), p.53. See also the essays in Stephen Hornsby, Victor A. Konrad and James J. Herlan (eds.), *The Northeastern Borderlands: Four Centuries of Interaction* (Fredericton, 1989), which includes my own 'The Borderlands Concept: A Critical Appraisal', pp.152–8.

15 McGregor, *Historical and Descriptive Sketches of the Maritime Colonies*, p.70. John Goldie makes a similar point about the Scots of Glengarry in *Diary of a Journey Through Upper Canada and Some of the New England States, 1819* (Toronto, 1897), p.8.

16 The best overview is J. M. Bumsted, *The People's Clearance: Highland Emigration to British North America, 1770–1815* (Edinburgh and Winnipeg, 1982), but see also Marianne McLean, *The People of Glengarry: Highlanders in Transition, 1745–1820* (Montreal and Kingston, 1991) and Marjorie Harper, *Emigration from North-East Scotland, I: Willing Exiles* (Aberdeen, 1988). For a critique of Bumsted's view that the movement across the Atlantic was voluntary, see T. M. Devine, 'Landlordism and Highland Emigration', in T. M. Devine (ed.), *Scottish Emigration and Scottish Society* (Edinburgh, 1992), pp.89–100.

17 Captain W. Moorsom, *Letters from Nova Scotia: Comprising Sketches from a Young Country* (London, 1830), p.308.

18 The quotation drawn from a local newspaper is cited in Graeme Wynn, '1800–1809: Turning the Century', in P. A. Buckner and John G. Reid (eds.), *The Atlantic Region to Confederation: A History* (Toronto, 1994), p.210.

19 James S. Buckingham, *Canada, Nova Scotia, New Brunswick . . .* (London, [1843]), pp.144–5. In fact, if Buckingham is correct about the date, the British in Montreal were in advance of their countrymen in England. In Great Yarmouth a column to honour Nelson was planned in 1805 but abandoned in 1807, when the subscription failed, and not finally

completed until 1819. See Alison Yarrington, *The Commemoration of the Hero 1800–1864: Monuments to the British Victors of the Napoleonic Wars* (New York and London, 1988), p.xii.

[20] Bumsted, 'The Cultural Landscape of Early Canada', 379, 392.

[21] The best overview of the emigrants remains Helen I. Cowan, *British Emigration to British North America: The First Hundred Years*, rev. and enlarged edn (Toronto, 1961). For the number of migrants, see p.288. Similar figures are given for 1815–1853 in N. H. Carrier and J. R. Jeffrey, *External Migration: A Study of the Available Statistics, 1815–1950* (London, 1953), but without explanation they give two figures for 1853 and lower figures than Cowan for every year after 1853.

[22] According to the 1871 census of Canada people of German origin (which would have included the descendants of the 'Foreign Protestants' and of some Loyalists and late Loyalists) formed 5·8 per cent of the Canadian population. The next largest groups were people of Dutch, Scandinavian, Italian and Polish origin, who formed only 0·9, 0·05, 0·03 and 0·02 per cent of the population. I have taken these figures from Madeline A. Richard, *Ethnic Groups and Marital Choices: Ethnic History and Marital Assimilation in Canada, 1871 and 1971* (Vancouver, 1991), p.44.

[23] I have taken these calculations from table I in Lloyd G. Reynolds, *The British Immigrant: His Social and Economic Adjustment in Canada* (Toronto, 1935), p.26.

[24] See Peter Moogk, 'Reluctant Exiles: Emigrants from France in Canada before 1760', *William and Mary Quarterly*, 3rd ser., xlvi (1989), 463–505.

[25] In making these calculations and those that follow, I have included only the totals for the colonies of PEI, Cape Breton (which would be reamalgamated into Nova Scotia in 1820), Nova Scotia, New Brunswick, and Upper and Lower Canada (which would be united into one province in 1841) in 1815 and 1861. In fact, I have excluded Newfoundland from the discussion because its history is entirely different from that of the other colonies, which is the main reason why it did not join Canada until 1949. Similarly I have excluded the area west of the Great Lakes because its formative period of development really began after 1860. Thus when I refer to British North America or the British North American colonies, I am using a restricted definition.

[26] Some estimates of return emigration are made in Frances Morehouse, 'Canadian Migration in the Forties', *Canadian Historical Review*, 9 (1928), 310–11.

[27] In his detailed analysis of *Immigration to and Emigration from Nova Scotia 1815–1838* (Halifax, 1942), J. S. Martell points out that the two groups most prone to emigrate to the United States were 'the descendants of the Pre-Loyalists and the newly arrived Irish' (p.30).

[28] In the Maritimes New Brunswick probably attracted the most American immigrants but even there the number of colonists who come from foreign

(i.e. non-British) territories – in fact, largely from the United States – formed a mere 3 per cent of those born outside the province in 1851. See Graeme Wynn, 'New England's Outpost in the Nineteenth Century', in Hornsby, Konrad and Herlan (eds.), *The Northeastern Borderlands*, p.71, n. 28.

29 See Reynolds, *The British Immigrant*, table II, p.27.

30 See, for example, Akenson, *The Irish in Ontario*, a detailed study of the settlement of Leeds and Lansdowne townships in Upper Canada.

31 For a more detailed examination of the Maritimes during this period, see my 'The Transformation of the Maritimes, 1800–1867', *London Journal of Canadian Studies*, 9 (1993), 13–30.

32 See T. W. Acheson, 'A Study in the Historical Demography of a Loyalist County', *Social History/Histoire Sociale*, 1 (April 1968), 53–65.

33 By 1851 the majority of the heads of households in the city were of Irish origin. See T. W. Acheson, 'The Irish Community in Saint John, 1815–1850', in P. M. Toner (ed.), *New Ireland Remembered: Historical Essays on the Irish in New Brunswick* (Fredericton, 1988), p.28.

34 Quoted in Murray Barkley, 'The Loyalist Tradition in New Brunswick: The Growth and Evolution of an Historical Myth, 1825–1914', *Acadiensis*, iv, 2 (Spring 1975), 20.

35 See Charlotte Erickson, *Invisible Immigrants: The Adaptation of English and Scottish Immigrants in 19th-Century America* (Ithaca and London, 1972).

36 See Charlotte Erickson, 'Emigration from the British Isles to the U.S.A. in 1831', *Population Studies*, 35 (1975), 182–3, 196.

37 D. Fitzpatrick, *Irish Emigration, 1801–1921* (n.p., 1984), pp.8–9.

38 Eric Richards, 'Varieties of Scottish Emigration in the Nineteenth Century', *Historical Studies*, 21 (1985), 492, and 'Voices of British and Irish Emigrants in Nineteenth-Century Australia', in Colin G. Pooley and Ian D. Whyte (eds.), *Migrants, Emigrants and Immigrants: A Social History* (London, 1991), p.21.

39 This is the theme of Peter A. Russell, *Attitudes to Social Structure and Mobility in Upper Canada 1815–1840: 'Here We Are Laird Ourselves'* (Queenston, 1989). See also his 'Upper Canada: A Poor Man's Country? Some Statistical Evidence', in Donald H. Akenson (ed.), *Canadian Papers in Rural History*, III (Gananoque, Ont. 1982), pp.129–47.

40 Even a glance at the volumes of the *Dictionary of Canadian Biography* reveals the extent to which the British emigrants and their offspring had come to dominate the provincial élites by the middle decades of the nineteenth century.

41 Buckingham, *Canada, Nova Scotia, New Brunswick*, p.128.

42 See my entry on 'Sir Charles Tupper', in *Dictionary of Canadian Biography*, XIV (forthcoming); John MacGregor, *Our Brothers and Cousins: A Summer Tour in Canada and the States* (London, 1859), p.30.

43 R. H. Girdwood, 'The Influence of Scotland on North American Medicine', in D. A. Dow (ed.), *The Influence of Scottish Medicine: An*

Historical Assessment of its International Impact (Carnforth, 1988), pp.41–2.

[44] MacGregor, *Our Brothers and Cousins*, p.13.

[45] J. G. Kohl, *Travels in Canada, and through the States of New York and Pennsylvania* (London, 1861), I, p.115.

[46] George Tuthill Borrett, *Out West: A Series of Letters from Canada and the United States* (London, 1866), p.169.

[47] Henry J. Morgan, *The Place British Americans Have Won in History: A Lecture* (Ottawa, 1866), p.10.

[48] Ibid., pp.3, 17–18; Andrew Learmont Spedon, *Rambles among the Blue-Noses: or, Reminiscences of a Tour through New Brunswick and Nova Scotia, during the Summer of 1862* (Montreal, 1863), p.50.

[49] [Egerton Ryerson], *Remarks on the Historical Mis-statements and Fallacies of Mr. Goldwin Smith* (Toronto, 1966), pp.3, 12, 15.

[50] Eva-Marie Kroller, *Canadian Travellers in Europe, 1851–1900* (Vancouver, 1987), p.4.

[51] A. W. Rasporich, 'Imperial Sentiment in the Province of Canada during the Crimean War, 1854–1856', in W. L. Morton (ed.), *The Shield of Achilles: Aspects of Canada in the Victorian Age* (Toronto, 1968), p.140.

[52] Gardner D. Engleheart, *Journal of the Progress of H.R.H. The Prince of Wales through British North America . . .* (privately printed, n.d.), pp.14–15, 21, 34, 42–4, 56, 69.

[53] Kinahan Cornwallis, *Royalty in the New World: Or, The Prince of Wales in America* (London, 1860), pp.39, 47–8.

[54] Many, but not all, Irish Catholics admired O'Connell and repeal associations existed in all the major urban centres. In 1843, for example, the repeal association in Halifax had 386 members and arranged for money to be sent to aid O'Connell. Terence M. Punch, *Irish Halifax: The Immigrant Generation* (Halifax, 1981), pp.32–3.

[55] G. Murray Logan, *Scottish Highlanders and the American Revolution* (Halifax, 1976), p.122.

[56] K. G. Pryke, 'John Boyd', in *Dictionary of Canadian Biography*, X (Toronto, 1972), p.85. I was directed to this source and to the next reference by comments in Ian Ross Robertson, 'The 1850s: Maturity and Reform', in Buckner and Reid (eds.), *The Atlantic Region to Confederation*, p.358.

[57] Ursula Bohman, 'The Germans: The Protestant Buffer', in Douglas F. Campbell (ed.), *Banked Fires: The Ethnics of Nova Scotia* (Port Credit, Ont., 1978), p.185.

[58] McLaughlin, *The Germans in Canada*, p.9.

[59] See Peter M. Toner, 'The Irish of New Brunswick at Mid-Century', in Toner (ed.), *New Ireland Remembered*, p.129 and Karen P. Corrigan, '"For God's Sake, Teach the Children English": Emigration and the Irish Language in the Nineteenth Century', in Patrick O'Sullivan (ed.), *The Irish World Wide: History, Heritage, Identity* (Leicester, 1992), I: *Patterns of Migration*, ch. 6.

[60] R. MacLean, 'The Highland Catholic Tradition in Canada', in W. Stanford Reid (ed.), *The Scottish Tradition in Canada* (Toronto, 1976), p.110.

[61] Kohl, *Travels in Canada*, I, pp.135, 202.

[62] See Graeme Wynn, 'Settler Societies in Geographical Focus', *Historical Studies*, 20 (1982–3), 353–66.

[63] See Allen P. Stouffer, *The Light of Nature and the Law of God: Antislavery in Ontario* (Montreal and Kingston, 1992), esp. pp.4 and 172.

[64] See Daniel John Keon, 'The "New World" Idea in British North America: An Analysis of some British Promotional, Travel and Settler Writings, 1784–1860', Ph.D. thesis, Queen's University, 1984.

[65] A breakdown of the pattern of emigration is given in my *English Canada: The Founding Generations, 1815–1860: British Migration to British North America*, Canada House Lecture no. 54 (London, 1993).

[66] Akenson, *The Irish in Ontario*, p.6. Akenson makes the same point even more forcefully in *Half the World from Home: Perspectives on the Irish in New Zealand 1860–1950* (Wellington, 1990), pp.7–10 where he declares that the term 'British' is of 'limited value' and its use 'inhibits specificity of thought'. Yet his decision to avoid the term forces him to fall back on the less precise and utterly ahistorical term 'Anglo-Celtic'. However, in a more recent study on *Occasional Papers on the Irish in South Africa* (Grahamstown, 1991), which I only had a chance to read after completing this chapter, Akenson accepts that there did exist in the colonies something 'not found in Britain' – 'a new synthetic "British" (or "English") culture' (pp.46, 99–100).

[67] Linda Colley, *Britons: Forging the Nation, 1701–1837* (New Haven and London, 1992).

[68] For fuller discussion of these issues, see my 'Whatever Happened to the British Empire', Presidential Address delivered to the Annual Meeting of the Canadian Historical Association (Ottawa, 1993), *Journal of the Canadian Historical Association*, 4 (1994), 3–32.

[69] See P. A. Buckner, *The Transition to Responsible Government: British Policy in British North America, 1815–1850* (Westport, Conn., 1985).

[70] Hugh Seymour Tremenheere, *Notes on Public Subjects, Made during a Tour in the United States and Canada* (London, 1852), p.232.

[71] Akenson, *The Irish in Ontario*, p.23.

[72] J. M. S. Careless, *Brown of the Globe*, I: *The Voice of Upper Canada, 1815–1859* (Toronto, 1959), p.23.

[73] Patrick A. Dunae, *Gentlemen Emigrants: From the Public Schools to the Canadian Frontier* (Vancouver, 1981), p.31.

[74] Stuart, *United States Expansionism and British North America*, pp.64, 83.

[75] See C. P. Stacey, *Canada and the British Army, 1846–1871*, rev. edn. (Toronto, 1963).

[76] As John Goldie found when he visited Upper Canada in 1819. See his *Diary of a Journal*, p.16.

[77] John Robert Godley, *Letters from America* (London, 1844), I, p.146.

The same point was made by Charles Richard Weld in his *A Vacation Tour in the United States and Canada* (London, 1855), p.158.

[78] An index of dissimilarity for 1871, which reveals the percentage of one population that would have to be relocated to produce a national distribution identical to that of another population, shows clearly that the bulk of the British immigrants lived in overlapping jurisdictions, compared with the much higher degree of concentration of other ethnic groups, particularly the French Canadians. See Richard, *Ethnic Groups and Marital Choices*, table 2, p.74.

[79] D. G. Boyce, '"The Marginal Britons": The Irish', in Robert Colls and Philip Dodd (eds.), *Englishness: Politics and Culture 1880–1920* (London, 1980), p.231.

[80] For example, see Nicholas Flood Davin, *The Irishman in Canada* (Toronto, 1877) and W. J. Rattray, *The Scot in British North America*, 4 vols. (Toronto, 1880). As far as I am aware no similar book was produced on the English.

[81] Bridget Lacey to Mary Thompson, August 1832, printed in the Revd Thomas Radcliff (ed.), *Authentic Letters from Upper Canada* (Toronto, 1953), p.99. The editor points out the name Bridget Lacey is a pseudonym but insists the letter is authentic.

[82] Printed ibid., pp.67–8.

[83] Patrick O'Farrell, *The Irish in Australia* (Kensington, NSW, 1987), p.5.

[84] See T. W. Acheson, 'The Irish Community in Saint John' and Scott See, 'The Orange Order and Social Violence in New Brunswick', in Toner (ed.), *New Ireland Remembered*, pp.32–9, and Michael Cottrell, 'St. Patrick's Day Parades in Nineteenth-Century Toronto: A Study of Immigrant Adjustment and Elite Control', *Social History*, xxv (May 1992), 60–1.

[85] See Cecil J. Houston and William J. Smyth, *Irish Emigration and Canadian Settlement: Patterns, Links and Letters* (Toronto and Belfast, 1990), pp.180–7.

[86] Bruce S. Elliott, *Irish Migrants in the Canadas: A New Approach* (Kingston and Montreal, 1988), pp.242–3.

[87] Quoted in Edward J. Cowan, 'From the Southern Uplands to Southern Ontario: Nineteenth-Century Emigration from the Scottish Borders', in Devine, *Scottish Emigration and Scottish Society*, p.74.

[88] William H. G. Kingston, *Western Wanderings: Or, A Pleasure Tour in the Canadas* (London, 1856), I, p.145.

[89] Cowan, 'From the Southern Uplands to Southern Ontario', 75.

[90] Cozzens, *Acadia*, pp.199–200.

[91] Peter M. Toner, 'The Irish of New Brunswick at Mid-Century: The 1851 Census', in Toner (ed.), *New Ireland Remembered*, p.115.

[92] See Richard, *Ethnic Groups and Marital Choices*, tables 10 and 14, pp.109 and 116.

[93] For some useful comparisons, see Oliver Macdonagh, 'The Irish in Australia: A General View', in Oliver MacDonagh and W. F. Mandle

(eds.), *Ireland and Irish-Australia: Studies in Cultural and Political History* (London, 1986), pp.155–74. Unfortunately MacDonagh tends to treat North America as a unit and thus fails to see the parallels between the Australian and Canadian Irish experiences. On Irish attitudes in the United States, see Kirby Miller, *Emigrants and Exiles: Ireland and the Irish Exodus to North America* (Oxford, 1985).

[94] Allan Smith, 'Old Ontario and the Emergence of a National Frame of Mind', in F. H. Armstrong, H. A. Stevenson and J. D. Wilson (eds.), *Aspects of Nineteenth-Century Ontario* (Toronto, 1974), p.194.

[95] See ibid., pp.204–10.

[96] Ibid., p.194.

[97] For a discussion of the attitudes of Maritimers to Confederation, see my 'The Maritimes and Confederation: A Reassessment', *Canadian Historical Review*, lxxi (1990), 1–30, and 'The 1860s: An End and a Beginning', in Buckner and Reid (eds.), *The Atlantic Region to Confederation*, pp.360–86.

3

Maps and Boundaries: Canada in Anglo-American Relations

M. E. CHAMBERLAIN

This chapter could perhaps be more accurately entitled 'Canada in Anglo-Franco-American Relations' because it is a study of the role Canada played in the complex web of British diplomatic relations in the middle of the nineteenth century when Britain was both an important player in the delicate balance of power in Europe and the centre of a world-wide Empire with global commitments. It also, incidentally, reveals something of the underside of European diplomacy in early Victorian times which, far from being more gentlemanly or more straightforward than that which emerged in the era of Bismarckian *realpolitik* or the ideological conflicts of the twentieth century, was often Byzantine in its complexity. This is rarely apparent from the official records alone but, when these are brought together with private papers, the truth often begins to appear.

Its history means that Canada cannot escape from relations with France, with Britain and with the United States. When I first visited the restaurant at the top of Mont Réal (the 'Mountain') in Montreal, I was startled by the murals which depicted French North America – startled because I had been brought up in the English tradition which did not recognize many of those claims. The English, in fact, had spent much of the eighteenth century fighting such pretensions. The last thing they wanted was French territory stretching down behind their Thirteen Colonies, with the French poised to push the English colonists into the sea. It was therefore ironic that, in the nineteenth century, the English were very happy to accept the full extent of the French claims in certain vital border areas in their disputes with the United States.

I first became interested in the north-east boundary dispute when I was writing my doctoral thesis in Oxford on the policy of the fourth Earl of Aberdeen as Sir Robert Peel's foreign secretary in the early 1840s. My interest then was in whether there was any truth in Lord Palmerston's charges that Aberdeen was a weak foreign secretary, who allowed British interests to be trampled on by foreigners. At the time, Palmerston had little success in pressing the charge. When the Ashburton–Webster Treaty, which settled the north-east boundary dispute among other things, came up for debate in the House of Commons, Palmerston had the humiliation of seeing the House 'counted out' (adjourned for lack of a quorum) while he was trying to make his case.[1] Later, however, when I came to work on colonization in general, and the case of Canada in particular, my interest shifted to the question of whether there was any justification for Canadian suspicions that their interests were always likely to be sacrificed for more general foreign-policy considerations. Such suspicions played their part both in Canadian Confederation in 1867 and in Canada's later wish to develop her own diplomatic service and control of foreign policy.

Anglo-American relations were certainly fraught in 1841. Aberdeen's predecessor at the Foreign Office had been Palmerston himself and Palmerston had contrived to embroil Britain in serious quarrels with both France and the United States. The quarrel with France had centred on the Eastern Question and rival claims to exercise influence in the declining Turkish Empire. Simultaneous quarrels with France and the United States, both significant naval powers, raised fears in some quarters of the revival of the coalition of 1778, which had led to Britain's defeat in the American War of Independence.[2]

Difficulties with the United States were more diverse than those with France but came together about 1840 to create a general crisis. Apart from the boundary questions (the so-called 'Oregon' boundary – that is, the frontier west of the Rocky Mountains – was in dispute as well as the north-east boundary), there was the problem of the slave-trade. Both Britain and the United States had independently prohibited the slave-trade in 1807. Slavery had been abolished in the British Empire in 1833 but, in the 1840s, it was still legal in the United States. There were always suspicions among British abolitionists that American opinion, and even the American government, were prepared to turn a blind eye to the trade to keep their plantations supplied. The Americans on their side suspected that, in the event of war, the British would not scruple to try to raise a slave revolt in the southern states. One belligerent Englishman did indeed write that they would need to send few troops, if they sent a good supply of guns to Kentucky.

There was also the question of who would actually hunt down the slave vessels, which still left West Africa. Of the European powers, despite the general condemnation of the slave-trade at the Congress of Vienna in 1815, only Britain consistently kept a naval squadron on the West Africa station. But, under international law, British warships could only intercept and arrest British slavers. Attempts to get slave trading equated with piracy – international law allowed any warship to arrest a pirate, whatever flag he was flying – failed, partly because of American opposition. Britain did manage to sign right-of-search treaties with most European powers which at least allowed British warships to intercept foreign slavers and hand them over to the nation under whose flag they claimed to be sailing. What was particularly galling to British naval officers was that obvious slavers of various nationalities would run up the Stars and Stripes on the approach of a British warship, which made it illegal for the British ship to stop them. Individual British and American officers tried to get round this by common-sense arrangements on the spot. The Americans did, at least intermittently, keep warships on the African coast, and it would be grossly unfair to suggest that all Americans connived at the trade.

One such local arrangement was arrived at between Captain Tucker RN and Lieutenant Paine of the American navy in 1840. What the British were now asking for was what they called 'right of visit', that is, a limited right to stop a ship and check whether it was entitled to the flag it was flying. Unfortunately, the Tucker–Paine arrangement was repudiated by the American government, and it actually exacerbated the situation because, on the strength of it, the Royal Navy had stopped several ships which turned out to be American. The question became the subject of an acrimonious exchange of notes between Palmerston and Andrew Stevenson, the American envoy in London, himself a Virginian and a slave owner. In the course of it, Palmerston protested that, although Britain conceded she had no right to search an American ship, it was intolerable that 'a merchantman can exempt herself from search merely by hoisting a piece of bunting with the United States emblems and colours upon it'. Unfortunately, this came to be reported in the United States as Palmerston calling the American flag 'a piece of bunting'.[3]

Fuel was added to the flames, as so often at this time, by a fortuitous event. The British had never suggested that they had any right to interfere in America's purely domestic slave-trade, by which slaves might be shipped from one American port to another. In October 1841 a ship called the *Creole* sailed for New Orleans from Virginia with 135 slaves on board. The slaves mutinied, killed one white man and took the ship into Nassau in the Bahamas. The British detained the mutineers but set the other slaves free. Even the mutineers were eventually released.[4]

Equally exciting events had occurred on the Canadian borders. Some Americans still resented the presence of any British colony on the soil of North America and had no trouble persuading themselves that the Canadians wanted to be liberated. Their moment seemed to have come with those small-scale rebellions in Canada in 1837–8. There were a few filibustering raids over the border and, more importantly, some gun-running. In December 1837 the Canadians surprised an American steamer, the *Caroline*, suspected of gun-running, on the American side of the Niagara River. There was a fight. The *Caroline* was sunk and an American called Amos Durfee was killed. Both governments (that is, the British government in London and the federal government in Washington) were embarrassed about the matter and let it drop until, in November 1840, a Canadian, Alexander McLeod, was arrested in New York State, where he had gone on business, and accused of being concerned in the murder of Durfee. The British government then communicated a statement, which had been prepared at the time but not delivered because the Americans had been disinclined to press the matter, saying that the sinking of the *Caroline* was an act of state for which individual British citizens could not be held responsible. The matter then became entangled with states' rights, the Federal government protesting that they could not intervene because it was within the jurisdiction of New York State. Palmerston ordered the British minister in Washington, Henry Fox, to demand his passports and leave at once if McLeod was executed. In the end McLeod was acquitted but war had been very near.[5]

During the McLeod case, the government had changed in both Britain and America. Peel and Aberdeen had replaced Melbourne and Palmerston, and John Tyler and Daniel Webster had replaced Martin Van Buren and John Forsyth. Both new administrations were more conciliatory than their predecessors and the Americans signalled this when Webster replaced the intransigent Andrew Stevenson with Edward Everett, an Anglophile and a cultivated man, who formed a genuine friendship with the scholarly Aberdeen. Peel and Aberdeen resolved to put Anglo-American relations on a better footing and decided to send Lord Ashburton to Washington to try to settle all outstanding issues. Ashburton was an interesting choice of envoy. He was a banker, not a regular diplomat, a member of the House of Baring, with extensive American interests and himself married to an American wife. There had been some discussion as to whether the negotiations should take place in London or in Washington. Washington had been decided upon because the north-east boundary was now regarded as top of the agenda and it was recognized that easy communication with representatives of the states of Maine and Massachusetts might be important.

There is an interesting contrast to be made between Washington's attitude to Maine and Massachusetts and London's attitude towards New Brunswick, the other primarily interested party. Washington, recently reminded of the states' rights issue by the McLeod case, did not doubt that it would have to win the support of the two states. Maine and Massachusetts were invited to send delegations to Washington to take part in the negotiations, and Ashburton found the leader of the Maine commissioners, William Pitt Preble, who had many years experience of the dispute, his toughest adversary. The British government felt under no similar obligation to consult New Brunswick – not because it was indifferent to New Brunswick's interests but because it felt that they could be adequately spoken for by officials, military men and the British government itself. It was Ashburton, apparently acting largely on his own initiative, who asked for some New Brunswickers to come to Washington to brief him on the situation. The consultation was an entirely informal one. The New Brunswickers were more flexible on some points, such as freedom of navigation on the St John River, less so on others, such as jurisdiction over the Madawaska Settlements, than the British government. It would be untrue to suggest that the New Brunswickers had no influence but at the end of the day it was London's views which prevailed – although it is fair to remember that Preble too went home deeply disgusted at the settlement.[6]

What exactly was the north-east boundary? At the time of the Quebec Act in 1774, with French Canada safely in its hands and wishing to curb the rebellious Thirteen Colonies, the British government had extended Quebec to its furthest possible limits, pushing its southern boundary to the confluence of the Ohio and Mississippi rivers. This definition had not survived the American War of Independence. The boundary between Massachusetts and British North America was described in both the preliminary peace treaty of 1782 and the definitive treaty (the Treaty of Paris) of 1783. The boundary was described in words but no official map was annexed to either treaty. It was generally agreed that the negotiators in Paris had used an edition of Mitchell's map, first compiled in 1755, but which edition was uncertain.[7]

The relevant section of the Treaty of Paris laid down that the boundary was to run

> From the North West Angle of Nova Scotia, viz. That Angle which is formed by a line drawn due North from the Source of the Saint Croix River to the Highlands, along the said Highlands which divide those Rivers that empty themselves into the River St Lawrence from those which fall into the Atlantic Ocean, to the Northwesternmost Head of the Connecticut River; thence along the middle of that River to the 45th degree of North Latitude; from thence by a Line due West on the said latitude until it strikes the River Iroquois or Cataraquy; thence along the middle of the said River into Lake Ontario.

It sounds very precise but, in fact, the area was neither settled nor fully explored – by Europeans – in 1783. When the region became better known, it was difficult to reconcile the wording of the treaty with the geographical realities. The original negotiators must have had some doubts because, later in the treaty, they added further directions for finding the vital 'North West Angle of Nova Scotia', which, unfortunately, only served to further obscure the matter.[8] The first source of confusion was that no one was sure which of three rivers, running into Passamaquoddy Bay on the Bay of Fundy, was meant by the St Croix. There was also doubt as to which line of Highlands had been regarded as forming the watershed, although there was probably some deliberate obfuscation by the British, who claimed that rivers flowing into the Bay of Fundy could not be regarded as flowing into the Atlantic Ocean for the purposes of the treaty.

There had been a number of attempts to determine the meaning of the treaty. Negotiations under the terms of Jay's Treaty of 1794 reached a compromise about the identification of the River St Croix.

The British contention that the River Schoodic was meant was accepted, but its source was defined as being on its north-east branch, as the Americans wished. Unfortunately, a line drawn due north from this point did not meet the Highlands. (Only later did the Americans realize that, if they had accepted the British definition of the source on the western branch of the St Croix, their contention as to the location of the 'North West Angle' of Nova Scotia would have been strengthened.) Commissioners who met under article 5 of the Treaty of Ghent of 1814 failed to reach agreement about anything. In 1828 the matter was referred to the arbitration of the king of the Netherlands. He decided it was impossible to determine the intentions of the original negotiators and, in 1831, announced a compromise line. The British would have reluctantly accepted it, but the American government, under pressure from Maine and Massachusetts, rejected it.

During the 1830s, as the area began to be opened up, the matter became more urgent. It reached a climax in 1839 when American and Canadian lumberjacks confronted each other across the Aroostock River, a tributary of the St John within the disputed area, the Americans singing,

> Britannia shall not rule the Maine,
> Nor shall she rule the water;
> They've sung that song full long enough,
> Much longer than they oughter.[9]

The Nova Scotian legislature voted Credits and sang 'God Save the Queen', and New Brunswick and Maine mobilized their militias. By this time London and Washington were getting worried. The immediate crisis was smoothed over by a standstill agreement, but it was generally agreed that a long-term solution must be found.

When Aberdeen, who as the duke of Wellington's foreign secretary, 1828–30, had been concerned with preparing the papers for the king of the Netherlands' arbitration, returned to the Foreign Office in 1841, he was convinced that little more could be done to find out the intentions of the original treaty-makers. They must look for a compromise. (There is a story that Aberdeen's second son, Alexander, who had been sent to Canada with his regiment after the 1837 rebellion, told his father that the territory was useless because there were no salmon rivers in it. Alexander was a fanatical fisherman and his father did value his advice on various subjects, but it seems unlikely that this played much part in his opinion.)

In his original instructions to Ashburton, Aberdeen encouraged him to seek a conventional, that is, a compromise, line which would preserve the two points Aberdeen had identified as British interests, that is, the navigable portion of the St John River and control of the Madawaska Settlements, where Canadian jurisdiction was already established.[10] He does not seem to have shown these instructions to anyone but Peel, and when the duke of Wellington saw them, there was an explosion. The duke sat up all night writing three letters. The first asked for the recall of the instructions before Ashburton sailed, the second expressed the duke's indignation at not being consulted, but the third was a cogent and detailed criticism of Aberdeen's approach. The foreign secretary, he contended, had missed the whole strategic point of the dispute, the importance of which had been underlined by the rebellions of 1837–8. The Americans must be removed from the Highlands 'overlooking Quebec', and the road from Halifax, Nova Scotia, to Quebec, which was a vital line of communication when the St Lawrence was frozen in winter, must stay in British hands.[11] Faced by this barrage Aberdeen gave in and wrote to Ashburton, who was detained by bad weather in Yarmouth Roads, cancelling his instructions on the north-east boundary and telling him to await further instructions on that subject.[12]

The matter now came forward for the consideration of the whole British cabinet. Aberdeen, a conscientious man, went through all the material in the Foreign Office and, at the suggestion of the Cabinet, consulted various 'military authorities', Sir George Murray, the master general of the Ordinance, and three professional soldiers who had served in Canada, Sir James Kempt (governor-general, 1828–30), Sir Howard Douglas (governor of New Brunswick, 1823–31) and Lord Seaton (lieutenant-governor of Upper Canada, 1828–38). They did not entirely agree with Wellington. All wanted to keep the Americans off the Highlands south of Quebec, but Kempt, for example, thought that the road from Fredericton along the north bank of the St John would be too exposed in the event of hostilities to be of much use.[13]

With all this contradictory advice, Aberdeen was not ready with Ashburton's new instructions until the end of March. When Ashburton received them, he was reduced to despair. He felt that British demands had been tightened up to the point where there was no chance of success. He emphasized the precarious nature of the new administration and the need to get a settlement while Tyler and Webster were still in control. When the delegates of Maine and Massachusetts arrived they proved to be as intransigent as Ashburton had feared. Perhaps to counter this, Ashburton had listened to the New Brunswickers and was taking a stiffer line on the Madawaska Settlements (this 'happy and contented village' he called it to Webster on 21 June) than his home government had envisaged. Negotiations went on through a very hot Washington summer, which nearly killed Ashburton – at least if his own letters are to be believed.[14]

What finally broke the logjam? In a real sense, it was the affair of the maps, that is, the discovery of a number of maps, with apparent claims to authenticity, which supported the contention of one side or the other. Both governments were sceptical but both were obviously alarmed by the possibility that the other might be able to prove its case. There is little doubt that this played an important part in overcoming the intransigence of Maine and Massachusetts. The story is not new. A great deal leaked out at the time and fuelled the debate on whether the treaty had been a sell-out. The matter has been debated ever since, both by the actors in the drama and by historians, fascinated by a mystery story.[15]

Even so there remain some international aspects of the affair which have still not been fully told. For our present purpose, the important map is that which became known as the 'Red Line Map'. A distinguished American historian, a Harvard professor, Jared Sparks, who was pursuing his own researches into the history of the American War of Independence in the French official archives in Paris, found a letter from Benjamin Franklin to the comte de Vergennes dated 6 December 1782, that is six days after the signature of the preliminary peace treaty by the British and American negotiators. The letter read, 'Sir, I have the honour of returning herewith the Map your Excellency sent me Yesterday. I have marked with Strong Red Line, according to your desire, the Limits of the thirteen United States, as settled in the Preliminaries between the British and the American Plenipotentiarys.'

Ashburton told Aberdeen,

> On reading this letter Sparks went to the topographical department where there are 60,000 maps & charts but so well indexed & catalogued that he had no difficulty of finding the map. It is by d'Anville dated 1746 – and of size of about 18 inches – and has the red mark, referred to by Dr

Franklin of the exact boundaries of the United States, marked apparently by a hair pencil or a blunt pen. The line marked gives Great Britain more than what is claimed by our line, for beginning at the St Croix it runs carefully round all the tributaries of the St John so as to throw even the country round about Honeton into New Brunswick. It is evident that the division was by *rivers* and that, as we always maintained, the waters of the St John were intended to belong to G. Britain.

Sparks, who had rather expected to find evidence favouring his own government, was pardonably disconcerted by this discovery and hesitated for some time before taking any action. Eventually, he decided to lay the whole matter before Webster, which he did in the middle of February 1842.[16]

The map has now disappeared and American historians have tended to take the line that there is no firm evidence that it was Franklin's map. But people at the time certainly took it seriously and, in the spring of 1843, when the secret was beginning to leak out and the Ashburton–Webster Treaty (finally concluded in August 1842) was under attack, Aberdeen asked Henry Bulwer, the British charge in Paris, to try to find the map.[17]

At first Bulwer could find neither Franklin's letter to Vergennes nor the map. Aberdeen urged him to try again and this time the letter turned up, apparently misplaced in a file of correspondence between England and France instead of that between France and the United States. Armed with this, Bulwer went to the Map Department and, with M. Barbier, the head of the department, looked through every map 'three times'. But he could find only one d'Anville map of 1746. This certainly had the frontiers of the United States marked with a red line but, remarkably, the disputed part of the boundary was omitted altogether. 'The line', he told Aberdeen 'stops where the dispute begins, & yet this is the only map that corresponds as to date & authorship with the one described by Mr Sparks.' Barbier insisted that Sparks must have been mistaken since all their maps were complete and there was nothing corresponding to Sparks's map in the catalogue. Bulwer was driven to the conclusion that either Sparks had used a copyist, who had made a mistake or been guilty of deliberate misrepresentation, or the map Sparks had seen had been removed and the map shown to Bulwer substituted. The first possibility – the careless or dishonest copyist – seemed very unlikely given Sparks's reaction and his desire to serve his own country. Bulwer hinted that the alternative possibility, the deliberate substitution, was more likely. The suggestion was naturally coldly received by the French.[18]

Aberdeen thought the whole story 'singular', especially as Sparks had specifically said that the keeper of the archives had helped him to find the map. Aberdeen was now beginning to suspect an intrigue by the American minister in Paris, General Lewis Cass, an ambitious man, very prone to follow his own policy and a sworn enemy of Britain, who never forgot that he had fought against Britain in the War of 1812. He never achieved his ambition of becoming president, although he was secretary of state from 1857 to 1860. He felt particularly strongly on the freedom of the seas issue and had recently published a notoriously belligerent pamphlet on the right of visit.[19]

Bulwer, on Aberdeen's advice, asked Barbier for a formal written statement of the whole matter. Barbier protested that he could not give that without the consent of his superior, M. Miguet, the head of the Record Department. Bulwer, the bit now between his teeth, said that he would call on Miguet but, before he had a chance to do so, Barbier sent a message asking to see him again. Bulwer happened to be unwell, but a colleague went and was told that Barbier had found another map of 1746 which 'had been doubled into other maps differently headed'. When Bulwer was able to get to the office he was shown a 1746 map with a line on it which did correspond to that described by Sparks but differing in other respects. Sparks had specifically said that his map had no colouring on it, but this map had the Spanish possessions marked in yellow and the French in green. Bulwer spoke to Miguet, who said that Barbier was an honest man but had little method, and he (Miguet) believed his story that it had all been a muddle.[20]

Bulwer, after a careful study of the subject, decided that the map he had just been shown was unlikely to be Franklin's and he now doubted whether Franklin had been referring to a d'Anville map in any case. He based this argument on the contention that a d'Anville map would have been awkward for Franklin's purpose and would have been too large to be enclosed in a letter. But there had certainly been some concealment by what Aberdeen had termed 'the subordinate Gentry in the French office'. Bulwer was now being given yet another version of events. The map had not been inadvertently folded into another as he had been told. It had been put aside for someone who was looking at old maps of Louisiana, and forgotten. Bulwer was now coming to the conclusion that the map had belonged to Reynaud, but this would be 'as good authority as Franklin's' and must therefore be for Aberdeen's ear alone.[21]

The British government, having agreed a compromise line, certainly had no interest in proving that the original British claim was justified. In fact, by this time all sorts of maps were turning up with some plausible claim to relate to the 1782–3 negotiations. Some supported the British case such as the so-called Steuben–Webster map, which had belonged to Baron Steuben, who had been sent by George Washington to plan the taking over of the British posts on the Great Lakes. It subsequently came into the possession of Webster, who used it along with Sparks's map to put pressure on the commissioners of Maine and Massachusetts. Aberdeen instituted further enquiries and three maps came to light. One in the State Paper Office (now the Public Record Office) favoured the British claim; two, one in the King's Library (George III's Library which formed the nucleus of the British [Museum] Library) and one drawn by Faden, George III's geographer, in the Paris archives, favoured the American claim. It also came out that Palmerston had known of the existence of the map in the King's Library (usually then referred to as the British Museum map), which effectively spiked the Whigs' guns when they attacked Webster for concealing the Red Line Map and the conservatives for being deceived about it.

Who knew about the Red Line Map and when? One can dismiss the wilder charges of layer upon layer of intrigue within American politics, although plainly in an unstable administration everyone was manoeuvring for position.[22] But it is apparent both that British Secret Service money was involved and that Ashburton knew of Sparks's map before the date given in the official version of events. Officially, he was supposed to have learnt of it on 9 August, when the terms had been agreed and when it would have been absurd to have wrecked the whole treaty (which covered much more than the north-east boundary) to reopen a historical enquiry, which everyone had agreed could not be finally resolved.

Ashburton's letters of 9 and 13 August giving Aberdeen details of both Sparks's map and the Steuben–Webster map clearly refer back to other letters no longer extant.[23] This is very unusual. Aberdeen, the classicist and scholar, was most punctilious in preserving all his letters for posterity (much more so than Palmerston) but he did weed some of his correspondence before his death – and left careful instructions to his youngest son, who was his literary executor and had previously been his private secretary.[24] There was clearly an important postscript to Ashburton's letter of 14 June. The letter still exists but not the postscript apart from an innocuous first sentence, 'My business is likely to move fast in about a fortnight', which comes at the bottom of a page. Aberdeen's reply of 2 July promised the utmost secrecy about the matters referred to in the postscript and assured Ashburton, 'you need not be afraid of employing the same means to a greater extent in any quarter where it may be necessary.'[25] This reference to 'means' is made clear in Ashburton's letter of 9 August, in which he informed Aberdeen that he had served a bill for £2,998 1s. 0d. on him (for secret service funds on which Ashburton was authorised to draw if necessary) and explained, 'The money I wrote about went to compensate Sparks and to send him, on my first arrival, to the Governors of Maine and Massachusetts.'[26]

What does all this mean for Anglo-Canadian relations? In fact, Canada probably got quite a good deal on the north-east boundary. The battle of the maps was fairly equal and, in the last resort, no map not formally annexed to the treaty had any legal validity. Most of Canada's real interests in the region were preserved, although more was surrendered on the Madawaska Settlements than New Brunswick wished. But the whole negotiation does tend to confirm Canadian suspicions that London would always see such issues in the light of more general foreign-policy considerations, including the need to restore good working relations with the United States. In the 1840s, the Canadians could do little more than grumble, but such memories played their part in the movement for Confederation in the 1860s.

Notes

[1] *Hansard*, 3rd ser., lxvii, 1313 (23 March 1843). His press campaign was equally unsuccessful. Charles Greville, the diarist, was right in saying, 'There is a very general feeling of satisfaction at the termination of the boundary dispute with the Americans, and it will be impossible for Palmerston . . . to carry public opinion with him in attacking this settlement', but he was deceived by popular rumour about the maps question. H. Reeve (ed.), *The Greville Memoirs* (London, 1888), V, pp.103–8, 113, 150–1.

2   The British ambassador in Paris, the Duke of Wellington's brother, Lord
    Cowley, sent home a secret report of French plans to capture British
    colonies in the event of an Anglo-American war, B(ritish) L(ibrary) Add
    MSS 43129, 'Rapport particulier', encl. in Cowley to Aberdeen, 31 Janu-
    ary 1842. Wellington himself returned to this theme at the time of the
    Oregon crisis three years later; cf. Add MSS 40461, Wellington to Peel,
    8 April 1845.

3   P(ublic) R(ecord) O(ffice), FO 84/376, Palmerston to Stevenson, 27 August
    1841.

4   For a detailed analysis, see Howard Jones 'The Peculiar Institution and
    National Honor: The Case of the Creole Slave Revolt', *Civil War His-
    tory*, 21 (1975), 28–50.

5   PRO FO 5/358, Palmerston to Fox, 18 August 1841. Peel's government,
    although generally more conciliatory, was equally firm on the McLeod
    case. On 18 October Peel met with senior ministers to discuss the deploy-
    ment of the British fleet in the event of war. Cf. Add MSS 40459, Peel to
    Wellington, 18 October 1841, and K. Bourne, *Britain and the Balance
    of Power in North America, 1815–1908* (London, 1967), pp.86–105.

6   Peel objected, as Palmerston had done before him, that the association of
    'commissioners' from Maine and Massachusetts with the secretary of state
    would be unconstitutional since Britain could only negotiate with a sovereign
    government. Aberdeen was prepared to accept them on grounds of practical-
    ity. BL Add MSS 43062, Peel to Aberdeen, 27 March 1842; Add MSS
    43123, Aberdeen to Ashburton, Private, 1 April 1842. For Ashburton's
    comments, see BL Add MSS 43123, 14, 29 June, 13 July 1842. For New
    Brunswick input, see for example PRO FO 5/379, Ashburton to Aberdeen,
    28 April 1842, enclosing opinion of John MacLauchlan (warden of disputed
    territories), 8 April 1842. The whole matter is discussed in Howard Jones,
    To the Webster–Ashburton Treaty (Chapel Hill, 1977), pp.122–6.

7   To add to the confusion, the province of New Brunswick was not carved
    out of Nova Scotia until 1784 and Maine was not separated from Mas-
    sachusetts until 1820.

8   *British and Foreign State Papers*, I, pp.780–1.

9   Quoted in T. A. Bailey, *A Diplomatic History of the American People*
    (New York, 1958 edn), p.208.

10 PRO FO 5/378, Aberdeen to Ashburton, no. 2, 8 February 1842.

11 BL Add MSS 43060, Wellington to Aberdeen, 8 February 1842 (3 let-
    ters).

12 BL Add MSS 43123, Aberdeen to Ashburton, Private, 9 February 1842.

13 BL Add MSS 43123, Memo^m N Eastern Boundary, FO 19 February
    1842; Aberdeen to Kempt etc., 24 February 1842; Kempt to Aberdeen,
    1 March 1842; Douglas to Aberdeen, 7 March 1842; Seaton to Aberdeen,
    9 March 1842; Murray to Aberdeen, 6 March 1842; Add MSS 43062,
    Abstract of Boundary Correspondence, 26 March 1842.

14 PRO FO 5/378, Aberdeen to Ashburton, no. 6, 31 March 1842; FO
    5/379, Ashburton to Aberdeen, no. 3, 25 April 1842; BL Add MSS,

43123, Ashburton to Aberdeen, Private, 26 April, 14, 29 June, 13 July 1842; FO 5/379, Ashburton to Aberdeen, no. 10, 29 June 1842 encl. Ashburton to Webster, 21 June 1842.

[15] Apart from the revelations in Parliament (*Hansard*, 3rd ser., LXVII, 1162–1252, 21–2 March 1843), see, for example, 'A Memoir of the North-Eastern Boundary in connexion with Mr Jay's Map by the Hon Albert Gallatin Ll.D., President of the New York Historical Society, formerly one of the Commissioners under the Treaty of Ghent, Minister to Great Britain etc. etc. Together with a speech on the same subject by the Hon. Daniel Webster Ll.D., Secretary of State etc. etc. Delivered at a Special Meeting of the New York Historical Society, April 15th 1843. Illustrated by a copy of the "Jay Map", New York, Printed for the Society, 1843'. The British Library copy is annotated in ink, 'For the British Museum with the compliments of the American Minister'. Later studies include J. Winsor, *Cartographical History of the North East Boundary Controversy.* (Cambridge, Mass., 1887); W. F. Ganong, Monograph on the Evolution of the Boundaries of the Province of New Brunswick, *Transactions of the Royal Society of Canada* (1901–2), 140–447, and C. P. Lucas, *The Boundary Line of Canada: Memorandum for the Colonial Office* (London, 1906). Howard Jones, *To the Webster-Ashburton Treaty* provides a modern summing up.

[16] Ashburton recounted the story to Aberdeen, BL Add MSS 43123, Private, 9 August 1842.

[17] BL Add MSS 43131, Aberdeen to Bulwer, Private, 17 February 1843.

[18] BL Add MSS 43131, Aberdeen to Bulwer, Private, 21 February 1843; Bulwer to Aberdeen, Private, 17, 18, 20, 24 February 1843.

[19] BL Add MSS 43131, Aberdeen to Bulwer, Private, 24 February 1843. It was partly Ashburton who had suggested to Aberdeen that Cass was intriguing against the treaty in America (BL Add MSS 43123, Ashburton to Aberdeen, Private, 28 May 1842) but the British government also had plenty of information on Cass's activities in Paris. Some of it came from *The Times's* correspondent in whom Cass had rather rashly confided, e.g. BL Add MSS 43062, O'Reilly to Peel, 1 January 1842. Cass, on his own responsibility, had addressed a strong protest to the French prime minister, François Guizot, on the signature of the Quintuple Treaty, which would have given mutual right-of-search concessions between the leading maritime powers of Europe, D. Webster, *Diplomatic and Official Papers of* . . . (New York, 1848), pp.177–81. Cass's pamphlet, first published in French and also designed to impede the ratification of the Quintuple Treaty, was republished in English in Baltimore in 1842 (on both occasions anonymously) as *An Examination of the Questions now in Discussion between the American and British Governments concerning the Right of Search*.

[20] BL Add MSS 43131, Bulwer to Aberdeen, Private, 26 February 1843.

[21] BL Add MSS 43131, Bulwer to Aberdeen, Private, 27 February 1843.

[22] Howard Jones is convincing on this, particularly in his scepticism towards

S. F. Bemis's theories (Bemis, *John Quincy Adams and the Foundations of American Foreign Policy*, New York, 1949). *To the Webster–Ashburton Treaty*, pp.126–31.

[23] BL Add MSS, Ashburton to Aberdeen, Private, 9, 13 August 1843.

[24] M. E. Chamberlain, *Lord Aberdeen: A Political Biography* (London, 1983), pp.1–2.

[25] BL Add MSS 43123, Ashburton to Aberdeen, Private, 14 June 1842; Aberdeen to Ashburton, Private, 2 July 1842.

[26] BL Add MSS 43123, Ashburton to Aberdeen, Private, 9 August 1842.

4

'Our advices from Canada are unimportant': The Times and British North America, 1841–1861[1]

GED MARTIN

In the spring of 1849, journalists in London began to realize that a political storm in Canada had the capacity to trigger an upheaval in party alliances at Westminster. The *Morning Chronicle*, organ of the Peelites, was denouncing 'the French (or disloyal)' majority in the Canadian Parliament for legislation to pay compensation for losses incurred during the Lower Canadian rebellion of 1837.[2] Gladstone saw an opportunity to denounce Lord John Russell's Whig ministry for allowing the largest province in the Empire to transgress and trample upon the limits of colonial subordination. The Canadian issue was transformed from the constitutional to the sensational when a Tory mob burned down the parliament buildings in Montreal. Suddenly, noted *The Times*, 'there were a thousand questions, and not one to answer.' Even ministers 'professed to know nothing about the matter. Nobody knew anything about it . . . So slight is the connexion and communication between England its chief British colony!' Highly unreliable reports were 'filtered through the greedy comments of the New York papers, and dribbled in angry letters received from military gentlemen stationed in Canada'. For once, Canadian newspapers were not 'immediately committed, as heretofore, to the waste paper basket'. Unfortunately, even this source was 'found to contain whole pages of frantic nonsense'.[3]

Five years later, *The Times* once again ruminated on its ignorance of Britain's transatlantic Empire. 'It is the misfortune of the sort of connexion we keep up with British America that we seldom hear anything about it, unless it be something unpleasant.' If the imperial link operated at a level more profound than trade and emigration, the British public might take a real interest in colonial politics 'and, when debates at home were getting rather dull, we might fill up the void with examples of Canadian eloquence or intrigue'. In reality, 'we only hear of these provinces as we do of Mount Etna, that is, when there is an eruption.' The rebellions in 1837, the riots in 1849, the row over the Clergy Reserves in 1853 – each had led the quarrelling parties, 'otherwise caring about as little for us as we do for them', to rush to argue their case in Britain. 'For nine days at the outside – sometimes only for nine hours – a Canadian topic may be said to occupy the public attention, and people begin really to think they know something about Canadian affairs, and are interested in them.' Invariably, however, the sparks from the sudden rocket were snuffed into darkness again, 'and it will be a twelvemonth before any body remembers there is such a place as British America'.[4]

For the mid-nineteenth-century British, their Canadian colonies figured only intermittently on the public agenda, usually in the form of a problem. Sources of information about individual episodes were unreliable and partisan – allowing scope for preconceived notions to act as filters for the analysis of information – notably through the looming presence of the United States. Much of the information on Canada received by the British came either from New York journalists, the voice of American democracy, or from British army officers, whose social and political role in Canada was to act as bastions against American expansion.

A sagacious reviewer once objected to the assumption 'that safeguarding Canada was the only chore that really mattered' to British governments in the mid-nineteenth century.[5] In the wide gamut of issues confronting Britain, British North American questions occupied only a very small place. By and large, it seems fair to argue that the British – governments, opinion-formers and probably the politically aware general public – did indeed wish to prolong the imperial connection with Canada, preserving it as 'a huge breakwater between us and our nearest but most formidable rival'.[6] 'Not one man in a thousand cares whether the Canadians prosper or fail to prosper', said Anthony Trollope's Phineas Finn. 'They care that Canada should not go to the States, because, – though they don't love the Canadians, they do hate the Americans.'[7] The imperial connection with British North America was valued in the abstract, but little was known of the provinces in reality.

The priority assigned to the colonies of British North America may be measured by the quality and nature of the governors they received. Until the mid-1830s, the provinces were almost exclusively ruled by military men: Sir Francis Bond Head could still speak of being 'stationed' in Upper Canada.[8] Briefly, in the aftermath of the rebellions, Lord Melbourne's Whig ministry sent out two high-ranking civilian governors, both former Cabinet ministers. Durham's appointment was a response to the crisis of the rebellions, if also perhaps a manoeuvre to remove him from the centre of events. Thomson was charged with the specific mission of carrying through the union of the Canadas. Thereafter, no pre-Confederation governor-general was a front-rank public figure, however much their names may now resound in the pages of Canadian history texts.

Bagot was a career diplomat and – incidentally – probably the first university graduate to govern Canada, Metcalfe a veteran of India, Cathcart a military stopgap for the duration of the Oregon crisis. Cathcart's successor, Elgin, was prickly in awareness of his own marginality at home: he even thought of settling in Upper Canada at the close of his term of office.[9] In the event, he returned to Britain, to become the only pre-Confederation governor-general to achieve Cabinet office, but only in the lowly position of postmaster-general and that but briefly. Sir Edmund Head had been a Poor Law commissioner, while Lord Monck – Newcastle's fifth choice[10] in 1861 – had held minor office.

It did not escape the notice of Canadians that their governors came from the secondary ranks of the British political world. The *Montreal Herald* greeted Elgin's appointment with the comment that he was 'a distant relation of some marbles in the British Museum – and that is nearly all'.[11] Newcastle was angry – and embarrassed – at press disparagement of Monck's appointment, suggesting that 'the Canadians were offended by the choice of an inferior man'.[12] The protest could not disguise the fact that Monck had very little experience, and that his only connection with the colonies was that he had previously declined to go out and govern New South Wales.[13]

> I am confident he will make his way and that quickly, for he is a man of thoroughly good sense combined with considerable ability, much activity and a hearty manner; in fact, his geniality is almost the only part of the Irish character he shows.[14]

There was no pretence that Monck had the slightest understanding of Canada.

Elgin was surely right to describe his office as 'one of the most responsible and least coveted under the Crown'.[15] The only high-ranking peer to hold the office before Confederation was the duke of Richmond, who owed his appointment in 1818 both to its military character and his relative poverty. Thereafter, even titled governors came mainly from the margins of the aristocracy. Aylmer, Gosford and Monck were Irish peers, an embarrassingly oversupplied category. Gosford and Monck managed to earn British titles, as did Elgin, whose two Scottish earldoms were still insufficient to seat him in the Lords. Colborne, Thomson and Metcalfe received peerages for success in Canada, although in Metcalfe's case the fact that he had no legitimate son to inherit the title probably smoothed his elevation. No British peer was sent to Canada between Durham in 1838 and Dufferin in 1872.

It is striking that no peerage was conferred upon Sir Edmund Head, a meticulous and judicious viceroy, and the kind of intellectual statesman whom Prince Albert had certainly hoped to see recruited to the upper house. Head's success in Canada was acknowledged in 1857 when he was made a knight commander of the Bath – then generally considered the order reflecting merit – and sworn of the Privy Council. Cambridge and Oxford followed with honorary degrees. The death of his only son meant that a peerage for Head would in practice have been limited to his own lifetime, but lack of broad acres ensured that the Right Honourable Sir Edmund Head remained – as even the first post-Confederation governor-general, Sir John Young, modestly styled himself – a 'mere Bart.'

If the province of Canada ranked relatively low in the British hierarchy, the rest of British North America was practically invisible. New Brunswick received three successive governors of ability and standing in the two decades before Confederation – although the last of them, Arthur Gordon, seemed to find it hard to grasp that the mere fact of being son of a former prime minister did not entitle him to act as an autonomous potentate in his own right. The succession of distinguished personalities may have been accidental: Sir Edmund Head took New Brunswick simply because the Poor Law Commission had been abolished and he needed a job. Head's predecessor, Sir William Colebrooke, had displayed a disastrous combination of 'sleepless activity'[16] and poor judgement. His successor, J. H. T. Manners Sutton, came to the colony with the most impressive political career of any British North American governor,

Durham and Thomson apart, having served as under-secretary at the Home Office for five years under Peel. His pedigree was even more resplendent, for he was the grandson of an archbishop and son of the Speaker of the House of Commons. Like Edmund Head, he was a scholar of some note. It is understandable that he seems to have been offended at being passed over for Canada in 1861.[17]

The governors sent to preside over the rest of British North America were for the most part men who had achieved little at home before their appointment and who would be barely heard of after their term of office. As *The Times* put it, 'there cannot be a greater mistake than to suppose that a ten years' residence in the Falkland Islands or Tasmania puts a man into a better position for English society so far as regards all kinds of preferment.'[18] Ex-governors were indeed 'to be met everywhere in London society',[19] but they were usually poor, for 'after a life spent in playing the Viceroy there is no pension to provide even a pittance for old age.'[20] The only aristocrat to preside in the Maritimes during the mid-century period was Lord Mulgrave, who was governor of Nova Scotia from 1858 to 1863. When his father, the marquess of Normanby, died in 1863, he was immediately granted permission to go home and take up his inheritance even though he was then close to the end of his normal term of office. While this was a convenient device for placing an entire ocean between himself and Charles Tupper, there was an evident assumption that a third of a million Nova Scotians could manage in the absence of a governor more easily than the Normanby estates could dispense with the presence of their marquess.[21]

Mulgrave had briefly visited Canada before, serving as an aide-de-camp to Durham in 1838, at a time when his father was a member of the Cabinet. As *The Times* had commented in 1849, most army officers were 'furiously "loyal"'[22] and probably few possessed the social sensitivity to gain real insight into colonial society and politics. None the less, while the impact of their perceptions of Canada cannot be quantified, they surely played a role in shaping the attitudes of the British élite to their transatlantic colonies. There were 417 officers in Canada in November 1838, and 924 were envisaged for the whole of British North America after the *Trent* reinforcements in 1862.[23] Many of the most influential families in the land numbered among their siblings and offspring somebody who had served in British North America.

At Bytown in 1839, Colonel Charles Grey had noted enthusiastically that 'such a place for the Capital of a Country never existed . . . It seems intended by nature from its magnificent situation . . . to be the first place in British North America.' Two decades later, as Prince Albert's secretary, he drafted the memorandum giving royal approval to the selection of Ottawa as Canada's seat of government.[24] This was probably little more than helpful coincidence: Ottawa was chosen because Sir Edmund Head masterminded a compromise equally acceptable (or unacceptable) to the other contenders. Nor is there any trace in the policy of his brother, the third Earl Grey, as colonial secretary, of the distrust of French Canadians which characterizes Colonel Grey's Canadian diaries.

While Peel and Aberdeen confronted an expansionist American administration which demanded British withdrawal from the entire Pacific coast in 1845–6, British claims on the ground were being upheld by the prime minister's son, Lieutenant William Peel, and the foreign secretary's brother, Captain John Gordon. Gordon made no secret of his belief that Vancouver Island was not 'worth five straws'. He placed little value on a country 'where the salmon will not take the fly', nor would he swap 'one acre of the barren hills of Scotland for all that he saw around him'.

The presence of the two men on the North Pacific station may not have been entirely accidental – Gordon had not been to sea at all for twenty-six years – but it is likely that in their family connections they were reflecting as much as contributing to the formation of policy, warning local Hudson's Bay Company officials that 'we could not expect to hold the entire country'. It would be exceeding the evidence to argue that Gordon's views on salmon fishing shaped the western side of North America – James Douglas, who reported the comment, may not have realized that even the brother of an earl might have a sense of humour – but it is a dimension of the Oregon diplomacy worth bearing in mind that even in so remote a corner of the world, the two key British statesmen had their own sources of information. The two officers agreed that if the forty-ninth parallel were accepted as a compromise boundary, southern Vancouver Island should be retained for its harbours, and Lieutenant Peel arrived back in London in time to make his report before the final resolution of the Oregon dispute.[25]

In some cases – Captain Millington Synge and his pioneer enthusiasm for a transcontinental railway would be one example[26]

– army and naval officers may have exercised a positive and even inspirational effect on British views of the provinces. In others, the social gap between officers and colonists – compounded by the ordinary discomforts of exile – was probably less helpful. The high-ranking Guards did not enjoy being sent out in the aftermath of the *Trent* crisis: *The Times* correspondent, W. H. Russell, ingeniously suggested that otherwise well-disposed Montrealers 'were deterred by the very prestige of the Guards' social position from offering them ordinary civility'. Russell was well aware that 'a common expression of dislike on the part of men who exercise a great influence on the most powerful classes in this country' was dangerous to the prospects of a continuing imperial connection with Canada. 'Our soldiers must be taught to respect the people of Canada as their equals and fellow-subjects – a hard lesson perhaps for imperious islanders, but not the less necessary to learn, if we would preserve their attachment and our territories.'[27] A despairing Joseph Howe was convinced that when the Guards returned to Britain, 'the higher classes appear to have been convinced that the Canadian frontier was indefensible' and threw their weight behind Confederation as a face-saving means of withdrawal.[28] Howe misread much of the British attitude to Confederation, but he may have been right in concluding that army officers framed the attitudes within which articulate British opinion – including the press – formed policy towards North America.

'*The Times* is very powerful, and it has got a great hold upon the public mind', lamented Charles Greville in 1855, adding that 'once this sort of power is established, it is difficult to undermine it'.[29] Its ascendancy had not been achieved overnight. In 1831, Sydney Smith had argued that Britain was governed by 'an heptarchy' of newspapers, of which he placed *The Times* first. Only by reforming the system of representation, he claimed, would their power be reduced.[30] If anything, the reformed Parliament, with its need to reach out to a wider electorate, only made the press more important, and accentuated the power of its strongest voice. In 1835, Lyndhurst urged Peel to make special efforts to supply *The Times* with information to secure its good will, since it was 'worth *all* the other papers put together'.[31] *The Times* was ingenious in securing *coups* – one of its most notable was the purloining of the Durham Report in 1839 before ministers could censor it[32] – and in the exploitation of new printing technology. In 1842, its circulation was double its 1836 level, and by 1850 it had doubled again. In 1841, its daily sale was twice the combined circulation of the *Morning Chronicle* – the *Grunticle* as *The Times* sometimes dubbed it – the *Morning Herald* and the *Morning Post* combined; by 1855 it had a threefold lead over the next six London competitors.[33] A year earlier the Tory J. W. Croker could offer the sardonic suggestion that the Speaker of the House of Commons should dispense with the traditional petition to the sovereign to allow members of Parliament freedom of speech, and plead with *The Times* instead.[34]

Many of the most exaggerated statements about the power of *The Times* date from close to its dazzling ascendancy of the mid-1850s. Lord Stanley reckoned that the sole post to equal the power of its editor would be that of governor-general of India, while Anthony Trollope drew a parallel with the tsar of Russia.[35] Abraham Lincoln joked that only the Mississippi River conveyed a greater impression of power.[36] Lord Shaftesbury could think of no earthly equivalent. 'Millions on Millions of Christian people should meet to "pray down" that paper', he urged in 1855, 'and implore God to stop its wicked course.'[37] It seemed that even the Almighty would need a good deal of encouragement to take on the Thunderer of Printing House Square. Its readers might not always agree with everything *The Times* said, but nobody who aspired to influence could afford to ignore its existence. (Even Richard Cobden, perhaps its deadliest foe, who never allowed *The Times* into his house, took care to read it in his club and was highly sensitive to its slights.) On hearing Sir Richard Mac-Donnell, Nova Scotia's pompous governor, claim in 1864 that he never read *The Times*, Lord Monck's sister-in-law wondered 'how they could entrust any government to him!'[38]

When *The Times* had broken with the Whigs in the mid-1830s, the Radical MP Benjamin Wood condemned its ingratitude in abandoning 'the people at large who had raised *The Times* to its importance'. *The Times* was brutal in its direct response: 'our circulation, even on the day on which we published these your falsehoods, was something which . . . almost surprised ourselves.'[39] The relationship between the newspaper and its readers was complex: as Lord Clarendon put it in 1849, *The Times* 'forms or guides or reflects – no matter which – the public opinion of England'.[40]

The power of *The Times* was the power of its leading articles, which imparted an *ex cathedra* status to the anonymous voice of its editorial.[41] Only rarely did a Radical voice refuse to speak 'of the mysterious *Times*' and attack its leader writers as named individuals, as Roebuck tried to do in 1835.[42] Thirty years later, refusing to treat *The Times* 'as an impersonal myth', Cobden determined to unmask its editor 'and hold him up by name to the obloquy which awaits the traducer and calumniator in every other walk of social and political life'. Unfortunately revenge was more easily threatened than executed. Not only did the editor, J. T. Delane, decline 'to publish a series of most offensive and unfounded imputations upon himself and his friends', but even the normally sympathetic *Daily Telegraph* patronizingly announced that it had too much respect for Cobden's reputation to open its columns to his diatribe. The veteran Radical was obliged to vent his fury in the *Rochdale Observer* and comfort himself with the reflection that 'you can never be in the path for success, in any great measure of policy, unless you are in opposition to that journal'.[43]

Paradox did not sit comfortably with the severely practical mind of Richard Cobden. As even he admitted, the plain fact was that at the height of its power, *The Times* had 'possessed almost a monopoly of publicity'.[44] The blanketing influence of its editorials was witnessed by the young barrister Frederic Rogers, who eked out his income by writing for the paper in the 1840s. He would receive general instructions on how a subject was to be handled, and would then be left to consider and discard various approaches before determining the best way of arguing the case. For days afterwards, he would find that conversation among the politically aware was dominated by the rehashing of his phrases and the recitation of his arguments. 'They *talked* my article, as if there was no other point in the debate than that which I had selected, and no other conceivable opinion but that which I had, perhaps doubtfully, adopted.'[45]

Cobden argued that the leading article interposed a distorting medium between the reader and the real news which made up nineteen-twentieths of each day's newspaper. *The Times*, naturally, disagreed, arguing that the verbatim reports of speeches and letters from correspondents which it printed were just as much statements of opinion on which comment was appropriate.[46] In truth, the sheer bulk of material in a mid-Victorian newspaper made the leading article a necessary feature, even if it did telescope the functions of reporting and commentary. 'We give these documents as part of the history of the times, not that we believe they possess any particular interest here', *The Times* haughtily remarked as it published correspondence between Papineau and the Lower Canadian administration in September 1837.[47] *The Times* did not like Papineau even in small doses, but it found itself overwhelmed by the Durham Report, one of its most celebrated journalistic scoops. 'We have even yet hardly had time to do more than cursorily glance over it once', it confessed editorially: there were, after all, '119 closely printed folio pages' which the paper had rushed into print immediately on receiving a copy.[48] If even the professional commentators who wrote *The Times* required an interval to digest (and then spit out) the Durham message, then it was utopian for Cobden to hope that leading articles could be dispensed with altogether; after all, Cobden himself estimated that a busy man might glance over 500 newspapers in a year.[49] If leading articles distorted, they might also highlight: in 1854, for instance, *The Times* thought it 'scarcely possible to overrate' the importance of the Reciprocity Treaty, even though it might seem 'uninteresting to the general reader'.[50]

If anything, the leading article became even more important after 1849, partly because the growth of agencies encouraged the pooling of actual news gathering – Reuters was founded that year – thereby forcing newspapers to differentiate their product in other ways. On 8 May, during a Lords debate on the repeal of the Navigation Laws, Abraham Hayward of the *Morning Chronicle* broke new ground by scribbling an immediate reply to a speech by Stanley for publication in the next day's paper. Hayward 'revolutionised at a stroke the whole art of leader writing', for previously editorial comment had appeared a day or so later 'when the speeches had done their work'.[51]

The increasing immediacy of leader comment was not without its complications: in the heat of debate, it was easy for the paper to contradict itself: Charles Greville, clerk to the Privy Council, complained that *The Times* was 'famous for its versatility and inconsistency'.[52] Examples abound. When the *Colonial Magazine* complained that while Manchester could decide to spend almost half a million pounds on its water supply, the Colonial Office would not allow distant colonies to spend even one tenth of that sum without its express permission, *The Times* sharply commented that it would need 'a column to expose all the absurdities of this short paragraph'. Yet eighteen months later, it could sneer that the Colonial Office 'will not allow a colony, however remote, to build a slaughter-house or to take up a vagrant without the assistance of Downing-street'.[53] The contradictions were especially striking in references to the United States: selective quotation can portray *The Times* either as thirsting for war with the Americans or as a celebrant of Anglo-Saxon kinship.[54] The historian can attribute these shifts, as Cobden bluntly alleged, to 'a shameless disregard of the claims of consistency and sincerity',[55] but it is probably fairer to regard them as expressions of the extreme ends of a spectrum of attitudes, evidence of Clarendon's view that *The Times* both reflected as well as shaped public opinion.

The two decades between 1841 and 1861 constitute a convenient unity for the discussion of the attitudes of *The Times* to Canada and its position in North America. The establishment of the united province of Canada in 1841 seemed to open a new chapter in colonial policy, but the year was also marked by two important changes in Britain, the formation of a Conservative government under Peel and the unexpected death, at the age of fifty-five, of Thomas Barnes, who in twenty years as editor had made *The Times* into the 'Thunderer' of legend. His colleague Edward Sterling 'never heard of him speak of anyone otherwise than depreciatingly'.[56] The diarist Creevey thought him 'at war with all the human race except Brougham' – a devotion which partially explains the hostility of *The Times* to Durham.[57] Barnes hid a generous private personality deep and effectively under a welter of venom, some of it admittedly triggered by his sympathy for the defenceless.[58] In the late 1830s, *The Times* had been implacably opposed to the Whigs, and frenzied in its antipathy towards Daniel O'Connell, upon whose Irish following the Melbourne ministry was dependent after 1835. The 'crawling, base-minded Whigs' it damned as 'impotent and shameless bipeds whom one blushes to call one's countrymen', while O'Connell was 'an unredeemed and unredeemable scoundrel' and 'the Papineau of Ireland'.[59] The Liberator gave no quarter, dismissing *The Times* as 'vile' and describing Barnes as 'the gin drinking-est editor in London'.[60]

The predominant misanthropy of Thomas Barnes reached its peak when confronted by Catholics or the French, a perspective which robbed the paper's analysis of Canadian affairs in the mid-thirties of any claim to objectivity. Papineau was simply another O'Connell, both 'representing one and the same principle – the subversion of British interests and the severance of British connexion'. The outbreak of rebellion only proved that Papineau was 'a fomenter of sedition and a crafty and cowardly conspirator' who could be 'compared to another agitator nearer home, in the recklessness with which he goads on his deluded followers to their destruction, and the cunning with which he contrives to secure himself from the consequences of his sedition'. Concession was pointless, as proved by that 'frivolous and toad-eating embassy', the Gosford mission. 'After wiping Papineau's hoof, they were rewarded, and justly, by repeated kickings.' His demands 'were manifestly not means of redressing wrongs, but of inflicting them – that is, of dismembering the British empire'.[61]

The Times of the 1830s can provide historians with plenty of eye-catching material, but there is hardly profundity of perception in allusions to 'our dear native countrymen in the Upper Province', 'our brave emigrated countrymen in that fine country' or – most bizarre of all – 'the ancient British province of New Brunswick'.[62] Indeed, in its contempt for the French as 'a perverse faction of ill-intentioned foreigners', *The Times* played its own part in goading Lower Canadians towards revolt. It saw the Russell resolutions of April 1837 as a riposte to threats of

> a rebellion of M. Papineau and his handful of dupes against Great Britain, should the Imperial Parliament dare to disobey the mandates of that Canadian agitator. The Imperial Parliament *has* resisted, and now let us see whether the rebellion will take place or not.[63]

In the decades after 1841, *The Times* under J. T. Delane could sometimes provide a reminder that there were limits to Victorian gentility, but it was rarely so consistently or so virulently opposed to any government as it had been to the Melbourne ministry.

If both for *The Times* and for Canada, 1841 may be taken as the start of a new chapter, a case may also be made for 1861 as its close. The outbreak of the American Civil War placed British North America firmly in a context of continental crisis which dominated the press for the next four years – especially after the vulnerability of the provinces was underlined by the confrontation with the United States in the winter of 1861–2 following the arrest on the high seas of the British steamer, the *Trent*, by a Northern warship.[64] Perversely, the provinces themselves were overshadowed to the point of obscurity:

'who is Minister, if any, at Quebec or any other seat of British Government in America, we none of us know', The Times confessed in June 1863.[65] 'Since the affair of Trent', it admitted a year later, 'we have had little attention to devote to the position of Canada.'[66] It might have been better had the statement been literally true. The *Trent* crisis had been followed in the spring of 1862 by the Canadian Assembly's rejection of the Militia Bill, and The Times had taken a leading part in lecturing a free province on the duty of self-defence. Twenty years later, J. C. Dent recalled that 'the tone adopted by the English press . . . during the summer of 1862, struck a blow at Canadian loyalty from which it has never fully recovered'.[67]

Not only did something of the warmth disappear from the British view of Canada after 1861, but The Times itself never fully recovered the awesome and despotic power it had wielded during the two previous decades. The abolition of the Newspaper Stamp Duty in 1855 opened the way to new competitors, and the process was speeded by the removal of duties on newsprint in 1861. Its ascendancy had not been without challenge between 1841 and 1861. The *Morning Herald* and the *Daily News* put the Thunderer on its mettle in the 1840s, while the new *Daily Telegraph* chased its circulation from 1855. That same year, the *Saturday Review* was founded, with the express purpose of challenging The Times in the realm of opinion.[68] Yet the competition served only to sharpen its writing and perhaps to moderate its excesses. Ministers took care to maintain contact. Lord Grey, colonial secretary from 1846 to 1852, used his under-secretary, Benjamin Hawes, as his line to Delane: after one briefing, Grey was able to record that 'two capital articles appear in consequence in today's Times'.[69] The duke of Newcastle, a master of tact, even thanked Delane for nominating Lord Monck as governor-general of Canada: The Times was soon forced to plead to 'about ten thousand gentlemen who have spent the last ten years in solicitations' that it had as much to say in appointing the bishop of Durham as in colonial patronage.[70]

The Times, then, may be taken as the voice of a confident mid-Victorian Britain (or, at least, England). In 1851, it hailed the second half of the nineteenth century, 'as far at least as this country and its offshoots are concerned' as 'the most prosperous – perhaps we may say the most imposing epoch in our national history'.[71] It was not clear whether those 'offshoots' included the United States of America: Bulwer Lytton's definition of civilization in 1854 as confined to western Europe and 'North-Eastern America' reflects the ambiguity.[72] The British were rarely accurate even in their basic information about the world across the Atlantic. An American student at Cambridge was disappointed in his confidence that 'an English gentleman who has attained his majority, might be expected to know that we have two houses of Congress and that New York is not a slave state'.[73] 'What territories exist I am at this moment unable to say', confessed J. A. Roebuck in his hastily written *Colonies of England* in 1849. 'Oregon is probably a state.'[74] In fact, Oregon did not enter the Union until 1858, the year in which *The Times* predicted that the population of the United States 'will soon equal our own'. The republic had overtaken Great Britain almost a decade earlier.[75]

Demographic defeat was made all the more galling by the fact that so much of the American gain was British loss. In 1849, *The Times* asked,

> what will be the fruits of a policy which is annually transfusing the sinews, muscles, courage, and intellect of British subjects into a foreign soil; and recruiting the stamina of a less masculine race, and the precocity of a presumptuous people, with . . . life-blood drawn from our own social body?

The fact too that so many of the migrants were Irish, 'and Irish only too glad to turn backs on the "old country"' sharpened the concern, since their resentments found a congenial home in their adopted country. 'They crown the bitterness of Celtic Papistry with the acrimony of American republicanism.'[76] As late as 1863, W. H. Russell could deny that Irish and German immigrants to the United States were 'really Americans in the proper sense of the word', but even he had to admit that war with the United States would be less 'unnatural' as American blood became progressively diluted by foreign immigration.[77] 'We are two people, but we are of one family', *The Times* could still proclaim in 1846 in announcing the end of the Oregon dispute.[78] By 1860, that sense of kinship was fading. 'An unaccountable cross has crept into the American breed, and we hardly know ourselves when we look at our second cousins.'[79] There was an uncomfortable reality in the images which Russell used to portray the two countries. The United States was 'a growing lad who is constantly testing his powers in competition with his elders'. England, on the other hand, was like 'an old Peninsula man . . . no doubt a very gallant fellow, and has done fine things in his day . . . but there is a secret belief that he will never do anything very great again.'[80]

Unease about the American people was increased by distaste for American institutions. Their operation, The Times claimed in 1842, had 'already done so much to strengthen the cause of limited monarchy and hereditary government, by contrasting them with the perversities and abuses of a republican frame of society'.[81] Even when a benign mood induced The Times to hail the American experiment as 'signally successful', it could warn Canadians that the example might be 'as dangerous as it is seductive', as the 'degradation and anarchy' of Latin America proved.[82] The election to the presidency of the 'gentlemanly' Zachary Taylor might prompt the more optimistic assessment 'that both in politics and in laws there is a much less interval between the Union and the mother country than is generally assumed'.[83] Yet recognizing the Americans as a kindred people was a short step to discerning them as a threat to British institutions. 'To some extent they indicate that to which we tend', The Times wrote in 1853, 'for the parts of England most like America are Manchester, Liverpool and Glasgow, and there are many who tell us the best thing we can all do is to be leavened throughout by these model cities.'[84] If The Times was poorly informed about the location of Glasgow, it was correct in perceiving that the American example would become the symbolic battleground for the future of British institutions of government in the 1860s.

An assertive people coupled with a democratic and even anarchic system of government constituted a dangerous combination. Condemning talk of the seizure of Cuba in 1849, The Times sombrely concluded that 'something is paid for that political independence of American citizens which is extolled as surpassing that of all the nations of the globe'.[85] The Times was not always so philosophical in its condemnation of democratic excess in foreign policy. The expansionist talk of the Oregon crisis aroused disgust among those who recalled that nine states had defaulted on their debts in the wake of the financial panic of 1837. 'It requires an almost preternatural impudence to threaten with future outrage the victims of perpetrated fraud, and to overpower with brutality the complaints of confidence abused.'[86] When an American warship bombarded the central American port of Greytown in 1854, The Times condemned 'one of the most extraordinary outrages ever committed by the commissioned officers of any civilized State'.[87] Occasionally there was a resort to irony. 'The diplomacy of the United States is certainly a very singular profession', *The Times* observed in 1855, following the publication of the Ostend Manifesto, in which three American ministers in Europe recommended the seizure of Cuba.[88] Dislike of democratic institutions fuelled condemnation of the way Americans pursued their external policies, but the lingering sense of kinship made it difficult to grasp that Americans had legitimate national interests of their own at all. *The Times* found it hard to forgive American reluctance during the Crimean War to support 'the cause of that country to which they owe their existence' – and in this case the bizarre entente between republican democracy and tsarist tyranny drew attention to Canada's loyal support for the allied cause.[89]

The excesses of American political debate made it difficult to read the future. 'A hundred times over, in the jargon of parties or the heat of battle, the union has been dissolved', *The Times* remarked in December 1849, urging its readers not to take such statements seriously.[90] Threats of secession, it concluded a year later, 'ought to be viewed simply as a specimen of the bad taste but too prevalent in all the writing and speaking of our American brethren', for 'with such a people talking and writing big words is, in fact, their constitutional safety valve.'[91] Consequently, *The Times* found it difficult to come to terms with the reality of secession in the aftermath of Lincoln's election. 'It costs a great effort of mind for any Englishman to enter into a question of national disunion.'[92] American statesmen surely supported the Union, but the question had fallen into the hands of 'vulgar demagogues and furious bar-room politicians'.[93]

Similarly, *The Times* normally discounted threats of war between the two countries.[94] Menacing references to the power of the Royal Navy or to invasion of the Southern states by Black troops from Jamaica were tongue-in-cheek responses from the early 1840s.[95] While there was recognition that the Mexican War changed the 'primitive integrity' of the republic into an imperial power, *The Times* felt no great respect for the successes of its undisciplined army.[96] It was not the immediate future of coexistence with the United States which alarmed *The Times*, but the longer term: a century ahead, there might be 200 million Americans.[97] This underlined 'the necessity of opposing the progress of the United States by a progress equally well conceived and energetic' – and that brought Canada into the picture.[98]

It was perhaps the only way that Canada could enter the British world picture. Elgin sourly suggested that *The Times* might 'condescend' to publish a favourable report on his province if Mississippi or Illinois were substituted for Canada. He complained that the British press often published as news items tendentious reports from the Montreal newspapers, many of them virulently opposed to the governor-general.[99] Even from a Montreal viewpoint, the British seemed ill-informed. 'Many . . . imagine Canada to be a hyperborean region, where the sun never shines and the snow never melts, and that it would be quite as profitable to throw money into the sea as to invest it in such a country', complained a Montreal correspondent of *The Times* in 1849.[100] While *The Times* itself from time to time deplored public and parliamentary apathy towards the colonies, it had no difficulty in accounting for the phenomenon. 'All Canada, New Brunswick, Australia and Cape Colony together', it noted in 1848, 'do not contain the population of London.'[101] A year later, it specifically placed the senior colony low in the hierarchy of nations – 'Canada, far larger than France, has a population not much greater than Wales.'[102] Five years later, Canada's size seemed more important, and even its population could be presented in a positive light.

> The colony in question is by far the largest in the world – the largest there ever was, so far as regards either the colonial population or the territory it occupies. It has a larger population than that of Scotland, and as large as that of many European states.

By that time, it had become evident that Canada was 'only dependent, if the term may still be applied, because she chooses to remain so'.[103]

'The commercial world in England knows of Canada and Australia as fields for exports, and the public in general has a vague feeling of pride at the world-wide propagation of our race', wrote *The Times* in 1860, 'but there is hardly yet a conception of the greatness of these settlements, their wealth and civilization, and the incalculable future which lies before them.' So far as Canada was concerned, British ignorance was largely a product of the social gulf between those who formed opinion and those who emigrated to colonies.

The Times indeed distinguished between Canada and the more recent success story of Australia: migrants to the antipodes 'are more thorough representatives of the mother country than the generality of immigrants to America', since they came from 'a wealthier and more completely English class'.[104] The equation of prosperity with Englishness is revealing. As the fifteen-year-old Arthur Gordon had put it in 1845, emigration to Canada was 'generally thought of as a last resource to people who have ruined themselves at home'.[105] *The Times* superciliously agreed. 'Across the Atlantic we have two or three millions of labourers and small farmers, with scarcely a gentleman or a good income among them.'[106] Colonies should not be allowed to 'degenerate into costly cesspools for the political and social refuse of the mother country'.[107] Emigration should be drawn from all classes. 'Do not turn the ignorant, the vicious, the helpless adrift to found states and direct legislatures', it urged in 1847.[108] By the middle of the next decade, the colonists seemed to be making a modest success of running their own affairs, but even then the Canadian remained something of an alien being: 'if you want to see the "British subject" in his most essential form', wrote *The Times* in 1856, 'you must go to Canada West.'[109]

From this lofty pinnacle of metropolitan superiority, *The Times* did not always feel the need to take Canadian politics very seriously. 'Our readers will often have been puzzled by the accounts which they read from time to time of Ministerial or Parliamentary crises in Canada', it acknowledged in 1856, adding that most amounted merely to personality squabbles.[110] To write that, in Canada, a politician 'sets about making a party as he would a salad' might have been the starting-point for a penetrating analysis of the politics of factional alliances. *The Times* did not make the effort, lamenting instead that it was easier to calculate the orbit of a comet than to 'predict the humours and vagaries of spoilt children'.[111] The annoyance could be forgiven as a condemnation of the naked selfishness of the Montreal annexationists, but *The Times* was often superficial in its judgements. When Metcalfe's ministers were sustained by a six-vote majority in the Assembly following the turbulent election of 1844, it concluded that in such a small house, the majority was 'amply sufficient for the working of the Government' – precisely the reverse of the moral which Elgin drew when he inherited this fragile situation two years later.[112] *The Times* showed some perspicacity in 1849 when it censured the ousted Family Compact as a selfish clique which could not accept the loss of its privileged position, but it was a gross exaggeration to claim that its members 'actually granted the greater part of Upper Canada to themselves, their fathers, their infant children, their cousins and connexions to the remotest degree'.[113] Even apparently good-humoured assessments contained deceptive exaggeration, such as the Christmastide reverie of 1856 which described Canada as 'nothing more than England reformed, with the addition of an unlimited supply of land'.[114] From these alternating moods of imperial euphoria and social disdain flowed the disastrous and abusive misunderstandings of 1862.

In comparison with its reporting of the United States, The Times gave relatively little space to the province of Canada. Other provinces received little attention and still less illumination. A rare reference to Prince Edward Islanders as 'an estimable body of men, who have never shown themselves deficient in loyalty to the crown of Great Britain' was at best a massive generalization derived from the small body of absentee proprietors, at worst a romantic stereotype.[115] The latter would seem to predominate in the claim that among Maritimers in general, 'the spirit of loyalty to the English throne and people burns with undimmed brightness'.[116] Reality was less arcadian. It was almost certainly Joseph Howe's 1854 speech calling for the integration of the empire that The Times dismissed as 'some of the most extraordinary specimens of transatlantic eloquence that it has yet been our lot to see'.[117] The best that can be said of the occasional discussions of the other provinces is that they were superficial. The Times got it right in explaining to its readers that life in Newfoundland was dominated by the fishery, although it was perhaps verging on the poetic to drag in the spice trade of Amsterdam and the wine exports of Gascony as parallels.[118]

The prairies were dismissed, in terms conventional to the 1850s, as 'an American Siberia'. The Times compared the Red River country unfavourably with the Ottawa valley, which in 1858 was still barely surveyed, let alone settled. Emigrants would hardly pass by 'this vast valley in order to bury themselves in a region cut off from the rest of mankind, without imports and exports, and in every respect inferior in natural advantages'.[119] However, this was not to say that Ottawa, 'a city that is to be rather than is now', should be chosen as Canada's seat of government. A theoretical case could be made out for Ottawa as a neutral centre, 'central not only for the river and the lakes, but also for that immense interior north and west of the lakes that may some day be peopled'. None the less, as a practical option, 'the choice of Ottawa would sacrifice the actual convenience of the majority to the ideas of a few.'[120]

In contrast to its lack of enthusiasm for the prairies, *The Times* showed some interest in the Pacific coast. A Commons debate on Vancouver Island in 1848 it hailed as 'of no ordinary importance'. The island was important for its 'great presumed resources, with a climate almost exactly assimilated to that of the mother country', and the fact the Americans had pushed so hard to acquire the whole of Oregon was enough to prove that the region had great potential. The Pacific coast of North America would become an important focus for the trade of Asia, but 'along the whole of this coast there are but two or three practicable ports for shipping.' Eighteen days' sailing from China and 'full of admirable coal', Vancouver Island would 'unquestionably . . . command the commerce of the coast; and if ever the North Pacific is indeed to become a Mediterranean, here will be its Tyre.'[121] Shortly after, the simile was varied: Vancouver Island was 'this Ceylon of North America'.[122] A decade later, it remained 'without exception, the most desirable portion of the surface of the earth'.[123] The nearby mainland was more of a mystery. 'What most of us know of these ultra-occidental regions may be summed up in a few words.'[124] *The Times* at first felt 'very little satisfaction' about the creation of a new colony as a result of the Fraser valley gold rush, although much of its annoyance was directed at Sir Edward Lytton's original intention to call it 'New Caledonia'.[125] Once the name was changed to British Columbia – and, indeed, once *The Times* caught up with the change and stopped calling the colony 'New Columbia'[126] – then 'the young establishment on the Pacific coast' became 'quite a favourite', even supplanting New Zealand as a destination for educated migrants.

> In days to come, when the Pacific coast is under Anglo-Saxon domination from the Frozen Sea to the Isthmus of Panama, when the Australians are a powerful community, when China and the whole of eastern Asia are penetrated by the enterprise of English-speaking races, the region now known as British Columbia will most assuredly rank among the most prosperous and powerful.[127]

Welcoming the idea of a union of British North America in 1858, *The Times* commented that the provinces were 'all, except Lower Canada, English in people, language, laws and institutions'.[128] French Canada, a threat in the 1830s, had gradually subsided through nuisance to marginal aside. In fact, even in its more Francophobe phases, *The Times* rarely seemed sure whether it was locked in conflict with the entire French population or merely determined to squash a minority of political agitators. Sir Charles Bagot was condemned for opening his Executive Council to LaFontaine and his allies in 1842 on the ingenious grounds that their selection was 'a libel on the French population of the colony'.[129] There was no objection in principle to bringing French Canadians into government.

> Their own simple and honest character – their mere numerical importance – their indisposition to the alliance of our encroaching and untrustworthy neighbours of the United States – all these circumstances point them out as fit recipients of a share, and a substantial one, of political power and influence.[130]

Surely, *The Times* insisted in 1842, there were loyal French 'who might have formed fit cases for evidencing this just impartiality.'[131] However, a year later it contradicted its own assertion. Some people were simply unqualified for politics. 'Such are the Irish populace – such in a less extravagant degree are the French Canadians. Political power they cannot exercise – they can but pass it on to the demagogue who happens to have their ear.'[132] In 1843 the spectre of Daniel O'Connell still loomed over British perceptions of French Canada.

In one respect, *The Times* may have been right in its analysis of the events of 1842, when it argued that there was 'no real community of interest or principle' between the French and the 'ultra-Reformers'.[133] Less happily, it derived this judgement in part from a highly bucolic portrayal of French Canadians, reinforced by a continuing desire to pursue its feud with Durham beyond the grave. Bagot's conclusion that the Canadian Union could only be made to work by bringing in the French 'reflects no great credit on the penetration of the late Lord Durham' whose prescription for their future had taken 'pretty much the stringent form of *delenda est Carthago*'. French Canadians were 'a *good* people' and did not deserve to be '*crushed*' merely because they refused to see themselves as 'wealth-creating machines'. Within five years of 1837 – and, perhaps more important, two years after the death of Barnes – *The Times* wished to distinguish between 'the French population' as a whole and 'those demagogues, few we believe, who are chargeable with the last outbreak'.[134]

When LaFontaine returned to office in 1848, *The Times* ranged deep into history to explain why the victorious French displayed 'all the bitterness of a sect and all the tactics of a party'. The seventeenth-century founders of French Canada had not turned their colony over to paupers and speculators. Rather, 'they sent from the shores of France a society, small in magnitude but perfect in its proportions and systematic in its organization – a society which was the archetype of provincial France, and stamped with all the lineaments of nationality.' The result was that while English-Canadian society was 'shifty, vague, and uncertain . . . slow in settling and slower in consolidating – this petty offshoot of Royal France has grown together in unity, in power and importance'.[135] By the end of the decade, *The Times* was 'anxious to believe that the French Canadians are a simple, quiet and orderly race', even if they were 'neither very enlightened nor very shrewd, nor yet very fond of Anglo-Saxons'.[136] Their traditions, their minority position and the warning of cultural extinction to be seen in Louisiana were all 'strong and reliable evidence that they will not commit the suicidal folly of merging themselves in the federal union of the American Republic'.[137]

French Canada became viewed as a bulwark against the United States at just the time when it seemed that the question of annexation might be settled by the defection of English-speaking Canadians. *The Times* placed the short-lived Montreal annexation movement of 1849 in a longer-term context as 'but the last move in a varied game begun at the capitulation of Quebec',[138] but it was less confident in extending analysis into prediction. In principle, *The Times* saw nothing wrong in open discussion of the issue. Happily the days had passed 'when every Englishman would have boiled with indignation at the presumption which complained of English dominion, and at the temerity which proposed to carry the presumption of language into action'.[139] Should the time arrive when 'an overwhelming majority in Canada' decide for annexation themselves, *The Times* asked only 'that our own loyalty may be spared a painful appeal'.[140] Less noble were the motives of the annexationists, 'disbanded hirelings' of the old protectionist system.[141]

Willingness to see the issue discussed did not imply that *The Times* wished to be rid of Canada. 'Could we give up to a rival and aggressive Republic a province as vast as France, without perilling our power and damaging our prosperity?' How would the loss of Canada affect Britain's relations with 'the brave loyalists of Nova Scotia', or the Empire's ability to retain 'the most valuable harbours on the globe? If Canada ceases to be British, must Nova Scotia, New Brunswick and Prince Edward's Island cease to be British also?'[142] A New York correspondent assured readers that the annexation of Canada was 'freely but coldly referred to' in the American press, and that public opinion seemed 'to regard it as an event which it is by no means desirable to hasten', one which would bring the United States little benefit at a cost of much sectional strain.[143] Editorially, *The Times* endorsed the reassurance. 'What is very remarkable is, that opinions are seriously divided upon the project in the States themselves.'[144] The territorial expansion of the United States had previously involved grabbing sparsely populated regions. 'But Canada is Canada, and would remain Canada.'[145]

Even at the time of the Montreal annexation movement of 1849, *The Times* found it hard to believe that Canadians would in the event decide to join the United States. While 'we cannot be blind to the tremendous pressure of circumstances ever dragging Canada into commercial and political unity' with its powerful neighbour, 'a transference of Canadian allegiance, painful as it would be to this country, would be far more painful to the Canadians themselves.'[146] Sentiment would not be the only casualty. Annexation would deprive Canadians of 'the benefit of a large British expenditure' on the colonial garrison, of protection on timber exports to the home market and the power to determine local tariff rates.[147] The threat of annexation seemed to fade with remarkable suddenness in the early months of 1850, partly overtaken by a sectional crisis in the United States. 'Whether Canada is one day to add her stars to the Union is as purely conjectural as the possible disruption of the Union itself.'[148] By 1856, *The Times* could confidently dismiss Canadian annexation as unlikely 'as the similar prospect of England, Ireland, and Scotland being one day added to the United States'.[149]

This was not to say that *The Times* thought Canada could stand alone in the world. In 1850 it bracketed 'annexation' with 'that independence which will infallibly lead to it'. British withdrawal would create only 'a tottering independence', in which Canada might not be able to 'avert a war of races, a financial brawl . . . and a final absorption in the dubious fortunes of an overgrown republic'.[150] In 1856, it still linked the two, although disagreeing with those who thought 'that the present political state of Canada is only a phase in the inevitable transition to independence, or to its almost certain consequence – annexation'.[151] Canada seemed to be doing well enough under the half-way system of responsible government.

The Times had been slow to embrace the idea of responsible government. Indeed, as it had noted in 1844, 'no two men . . . mean the same thing' when they used the term.[152] However, the policy of leaving Canadians to manage their own affairs seemed to have proved its worth in saving the province 'from insurrection and revolt' in the turbulence of 1848,[153] and throughout the Rebellion Losses bill affair *The Times* stood firmly against intervention. Support for colonial self-government was one thing; definition another. In 1850, *The Times* referred to 'the all but independent communities of British America'.[154] In 1852 it challenged the claim that colonial self-government fell 'little short of independence'.[155] In 1856, it noted that Canada's 'practical independence' was limited by an imperial veto on colonial legislation, 'a reserve which comes to very little'.[156]

Imprecision in the definition did not seem important. What mattered was that responsible government worked. 'It is now fourteen years since this country entered on a new course of policy with regard to the Canadas', *The Times* announced in December 1854, 'and the experiment may now be said to be fully and completely worked out.' Implicitly tracing the origins of responsible government to the Union of 1841, *The Times* rejoiced that colonial loyalty seemed stronger than ever at just the moment when most of the British garrison was being withdrawn for dispatch to the Crimea. 'At this period . . . the dismemberment of the empire ought to be complete, and Canada, freed from all shackles and bound by no material ties, might be supposed about to drift away from us for ever.' On the contrary, the province had just voted £20,000 to the Patriotic Fund, showing that 'there are beyond the Atlantic hearts that would feel for and hands that would aid us'. Moreover, such free and spontaneous support came from 'this same Canada – where, not twenty years ago, the people rose in armed rebellion . . . where the supplies used to be stopped every year, and a Governor was fortunate who escaped both mobbing and impeachment'.[157]

'We really seem at last to have solved the problem so long deemed insoluble', *The Times* remarked in 1856, 'how to retain a Colonial dependency under the dominion of the mother country, without violence and without coercion, by the mere strength of mutual interests and mutual benefits.'[158] There was, too, a practical and less high-flown argument in favour of responsible government: it ensured that Canadian quarrels found 'no home, no nest, in this country', leaving the British public to deal with 'our own share of troubles'.[159] Given its editorial potential for rhetorical exaggeration, The Times was remarkably restrained in its assessments of Canada's future. An underlying tone of imperial pride in an unprecedented partnership with such an unusual colony was surely pardonable. Outbursts of sentiment hailing the spread of Alfred's language and Chaucer's poetry across transatlantic wilderness were rare, and only once in these two decades can 'the blood of Wolfe' be found spattered across a Times leader.[160] Sober common sense was far more usual: 'the future importance of the United Provinces of Upper and Lower Canada to this country' made it 'highly to the interests of this country to cultivate their friendship and good-will'.[161] Nor did The Times actively disagree with those, like Cobden, whose 'preliminary point of faith' was that Canada 'cannot for ever be politically dependent on and governed by England'.[162] The remaining colonies might one day break away as the United States had done, but 'the question is not only what is probable thirty years hence, but what is prudent at the present hour. We need not hasten to realize even what we cannot but forebode.'[163]

'What are we to do with Canada?', The Times asked when Lord Ellenborough called for the province to become independent in 1854. 'Are we to go on for a generation or two more on a cold-blooded cork-jacket system, telling it coolly that it must manage for itself before long, and meanwhile we will help to keep it afloat?' The Times refused to answer its own question, urging Ellenborough to spare himself 'this load of fruitless enquiry' by using his heart rather than his head. 'A grain of common feeling will help you more than a ton of uncommon philosophy.' In the previous thirty years, there had been 'nothing ingenious and wicked, prescient and suspicious, elaborate and vindicative, pompous and mean, that we have not been asked to do in Canada'.[164] In place of 'logical alternatives and political impossibilities', it was better to accept that three million British North Americans, 'people of our blood and spirit, who may any day they please attach themselves to a neighbouring republic . . . are not to be treated like a handful of Englishmen dropped on a continent of savages or an island in the Pacific'.[165]

History, of course, should be written free of present concerns, and reflections across the span of time belong, if at all, in a tailpiece. A

century and a half later, Canadians alternately complain that the
British news media ignore their country or report it in a remarkably
superficial manner – sometimes by correspondents based south of
the border. Perhaps the major difference nowadays is that the British media are not only aware of the existence of a French-speaking
community in Canada, but have become fixated on the issue of
Quebec. As in the 1850s, the British public only hears about Canada
'when there is an eruption', but nowadays Mount Etna is called
separatism, and even minor tremors are eagerly hailed as lava flows
of Quebec sovereignty. When a Canadian political upheaval does
command attention, commentators ignore Prince Albert's warning
not to 'mix up Canadian *party* politics with general English *party*
politics'[166] – as happened when the routing of the Progressive
Conservative party in the 1993 federal election was widely urged as
a warning to the struggling Conservative government in Britain.

It may thus be worth closing this survey of the sometimes irritat-
ing pontifications of *The Times* by citing a piece of common sense
which it offered in 1861 as it deprecated the strengthening of the
British garrison at a time of violent internal discord – the less squeam-
ish called it a general election – in the province of Canada. *The
Times* wanted the troops kept out of any trouble:

> whatever the quarrels of the two races may be, it is clearly no part of our
> duty to take part in them. We are friends of both sides, and can act for
> or against neither . . . Canada has the power of shaping her own destinies,
> and it is neither possible if it were wise, nor wise if it were possible, to
> interfere with the gradual unfolding of events.[167]

The patronizing tone and the language of race are no longer appropriate, but the sentiment itself remains sound as events in Canada
continue to unfold to the bewilderment of distant observers.

Notes

Except where noted, biographical information is taken from the *Dictionary
of Canadian Biography*. Only direct quotations or extended discussions are
footnoted.

[1] The title is taken from *The Times* of 9 November 1846. All references
to *The Times* are given simply in date form, and refer to leading articles
unless otherwise noted.

[2] Ged Martin, 'The Canadian Rebellion Losses Bill of 1849 in British

Politics', *Journal of Imperial and Commonwealth History*, vi (1977), 3–22.

[3] 28 May 1849.

[4] 12 July 1854.

[5] C. M. Johnston, *American Historical Review*, lxxiv (1969), 1391–2.

[6] 31 October 1849.

[7] Anthony Trollope, *Phineas Finn* (first published 1869), ch.56.

[8] In his reply to the address of 25 March 1836 from 'the industrious classes' of Toronto, which he couched in 'plainer and more homely Language' than an official document. *British Parliamentary Papers*, 1839, xxxiii, Dispatches from Sir F. B. Head, p.168.

[9] University of Durham, Grey Papers, Elgin to Grey, 1 July 1854.

[10] So Newcastle reported to Queen Victoria and to Sir Edmund Head, Royal Archives, RA/P22/63, 27 August 1861; University of Nottingham, Newcastle Papers, NeC 10885, Newcastle to Head (copy), Private, 27 August 1861, quoted by J. A. Gibson, 'The Duke of Newcastle and British North American Affairs, 1859–1864', *Canadian Historical Review*, xliv (1963), 146.

[11] *Montreal Herald*, 12 September 1846, quoted *The Times*, 1 October 1846.

[12] University of Nottingham, Newcastle Papers, NeC 10885, Newcastle to Head (copy), Private, 28 September 1861, quoted Gibson, 'The Duke of Newcastle', 146.

[13] Royal Archives, RA/P22/18, Labouchere to Queen Victoria, 13 May 1856.

[14] Quoted, Gibson, 'The Duke of Newcastle', 146.

[15] University of Nottingham, Newcastle Papers, NeC 9552, Elgin to Newcastle (copy), 27 January 1854. The British system of titles can confuse the unwary. Automatic membership of the House of Lords was confined to those who held English peerages conferred prior to 1707, or United Kingdom ('British') titles thereafter. Holders of Scottish or Irish titles, however imposing, could sit in the Lords only if chosen as representative peers. The eldest sons of dukes, marquesses and earls were known by one of their families' lesser titles, but despite these 'courtesy titles', they too were commoners. Thus it was possible to be a Lord and also very short of money, a common condition among Irish peers and eldest sons.

[16] Description by James Stephen of the Colonial Office and not intended as a compliment, quoted *Dictionary of Canadian Biography*, IX, p.147.

[17] This seems a reasonable deduction from the tone of Newcastle's reply to a lost letter, University of Nottingham, Newcastle Papers, NeC 10885, Newcastle to Manners Sutton (copy), 23 August 1861, quoted Gibson, 'The Duke of Newcastle', 147–8.

[18] 22 August 1861.

[19] 26 March 1864.

[20]   22 August 1861.

[21]   University of New Brunswick, Harriet Irving Library, Stanmore Papers, Reel 2, Normanby to Gordon, 7 September 1863. The same assumption prevented Lord Chandos from becoming governor-general in 1861 on the death of his father: Newcastle commented that he 'is now out of the question for he became Duke of Buckingham yesterday'. University of Nottingham, Newcastle Papers, NeC 10885, Newcastle to Head (copy), Private, 31 July 1861, pp.187–9.

[22]   28 May 1849. Goldwin Smith vividly described the distaste which the British aristocracy felt for American democracy as 'a monstrous and unnatural birth, which, if we still only wait a little, will creep back into the womb'. G. Smith, *The Empire* (London, 1863), p.138.

[23]   J. Mackay Hitsman, *Safeguarding Canada 1763–1871* (Toronto, 1968), pp.136, 172.

[24]   W. Ormsby (ed.), *Crisis in the Canadas: 1838–1839. The Grey Journals and Letters* (Toronto, 1964), p.221.

[25]   Barry W. Gough, 'John Gordon', in *Dictionary of Canadian Biography*, IX, pp.326–7.

[26]   M. H. Synge, *Great Britain One Empire* (London, 1852). In 1851, Earl Grey called him 'a very clever fellow', A. G. Doughty (ed.), *The Elgin–Grey Papers 1846–1852*, 4 vols. (Ottawa, 1937), II, p.825. Synge was an officer of the Royal Engineers who had been stationed in Canada.

[27]   W. H. Russell, *Canada: Its Defences, Condition, and Resources* (London, 1865), pp.156, 122.

[28]   Howe to W. J. Stairs, 15 March 1867, in L. J. Burpee, 'Joseph Howe and the Anti-Confederation League', *Transactions of the Royal Society of Canada*, section ii, series iii, x (1917), 457.

[29]   Greville to Reeve, 19 October 1855, in A. H. Johnson (ed.), *The Letters of Charles Greville and Henry Reeve 1836–1865* (London, 1924), p.248.

[30]   [Sydney Smith], *Mr Dyson's Speech to the Freeholders, on Reform*, 2nd edn (London, 1831), p.14.

[31]   Quoted, *The History of The Times: 'The Thunderer' in the Making 1785–1841* (London, 1935), p.348 (cited as *History of The Times*, I).

[32]   According to H. R. Fox Bourne, *English Newspapers: Chapters in the History of Journalism*, 2 vols. (London, 1887), II, pp.104–5, the Report 'contained two paragraphs respecting church or crown lands to which the government objected, and which Durham consented to alter'. These paragraphs represented the views of Durham's associate Wakefield, 'who was determined that they should not be tampered with'. Accordingly, Wakefield sent a copy to *The Times*. Fox Bourne gave no source for the story, but as a member of a Whig clan he may have had some private knowledge.

[33]   *The History of The Times: The Tradition Established 1841–1884* (London, 1939), pp.196–7 (cited as *History of The Times*, II); A. P.

Wadsworth, *Newspaper Circulations, 1850–1964* (Manchester Statistical Society, 1955), esp. p.9.

[34] Quoted, *History of The Times*, II, p.200.

[35] J. Vincent (ed.), *Disraeli, Derby and the Conservative Party: Journals and Memoirs of Edward Henry, Lord Stanley 1849–1869* (Hassocks, 1978), p.104 (24 March 1853); Anthony Trollope, *The Warden* (first published 1855), ch. 7 (in which *The Times* is thinly disguised as *The Jupiter*).

[36] W. H. Russell, *My Diary North and South*, 2 vols. (London, 1863), I, p.57. Jefferson Davis actually offered Richard Cobden a current file of *The Times* when the two met on a Mississippi riverboat in 1859. Brian Jenkins, *Britain & the War for the Union*, 2 vols. (Montreal, 1974), I, p.10.

[37] Shaftesbury's journal, 27 June 1855, quoted B. Harrison, 'The Sunday Trading Riots of 1855', *Historical Journal*, viii (1965), 231.

[38] W. L. Morton (ed.), *Monck Letters and Journals 1863–1868: Canada from Government House at Confederation* (Toronto, 1970), pp.153–4. See also Cobden to Delane, 9 December 1863, in J. Morley, *The Life of Richard Cobden* (London, 1903 edn), p.890: '*The Times* never enters my house, except by rare accident . . . It is only during the [parliamentary] Session, at the Club, that I am in the habit of seeing your paper.'

[39] Quoted, *History of The Times*, I, pp.323–4.

[40] Clarendon to Reeve, 14 October 1849, in H. Maxwell (ed.), *The Life and Letters of George William Frederick Fourth Earl of Clarendon*, 2 vols. (London, 1913), II, p.292. It should be noted that both Clarendon and Lincoln addressed their comments to associates of *The Times*.

[41] G. C. Lewis, *An Essay on the Influence of Authority on Matters of Opinion* (London, 1849), pp.342–50.

[42] *History of The Times*, I, pp.420–4. Unluckily, it was not easy to unmask the anonymous. Roebuck was forced to partial retraction when one of his targets, Edward Sterling, dismissed his allegations by saying that there was 'only one word in the English dictionary by which they can be fitly characterized'.

[43] The controversy, in December 1863, is extensively documented in Morley, *Cobden*, pp.887–903.

[44] Ibid., p.890.

[45] G. E. Marindin (ed.), *Letters of Frederic Lord Blachford Under Secretary of State for the Colonies 1860–1871* (London, 1896), pp.112–15. Given the way in which leading articles evolved, it may not be entirely accurate to attribute the view of *The Times* in 1866 that the Welsh language was 'the curse of Wales' to Delane in person. K. O. Morgan, *Wales 1880–1980: Rebirth of a Nation* (Oxford, 1982 edn), p.4.

[46] 5 February 1853, commenting on Cobden's speech at Holmfirth.

[47] 13 September 1837.

[48] 8 February 1839.

[49]   Morley, op. cit., p.893.

[50]   29 September 1854.

[51]   Charles Pebody, quoted H. E. Carlisle (ed.), *A Selection of the Correspondence of Abraham Hayward, Q.C. from 1834 to 1884*, 2 vols. (London, 1886), I, p.138. *The Times* was collaborating with its London rivals to secure regular news overland from India as early as 1846. *History of The Times*, I, p.79.

[52]   C. F. Greville (H. Reeve, ed.), *Journal of the Reign of Queen Victoria from 1852 to 1860*, 2 vols. (London, 1887), I, p.74 (12 July 1854). *The Times* brushed such charges aside. *History of The Times*, I, p.211.

[53]   3 January 1850; 24 June 1851.

[54]   For celebrations of kinship, see e.g. 3 January 1836, 27 January 1838 and 3 January 1846, the last quoted by H. C. Allen, *Great Britain and the United States: A History of Anglo-American Relations (1783–1952)* (London, 1954), p.413.

[55]   Quoted, Morley, op. cit., p.887.

[56]   Quoted, Fox Bourne, *English Newspapers*, II, p.111n.

[57]   *History of The Times*, I, p.459. Brougham was one of the chief critics of Durham's mission to Canada. Durham also cultivated *The Times*, ibid., p.206. Brougham himself recalled that while Barnes called himself 'my debtor for life', he showed his appreciation 'by instalments of abuse – I won't say daily, but almost weekly'. Ibid., I, p.487.

[58]   His sympathy with the underprivileged even extended to Irish tenants – despite his antipathy to O'Connell – and was expressed in a celebrated description of Lord Limerick as a 'thing with human pretensions', for which comment James Lawson, printer of *The Times*, was summoned before the bar of the House of Lords in 1831. *History of The Times*, I, p.360.

[59]   20 December 1837, 2 February 1838, 29 August 1836, 25 December 1837.

[60]   Quoted, *History of The Times*, I, p.198.

[61]   13 July 1836, 27, 23, 20 December 1837, 15 January 1838.

[62]   25 December, 10 March, 20 December 1837.

[63]   10 March, 26 April 1837.

[64]   Jenkins, *Britain & the War for the Union*.

[65]   2 June 1863.

[66]   29 June 1864.

[67]   J. C. Dent, *The Last Forty Years: Canada Since the Union of 1841*, 2 vols. (Toronto, 1881), II, p.426.

[68]   See, generally, Fox Bourne, op. cit., II, and *History of The Times*, II. In its first number, on 3 November 1855, the *Saturday Review* wrote: 'No apology is necessary for assuming that this country is ruled by "The Times". We all know it, or, if we do not know it, we ought to know it.' It was hard to reconcile 'the magnificent spectacle afforded by British

freedom' with the fact that thirty million people were 'governed despotically by a newspaper'.

[69] University of Durham, Grey Papers, journal of third Earl Grey, 14 January, 12 May 1849.

[70] Newcastle to Delane, undated, in A. I. Dasent, *John Thaddeus Delane Editor of 'The Times': His Life and Correspondence*, 2 vols. (London, 1908), II, p.30 ('*Your* cock fights . . . Lord Monck has accepted Canada'), and cf. *The Times*, 22 August 1861. Cobden was unconvinced by the denial: 'I do not even say that the stream of patronage ought not to flow to the *Times* office; I only contend that it should not run underground' (quoted, Morley, op. cit., p.901).

[71] 6 January 1851.

[72] Speech at Leeds, reported 30 January 1854.

[73] C. A. Bristed, *Five Years in an English University*, 2 vols. (New York, 1852), I, p.38. See n.86 for the possible origin of the reference to two houses of Congress. The University was Cambridge.

[74] J. A. Roebuck, *The Colonies of England* (London, 1849), p.82n.

[75] 30 October 1858.

[76] 22 March 1849.

[77] Russell, *My Diary North and South*, II, pp.6, 37.

[78] 3 January 1846.

[79] 10 October 1860. See also M. Crawford, *The Anglo-American Crisis of the Mid-Nineteenth Century:* The Times *and America, 1850–1862* (Athens, Ga., 1987).

[80] Russell, *My Diary North and South*, I, p.42.

[81] 28 September 1842.

[82] 7 February 1850.

[83] 23 March 1849.

[84] 1 August 1853.

[85] 31 August 1849.

[86] 21 October 1845. This article was almost certainly influenced by the sarcastic tone of Sydney Smith's *Humble Petition to the House of Congress at Washington* (1843). Cf. Allen, *Great Britain and the United States*, pp.93–4.

[87] 9 August 1854.

[88] 24 March 1855. *The Times* did not accept that 'Mr Monroe's extravagant doctrine' gave the United States the right to intervene in its neighbours' affairs, 21 November 1849.

[89] 12 December 1854.

[90] 29 December 1849.

[91] 16 December 1850.

[92] 5 December 1860.

[93] 24 December 1860.

[94] E.g. 6 November 1855.

[95] E.g. 20 February 1844, 13 October 1842.

[96]   11 January, 31 August 1849.

[97]   27 January 1838.

[98]   3 September 1858.

[99]   Elgin to Grey, Private, 8 November 1850, 1 November 1849 in Doughty, ed., *Elgin–Grey Papers*, II, pp.737–8, 529.

[100]   16 August 1849, letter from Montreal correspondent, 26 July.

[101]   27 July 1848.

[102]   28 June 1849.

[103]   30 June 1854.

[104]   6 January 1860. The use of the term 'settlements' is in itself instructive.

[105]   Quoted, J. K. Chapman, *The Career of Arthur Hamilton Gordon First Lord Stanmore 1829–1912* (Toronto, 1964), p.6 (letter of 20 July 1845).

[106]   22 October 1844.

[107]   28 July 1848.

[108]   21 January 1847.

[109]   22 December 1856. Upper Canada (later Ontario) was often called 'Canada West' between 1841 and 1867.

[110]   1 December 1856.

[111]   26 January 1850.

[112]   1 January 1845. 'The defection of two or three individuals from the majority of ten puts the administration in peril.' Elgin to Grey, Private, 27 May 1847, Doughty (ed.), op. cit., I, p.46.

[113]   16 May 1849.

[114]   22 December 1856.

[115]   19 January 1848.

[116]   23 January 1847.

[117]   7 January 1856. For Howe's speech, see J. A. Chisholm (ed.), *The Speeches and Public Letters of Joseph Howe*, 2 vols. (Halifax, 1909), II, pp.268–95.

[118]   18 April 1859.

[119]   22 July 1858.

[120]   4 April 1857.

[121]   21 August 1848.

[122]   4 September 1848.

[123]   28 June 1858.

[124]   9 July 1858.

[125]   26 July 1858. Cf. Ged Martin, 'The Naming of British Columbia', *Albion*, x (1979), 257–63.

[126]   28 August 1858.

[127]   1 April 1859.

[128]   3 September 1858.

[129]   15 October 1842.

[130]   27 October 1842.

[131]   15 October 1842.

[132]   16 December 1843.

[133] 27 October 1842.

[134] 29 October, 1 November 1842. *Delenda est Carthago* ('Carthage must be destroyed') was the refrain of speeches by Cato the Elder in the Senate of Republican Rome. In an era when the classics dominated liberal education, the phrase conveyed the paranoid intolerance of power.

[135] 1 August 1848. It is hardly necessary to state that this was a romantic interpretation of the demographic origins of New France.

[136] 11 April 1849.

[137] 22 June 1849.

[138] 3 January 1850.

[139] 31 October 1849.

[140] 11 February 1850.

[141] 26 January 1850.

[142] 31 October 1849.

[143] 14 August 1849 (letter from New York correspondent, 31 July).

[144] 22 August 1849. *The Times* was also realistic in its recognition that the Americans would take the view that 'all is fish that comes into that net' (20 November 1849).

[145] 21 September 1849.

[146] 3 January 1850.

[147] 20 November 1849.

[148] 26 January 1850.

[149] 22 December 1856.

[150] 11, 7 February 1850.

[151] 22 December 1851.

[152] 2 January 1844.

[153] 5 February 1849.

[154] 23 April 1850.

[155] 11 October 1852.

[156] 22 December 1856.

[157] 12 December 1854.

[158] 5 March 1856.

[159] 12 July 1854.

[160] 4 May 1849, 4 July 1848.

[161] 6 May 1843.

[162] 24 December 1849, reporting speech at Bradford.

[163] 7 February 1850. *The Times* guessed that the province of Canada might contain between five and six million people by 1874, 11 May 1849.

[164] 17 June 1854.

[165] 30 June 1854.

[166] Albert to Grey, 3 August 1846, in K. Jagow (ed.) (tr. E. T. S. Dugdale), *Letters of the Prince Consort 1831–1861* (London, 1938), p.105.

[167] 17 June 1861.

5

Learning about Oneself: The Making of Canadian Nationalism, 1867–1914

JAMES STURGIS

Growing Up Dual

Margaret Prang lived in Edmonton. It was in the early 1930s. Relatives who visited her family from Ontario or elsewhere were usually taken for a drive along a street which, within its less than two-mile reach, held up to view some fifty ethnic churches. Quite naturally her life was affected by the presence of those whom she had learned to call 'new Canadians'. Later, and in her own words, she wrote:

> Dare I confess that in my first year of high school I won a public speaking contest with an oration on the role of the prairie provinces, with their mixed population, in the growth of Canada. My finest moment was the final peroration, borrowed, naturally, from D'Arcy McGee: 'I see in the not remote distance one great nationality bound like the shield of Achilles by the blue rim of ocean'.

Let us commend such astuteness (how natural that she should have eventually become a professional historian) in picking out the words of this martyred visionary, a former Irish rebel who eventually embraced the Crown after a short spell of journalistically rhapsodizing about the great Republic, and whose call for the creation of a 'new nationality' in British North America raised suspicions in many minds as to what the true intent of Confederation was. Did it signify the end of the imperial connection? Or was it possible that a loyalty to Crown and Empire was compatible with the project of developing a 'new nationality'?

If we return to the recollections of Margaret Prang, by now living in Ontario, then we can see how far the matter had advanced by the late 1930s.

Although I had nothing against the King, I always sang 'O Canada' with greater gusto than 'God Save the King', and if I had been asked at the age of fifteen to choose this country's national anthem I would not have hesitated for a moment. A little later, as part of a high school audience assembled in front of the Brantford Collegiate Institute listening to the Governor-General, Lord Tweedsmuir, extolling the glories of the land he had so quickly come to love, I sensed nothing unusual in his assurances that it was our first duty to understand and serve Canada. Such advice seemed quite unexceptional and I would have been shocked to have been told anything else. I was unaware, then, of the storm that such sentiments on the lips of the Crown's representative created in some sections of English Canadian society.[1]

So, as these words indicate, even upon the eve of the Second World War the relationship between Canadianism and imperialism in English Canada was far from settled. Indeed, in the opinion of another historian, Arthur Lower, writing in 1943, the balance was still all wrong:

A recent writer has termed this country [as] the 'unwanted step child' of England . . . [But it] is both less and more than a stepchild. From one point of view, it is the illegitimate offspring of a French mother by an English father: from another it is the child of a couple now divorced, England and the United States. Whoever its progenitors, none of them has ever wanted the baby. Though the father, John Bull, took it until it came to manhood, he carried out his duties with reluctance. Since even in extreme cases it is hard to extinguish filial respect, there have always been many of our citizens who deem the paternal establishment [as] more worthy of their affections than their own family hearth. Although we are now growing up, many of our people still hold this view.[2]

Did the persistence and longevity of such attitudes indicate a failure in Canadian statecraft? Or, considering the fact that many of the generation to whom Lower was referring grew up in the pre-First World War period, was this actually the desired result of the kind of socialization to which they had been subjected? Actually, the family metaphor used by Lower is highly appropriate to our purposes. In the latter half of this chapter we will look at the array of influences to which the English Canadian child in the period from 1870 to 1914 was subjected, as well as any other independent factors which might help to explain the cultural climate within which Prang and Lower grew to adulthood.

The argument of this chapter can be simply put. It is premised on the necessity of recognizing the many influences which created the

Britishness which in itself did so much to define English Canadian nationalism. The cultural impact of British immigration alone, the effects of which are set out by Phillip Buckner in this volume, helps to account for this Anglocentric outlook. So does the protective shield which the embrace of such values, and the power behind them, provided against an expansive America. But this chapter also argues that it would be a mistake to discount the reality early on of what can be called a Canadian territorial nationalism – a nationalism that prided itself on its own climate, vastness and potentialities. Often an independent northern theme, it could also segue effortlessly into more Elgarian realms. However, in a temporal sense, what is important to notice is the way in which a developing Canadian nationalism was to a great extent nipped in the bud by the force of what Benedict Anderson has more generically called a state-sponsored form of 'official nationalism'[3] (which in this context can be recognized as an insistent British imperial sentiment) in the late nineteenth century. Yet, despite this, Canadian national feeling, sometimes manifesting itself as nothing more noble than 'nativism', informed in an important way the attempts, for example, to assimilate the flood of immigrants into the West in the decade or so before the War of 1914. Recognition of the importance of this point helps to explain the impatience of individuals such as Margaret Prang and Arthur Lower with Canada's duality of outlook.

The Making of Nationalism

However fine a mesh used by the historian, the definition of nationalism has usually evaded capture. However, Benedict Anderson has recently provided some helpful guidelines. In his view it is better to think of nationalism as similar to religion or kinship rather than to political beliefs like liberalism or Fascism. His own phrase is that a nation is 'an imagined political community' which is always conceived of 'as a deep, horizontal comradeship' and for the sake of which people are ultimately willing to die. What, in Anderson's view, allowed the development of nationalism was a complex set of forces, most notable of which were the almost concurrent developments of vernacular languages, capitalism and printing. By the end of the nineteenth century most established regimes had learned, however unpredictable and dangerous nationalism might once have been, to contain and exploit it.[4]

One such technique was by means of what Eric Hobsbawm has called the invention of tradition. He has formulated the way in which the state could use devices such as national holidays or flags for purposes of integration and assimilation. He identifies invented tradition as consisting of a set of practices of a ritualistic 'or symbolic nature, which seeks to inculcate certain values and norms of behaviour by repetition' and which gains legitimacy in the eyes of the citizen by an implied continuity with the past. He gives the example of the Third French Republic where the celebration of the storming of the Bastille was deliberately set up in 1880 in order to stimulate republican sentiment.[5] Hobsbawm, it should be noted, does allow for an indigenous force of nationalism with which state power has to contend. This force was vastly strengthened during the course of the nineteenth century as a result of the democratization of politics – when, in other words, subjects became citizens and began to regard the state as in some respects their own. Nevertheless, governments knew the value of mobilizing national feeling and often did so by resort to racial or xenophobic appeals.[6]

In another attempt to account for the nature of nationalism, Ernest Gellner links it directly with the forces of modernization and industrialization. He refers to the 'basic deception' of the nationalization process whereby the pretence is followed that a culture of the people is being stamped upon the character of the nation. Instead nationalism 'usually conquers in the name of a putative folk culture' and represents 'the general imposition of a high culture on a society'. Even in those cases where one people is ruled by another, the forces which are deployed to combat the alien are but the revival or invention of a local high culture. As he says, it tends to be the 'great ladies' who go to town in what is claimed to be a peasant dress.[7] Gellner's reminder of the deliberate and manipulative element in the making of nationalism is a useful one. However, in Canada's case, the presence of Quebec within the Confederation meant that the federal state at least could not overtly turn itself into an apparatus for cultural change.

American Certainty

It could hardly be otherwise, considering the circumstances of Canada's birth, that a more than latent anti-Americanism was embedded within the Canadian central nervous system. Two elections, in

1891 and 1911, put the question of closer economic ties with the United States squarely to the electorate; both times they were rejected, mainly due to the fears that were aroused concerning the increased possibility of subsequent political union. The Toronto *Telegram* must be adjudged to have got it right when it editorialized in 1903 that 'Continentalism always and ever must be the enemy and assassin of Canadianism'.[8] In the late nineteenth century popular distrust of the Republic was added to by the view that the American system of government was inherently unstable and corrupt, that its society was increasingly plutocratic and that the American system showed too many signs of being unable to cope with the challenges of Black emancipation, urbanization and industrialization.[9]

However much Canadians and their newspapers bolstered their own self-confidence by deploring American political and social inadequacies, there was one aspect of the individual American's make-up that was much admired. Briefly, this trait concerned identity. An American knew who he or she was. Without doubt the way in which that badge was worn was much too blatant and uncritical, but Canadians nevertheless could not but be impressed by it. More than that, Americans knew how to celebrate their own self-declared greatness. But what happened when efforts were made by the 'Canada First' movement to replicate the American approach to national glorification? One Anti-Confederate newspaper in 1875 reported with glee that

'Canada First' tried to make a demonstration in Toronto on Dominion Day. It thought that the day should be celebrated in American fashion; that there should be a procession and one or more orations, and that the people should be told how happy they are, what a glorious constitution they enjoy, and all that sort of thing. The procession, according to the [Toronto] *Globe*'s description, was not very imposing in any way, and the meeting held in the Park was not very large.

The report put the point that one of the speakers, W. P. Howland, had nothing to say and that he 'dealt in declamation'. Its tart observation regarding another speaker, who avowed that he had driven ninety miles to get there, was that he would have been better advised not to have taken so much trouble. In the end, the whole affair had no meaning or impact.[10]

What seemed to be incontrovertible, however, was that American institutions were effective in terms of drawing out and enhancing the citizen's love of country. This was a theme to which Canadian nationalists of all persuasions would return to time and time again. It was as if they instinctively knew and understood how vigorously the attempts had been made in the early years of the Republic to create a sense of loyalty among its citizens. Intellectuals, ministers and politicians had all been participants. Devices ranging from formal schooling to the flamboyant celebration of holidays with their spread-eagle oratory, parades and pageants, not to mention the edification provided by monuments and statues for departed heroes, all played their part in creating a myth of American exceptionalism and providentialism. As one who lived through this pressure-cooker style of producing patriots, T. L. Nichols wrote:

> We were taught every day and in every way that ours was the freest, the happiest, and soon to be the greatest and most powerful country in the world . . . Our education was adopted to intensify our self esteem. Ours was the model government of the world; our institutions were model institutions, our country the model Republic. I do not in the least exaggerate. We read it in our books and newspapers, heard it in sermons, speeches, and orations, thanked God for it, in our prayers, and devoutly believed it always.[11]

British Superiority

After 1867 Canadian and British perceptions of the Empire and their own native land were quite different. An Englishman could feel perfectly secure in his identity but, as Sir John Seeley was to insist in his classic work of *The Expansion of England* (1883), he needed to become more aware of, and committed to, Empire. Canadians, on the other hand, had always been colonials and members of a protective Empire. Yet events such as Britain's open championing of Confederation, and even more, the withdrawal of the legions, highlighted for others the need to be more independent. With some success the process of Canadianizing a population began to take effect during the first two decades after Confederation. When the imperial federation movement, which started in Britain in 1884, spread its network of clubs to Canada it hardly made any headway at all. Indeed, according to its historian, the prospects in Canada by 1887 looked extremely 'gloomy' and only recovered when the controversy over commercial union with the United States emerged in that year.[12] Nevertheless, imperial sentiment was to grow apace during the 1890s until Sir Wilfrid Laurier as prime minister during the Boer War had to agree, against his better judgement, to dispatch volunteer troops to join the fray. Although the last few years of the nineteenth century were to be the high water mark of imperial loyalty in Canada, there was to be in succeeding years less of a complete cave-in than a slow subsidence.

Whereas there was some awareness as to how American loyalty was inculcated, Canadians assumed that British loyal and imperial sentiment had either come about as an entirely natural growth or by some form of providential intervention or a wonderful combination of both. In the Foreword to her book, *Stories of the British Empire*, the Canadian writer, Agnes Machar, wrote:

> No one, surely, with any adequate belief in the Divine Ruler of the Universe, can study the wonderful story of our British Empire without being impressed with a sense of its Divine purpose, its final mission to humanity, as the end for which the shoot of Saxon freedom, planted in British soil, has grown into the greatest Empire this world has ever seen.[13]

In fact, however, as a recent book reminds us, Britons and Canadians 'often had rather vague ideas of the realities on the other side of the Atlantic'. Canadians 'were prone to conjure up a somewhat romanticised image of British country life – of fox-hunting, muscular outdoor activities, and the intelligent squire surrounded by yeomen farmers', whereas Canadians to Britons were just as likely be stout-hearted but unsophisticated backwoodsmen.[14]

How were Canadians to know that the welding together of diverse peoples into personalities called British was the result of almost as much contrivance as the cloned everyday versions of Uncle Sam? In a remarkable *tour de force* Linda Colley has shown how, as she puts it, in

> the half century after the American war, there would emerge in Great Britain a far more consciously and officially constructed patriotism which stressed attachment to the monarchy, the importance of empire, the value of military and naval achievement, and the desirability of strong, stable government by a virtuous, able and authentically British elite.[15]

British achievement in so many fields of endeavour during the course of the nineteenth century could not help but fuel feelings of pride among an observant citizenry. That it could lead as well to insularity and complacency is also apparent. J. H. Grainger, in his study, *Patriotisms*, thinks that it was not until Britain's pre-eminence was challenged towards the end of the nineteenth century that it became 'obvious that in order to survive Britain must remake herself as a power', a major part of which would be to create a patriotic citizenry.[16]

Muted Beginnings

When British North Americans built a new nation in the 1860s emotion rarely got in the way. On one of the few occasions when it did, during the Charlottetown conference in 1864, the celebratory toasts led to such exuberant oratory that sober-minded Maritimers became immediately distrustful of the politicians who had allowed themselves to be levitated beyond the realms of the balance sheet. R. G. Haliburton, one of the members of 'Canada First', stated that Confederation had been put together with about as much excitement as if a joint-stock company had been formed. The historian, Arthur Lower, in the 1950s wrote that the two fathers of Confederation, John A. Macdonald and D'Arcy McGee, could say of their work: 'We have made Canada; now we must make Canadians.'[17] As if this were not problematical enough, Nova Scotia was openly disaffected by the terms of union and sent a solid phalanx of Anti-Confederates to Ottawa in 1867. Although Macdonald's polished powers of persuasion and canniness in the use of patronage overcame that problem, hard times in the 1880s were to cause the issue of separation to return to the political agenda. At the same time the execution of Louis Riel, the Métis rebel leader in the West, in 1885 did as much to cause serious divisions between French and English, as the completion of the Canadian Pacific Railway did to bind the country together.

Of course, not all the prognostications or prospects were gloomy. The aforementioned R. G. Haliburton, whose ill health caused him to write from a site in the tropics, believed that Canada's future was assured because the northern climate was an assurance of hardiness, energy and vigour among its people. A further advantage was that it deterred immigration from people of lesser efficiency. Another advantage enjoyed by northern people was that, as with the British, there was a natural desire for liberty and self-expression. This idea of the 'true north, strong and free' was to become a staple article in the articulation of Canadian nationalism in this period, and helps to account for the later popularity of the Group of Seven painters, as they took self-conscious shape in the early twentieth century.

Canadians also defined themselves as a people by giving their allegiance to a social Christianity which gave precedence to reform over doctrine. That Canadians, in addition, inherited all the privileges of free-born Englishmen, as well as the accompanying self-governing institutions, gave them a fair and benign breeze as they lifted anchor and left port as a new nation.

If we go back to the first few years after Confederation, what we find attempted at the celebratory level could hardly have been more symbolically disastrous. The decision was taken that the fact of the founding of Canada was going to be marked by a national holiday and festivities. It turned out to be flat champagne. Maybe one of the reasons for this was that the government bungled the arrangements. The following account of 24 June 1867, written admittedly from the standpoint of an Anti-Confederate newspaper in New Brunswick, allows us to understand why confusion reigned:

> It seems that the Government have actually proclaimed the First of July a holiday. To our mind it would have been much wiser, before ordering any Confederation celebrations, to try how it worked. We have yet to learn what there is to rejoice about. Our impression is that there will be a good many Union Jacks upside down next Monday. The Government papers here, and those in Nova Scotia, but particularly those of Canada – which appear to be ever ready for a spree or a jollification of some kind – have for some time been agitating and throwing out hints and rumours in order, apparently, to feel how some sort of celebration on the first of July, to mark the birth of the new Dominion, would take among the people ... At one time we are told our Government will proclaim a holiday and call out the Volunteers; at another the Governor General is represented to be the moving spirit in the matter, – although there is really no General Government. They were going to do the thing in good style; and their liberality was heralded as something extraordinary, because the volunteers ... were to be called out, and at 12 o'clock, or daybreak, or sunrise, or some other time of the day of the first of July a feu de joie was to be fired that would resound from Halifax to Sarnia. For this service the men were to receive a day's pay each.

However, continuing in the same vein, the editorial argued that when it was realized what the state of opinion was within the force in Nova Scotia, and to a lesser extent in New Brunswick, it was decided that the result would be a very 'sorry celebration'. Minds then turned to the possibility of a reciprocal and grand Inter-colonial visitation but that foundered on Bluenose opposition. However, the 'irrepressible Canucks', waving free passes from the Grand Trunk Railway were now attempting to lure members of the Saint John City Corporation to visit other parts of Canada. At the time of writing, the piece concluded, it was impossible to know whether a 'grand Intercolonial drunk' would take place or not.[18] Despite having committed the same error in the previous year, *The New Dominion* in Saint John, a less partisan journal, on 20 June 1868 was again critical of the government because of the late arrival of information as to whether 1 July was to be a holiday or not.[19]

One might be excused for asking how all this affected ordinary people of the time. A seven-year-old boy, living in a Highlander community in eastern Ontario, recalling 1 July 1867, wrote that it was another 'national event [which] barely made a ripple on the surface of our life in the backwoods'. 'I don't remember', he continued, 'hearing a word about the great achievement, even in the manse.'[20]

It would now seem appropriate to look at a few of the agencies of socialization, mainly the schools and holidays, to see whether the flatness experienced by the likes of the young Ralph Connor was ever likely to be modified or changed. The argument which is presented is that indeed during the period from 1870 to 1914 there were ever increasing and effective means adopted in order to indoctrinate the young Canadian. The general change of emphasis in tone in the press was from the search for the means of expression of a territorial nationalism towards an ever more insistent emphasis upon imperial loyalty. It would be a mistake, however, to underestimate, as does Joseph Levitt's otherwise ground-breaking book, *A Vision Beyond Reach*,[21] the degree to which a seam of territorial nationalism took shape in the new Dominion after 1867. Especially so was this true outside Ontario, even if for our purposes O. D. Skelton, university professor and later adviser to Mackenzie King, demonstrates that national sentiment was not always chained to the imperial lion.

The National Role of Provincial Schools

When the work of the provincial public schools in furthering patriotism is investigated, it must be concluded that they emphasized an imperial as opposed to a strictly defined Canadian nationalism. A further restraint was the fact that when educational systems were set up, as in Upper Canada in the 1840s, they were not charged with any national or imperial purpose. Instead the architect of the system,

Egerton Ryerson, saw the inculcation of morality as of uppermost importance in order that the school system could play its proper role in reducing levels of crime and social disorder as well as creating a disciplined work-force.[22] The recent occurrence of the rebellion in 1837 led to the suspicion that American textbooks might have been influential in leading people astray.[23] According to one member of the colonial executive committee, what a schoolboy would learn from studying American school geographies was:

> a smattering of Geography . . . in which England appears as a pitiful little island filled with tyrannical landlords and very fat clergymen, and a great number of squalid tenants and labourers. Ireland is a joyless land of bogs, pigs and catholics, and Scotland an out of the way place in which mountains and the men have a national and barbarous prejudice against decent covering.[24]

Thus the Irish national readers were chosen as the best medium of instruction in Upper Canadian schools. Besides being non-denominational, they also had the added advantage of teaching salient aspects of the Victorian moral code such as the idea that poverty arose entirely from the moral failings of the individual.[25]

In New Brunswick, schools were also seen as catalysts of moral rather than patriotic learning. According to the young R. B. Bennett there was, however, a daily diet of unprogrammed imperial loyalism. 'Students learned that the British Empire was the epitome of all that was good, true and beautiful.'[26] Because of a reliance on imported texts some absurdities could result, however. A school inspector in the county of Northumberland, in 1890, reported on the results of one classroom visitation:

> The lesson began: 'The country where you, children, live in, is called Ireland', and the teacher gave the explanations all on the assumption that the children did live in that country. The class was dismissed without any reference to the error, and, on examination . . . [I] found that the children actually believed they lived in Ireland.[27]

As a result there was in the province a growing feeling that the textbooks were unsuitable for nation-building. Inspector H. S. Bridges stated at a Teachers' Institute meeting:

> No one would question the patriotism of the 1600 teachers of the province who were inculcating patriotic principles in the minds of the children . . . [but] Our text books are not calculated to inspire patriotic feelings. Prizes for essays and original poems should be given. An accurate

knowledge of the resources of the country is indispensable to a pupil . . .
The national holiday should receive more attention from our teachers
and the national flag should float over every school house in our land.[28]

This sentiment was by no means confined to New Brunswick. Such
a concern led to a Dominion history competition in 1893 and the
offer of a prize to the writer of the most suitable high school text.
The young Charles G. D. Roberts offered his *History of Canada*
which, despite not winning, was superior in quality and eventually
published.[29] Broadly, the pattern of things in Nova Scotia was similar.
The teacher's primary duty was to instil notions of morality. By
1900 this was overlaid somewhat by a patriotic patina by which the
assumed link between imperial patriotism and good citizenship was
given more emphasis by the authorities.[30]

In British Columbia a study of the textbooks used in the schools
between 1892 and 1925 reveals, not unexpectedly, a strong moral
imperative upholding loyalty to, and love of, Britain and its Empire.
Any student might have been forgiven for thinking that it 'was not
God but the Union Jack that told pupils to be brave, pure and true'.
One set of readers in Ontario found no need for qualifications in its
statement that the 'British Empire was progressive, powerful and
the most enlightened of civilisations and that the British people were
brave, intelligent and moral'.[31] Robert Stamp has commented on
the manner in which Ontario's history and geography texts projected
an Anglo-Saxon racial superiority.[32] Despite an increasing demand
after 1900 for Canadian history, its usual appearance was as a
patched-on addition to British history.[33] Alberta was much influenced
by Ontario and used some of the same texts.

In Manitoba, the need to assimilate the large foreign element
demanded a wider range of approaches. Especially favoured was
the use of play and games as a way to get the foreigners 'to think
and act like Canadians'.[34] It was in Manitoba where the issue of the
right for publicly funded separate and bilingual schools was played
out, to the detriment eventually of all those who did not constitute
a part of the Anglo-Saxon majority. A spur to action to use the
schools as agencies of assimilation was the example set in the United
States and Germany. The Anglo-Saxon charter group set out in vigorous fashion to use the schools as part of a melting-pot approach to
cultural difference.[35] Symbolic of the drift of things was the enact-
ment in 1906 that all provincial schools had to fly the Union Jack

during school hours.[36] The deputy minister of education for a long number of years both before and after the First World War, Robert Fletcher, was an ardent upholder of the imperial connection. When the young Englishman, Fred J. Ney, launched the 'Hands Across the Sea' movement in 1910 he found 165 teachers from Manitoba anxious to go and, equally important, able to pay their fares for a summer tour of the 'old country'.[37]

Accompanying the burgeoning imperial faith in the 1890s was an advocacy of military preparedness. What was urged was an improvement in the standard of physical fitness, mainly by the introduction of callisthenics and physical exercises in schools. Even more important, it was argued, was cadet training. Although such corps had existed since before Confederation, it was J. L. Hughes who in the 1890s, as superintendent of schools in Toronto, established the practice of mustering the entire school population for annual military reviews.[38] In 1909 Lord Strathcona announced a contribution of $250,000 to encourage physical and military training across Canada. A more fully developed programme of cadet camps, begun in 1896, was made possible by the Strathcona money. In 1913 500 boys from Ottawa alone attended cadet camp. Finally, another subject which was perceived to have enhanced importance in an increasingly complex world was history. J. H. Putman, the superintendent of Ottawa schools, put pressure upon his teachers to improve the quality of teaching in this subject. He did so in response to the formation of local organizations anxious to see the schools do more to encourage patriotism.[39]

The British Public School Tradition

The way in which the British public schools dovetailed with the needs and values of the Empire has been well documented.[40] The ethic of muscular Christianity underscored both the value of team games, especially cricket, and the idea of service. The schools became the recruiting ground for the colonial service, the missionary field and, among other endeavours, overseas educational careers. At some major schools the average percentage of boys leaving for the colonies was as high as 33. One indicator of the impact of this migration was the discovery, after the setting up of the Western Canada Public Schools Association in 1909, that there were over a hundred such old boys in Winnipeg alone.[41] The aim of the Colonial College in

Suffolk, set up in 1887, was to provide courses for prospective public school emigrants. Not only would such an organization help to solve the 'younger son' problem of the British middle classes but also, by providing better training of intending emigrants, avoid the stigma of the public schools being associated in the public mind with remittance men and others unsuited to the rigours of colonial life.[42] This was followed by the appearance in 1904 of the British Public Schools Association, which had the specific aim of encouraging emigration to the dominion.

It was British Columbia which most keenly felt the influence of British emigration and education. In the years before the war the population grew from 130,000 to over 400,000. About 170,000 of these newcomers were British. As Douglas Cole says, 'the British element constituted itself as an aristocracy of talent and taste. They were literate, read *The Times*, and published in England.'[43] About fifty or sixty private schools were set up in conscious emulation of their British prototypes. As a result, the prefect system, school uniforms and the fetish for games all replicated themselves. There was no doubting the message imparted by these schools:

> Each headmaster was trying to create what most boys still recall as 'a little England,' an environment founded on the assumption that 'British,' or, possibly, 'British Empire,' was best; 'Canadian,' passable; and 'American' quite unacceptable. A University old boy has described the headmaster's unreasoning and unforgiving prejudice for everything English over anything that wasn't. 'Baseball, for example, was made to seem like an indecency.' One Vernon pupil has suggested that 'the two great supporting beams on which the framework of the school was raised' were the Christian religion and the British Empire.[44]

The story was the same elsewhere, even if the numbers were fewer. George Parkin, one of the founders of the Imperial Federation League, after he became headmaster of Upper Canada College in 1895, made an even more determined effort to use the 'best' British schools as a model for his own, one aspect of which was the desirability of employing some masters directly from the mother country. In his inspiring addresses to the boys, Parkin held up Wellington, Nelson, Gordon and Kitchener as heroes and role models.[45] Parkin, having been born in Canada, was something of an exception as a headmaster. J. A. Mangan has shown how these élite schools were usually governed by Englishmen – no doubt explaining why they became the life-support system of the game of cricket. In such an atmosphere it took a long time for the northernness of ice hockey to have an opportunity to express itself.[46]

Dominion Day

As we have seen, the fitting celebration of a holiday on 1 July as Dominion Day encountered problems from the very outset. A study by this author of the manner in which the day was observed in New Brunswick between 1867 and 1891 revealed that these difficulties were by no means just early teething problems. Lack of civic interest, fears of employers about loss of work time, as well as hard times in general, prevented a warm embrace of the day. The result was that Dominion Day began to acquire a reputation for dullness which even its biggest boosters and occasional one-off successes could not entirely dispel. One newspaper commented in 1874 that

> A holiday in St. John was one of the most miserable days of the year. Had the government wished to punish the people, it could scarce have hit upon a more cruel mode than a holiday . . . Just fancy forty or fifty thousand people . . . [on] a public holiday . . . and walking around the whole live-long day . . . doing nothing, thinking nothing, and wearing the forbidden aspect of semi-idiots.[47]

New Brunswickers could not help but be concerned about the apparent lack of exuberant celebration of their national feeling. This was all too apparent when public excitement was compared with the 'Glorious Fourth' across the border. However, while accepting that apathy was too often the prevailing attitude, newspaper editors were adamant in their refusal to accept the conclusion that this fact meant that Canadians loved their country any the less. As proof, they made the observation that Canadians had difficulty enjoying any holiday, including the birthday of the Queen on 24 May. Yet the worry could not help but persist. Was there something wrong? The most satisfying explanation, one often resorted to, was that it was due to the character of the Anglo-Saxon people and their habitual practice of understatement and uneasiness with the idea of self-enjoyment.

The conclusion of the study was that Canadians had been overly concerned about their nationalistic inadequacies and that there was much more celebratory pride exhibited than might be inferred from editorial jeremiads. And who can deny the educational qualities of celebratory events, especially for a people yet to experience shorter working hours or paid holidays? As the 1880s wore on there

> was more variety of entertainment and genuine street theatre than might be thought from the constant carping of nationalists. Yes, there was the mindless and aimless parading up and down streets that offered no gaiety. But there was also much to thrill the young and the over-worked adults. There were the ever present Calithumpians or Polymorphians who created a din and kept up a tradition of grotesque anonymity . . . Then too, there were the brass bands, torch-light processions as well as hops and dances.[48]

Of course, a lot of what occurred was bound up with party politics. Macdonald's National Policy, evolved as a nation-building programme during the 1870s, demanded that loyal Conservative newspapers adopt a nationalistic tone. Reform newspapers, on the other hand, due to the unfortunate fact that George Brown left the political coalition before the passing of the British North America Act, were almost by default cast as critics and complainers. Yet even Liberal newspapers gradually slipped on more nationalistic garb as time went on.

Empire Day

It was Canada which led the way in beginning the custom of marking the school day before 24 May as a designated day for the observance of a special school programme celebrating Canada's membership within the British Empire. It was started by an anti-suffragist from Hamilton, Ontario, by the name of Mrs Clementine Fessenden. During 1897 she began to work up a campaign in favour of the idea of 'a national patriotic scheme of education'. The target of her efforts was George Ross. He was a long-serving minister of education in the provincial Liberal government, with definite ambitions to become premier, something which he finally achieved in 1902. He was himself a firm imperial patriot. Since Mrs Fessenden's campaign was coincidental with the Jubilee celebrations of Queen Victoria and also Ross's own vigorous promotion of his political persona, she won his backing. He, in fact, took over the leadership of the movement in the following year, saying that there was 'no antagonism between Canadianism and Imperialism. The one is but the expansion of the other.' The first official day which was celebrated was on 23 May 1899, although the Hamilton schools had actually launched it at the local level in the previous year. Among the most notable presentations in 1899 was at Gladstone Avenue school in Toronto where principal Alexander Muir's 'The Maple Leaf Forever' was sung with 'much fervour'. But the message of Empire Day was more likely to take the tack of the governor-general in 1909. In his address at Toronto, Earl Grey said:

> I want you boys to remember what Empire Day means. Empire Day is the festival on which every British subject should reverently remember that the British Empire stands out before the whole world as the fearless champions of freedom, fair play and equal rights; that its watchwords are responsibility, duty, sympathy and self-sacrifice.[49]

Mother and the Home

It was in the late nineteenth century that important changes took place in society's views of children. Due to the influence of the theories of educational reformers such as Friedrich Froebel, the idea took root that a child was not a hardened or 'marble being' but a delicate plant whose upbringing required study, care and attention. The result was an enhanced role for mothers in the demanding business of bringing up children. This development was aided by a drift to suburban homes from which fathers were likely to be absent for long periods of time.[50] So far as the outlook of Canadian women is concerned, there is no reason to think that their views on nationalism and imperialism were any different from men's. That is, one can see within the temperance movement, for example, an emphasis on the North American nature of the idea behind the reform. The motto of the Women's Christian Temperance Union, which spread quickly into Canada after its founding in Ohio in 1874, was 'God, Home, and Native Land'. Typifying the outlook of Canadian temperance women was an article written in 1890 by Mrs D. Parker and entitled 'Making the Nation Pure'. She wrote:

> In every true Canadian woman's heart there is a strong aspiration after the ideal nation, built on the best foundation: God, Freedom, Righteousness, Love. Canada, our beloved land, favoured of God ... with the opportunity to graft upon our young national stock the best elements of the four or five nationalities that claim kinship with us; why should not

Canada lead the world to-day, in all that makes for human progress? May we not hope in shaping our national life to avoid the mistakes of older nations? . . . We want to grow a patriotism of that holy type which shall harmonize with all the claims the God of nations makes.[51]

It is also true that there were organizations devoted much more to the Empire. The Imperial Order of the Daughters of the Empire was established in the full flood of imperial feeling in 1900. Its purpose was stated to be primarily the attachment of women and children to the throne and to the 'bettering of all things connected with our great Empire'.[52] Carol Lee Bacchi in a study of Canadian suffragists has shown how uppermost in their minds were fears concerning the fate of the Anglo-Saxon race and the need for measures to ensure a healthy race.[53] Reinforcing an imperial outlook was the very substantial number of British emigrants during this period. The census of 1921 revealed that, leaving aside the 27·9 per cent of the population who were of French Canadian origin, 55·4 per cent of people traced their ancestry to the British Isles. No other group accounted for more than 3·3 per cent of the total.[54] What is also very clear from the work of Ross McCormack is the strong imperial loyalties which he found among English immigrants in Winnipeg prior to the First World War.[55]

Canadian Protestantism

Another socializing and nationalizing agency of importance was the churches. By the mid-nineteenth century evangelical Protestantism had established a hegemony over the cultural life of English Canada. In Ontario, for example, where once there had been bitter strife between Anglicanism and other churches, there was now a growing consensus on the need for Christian action to help realize God's Kingdom on earth. In this post-millennialist scheme of things the education of the child would be of vital importance in creating a person of religious and social awareness.[56] The Methodist Church, the largest single body within Protestantism, in its hopes to 'shape society' in its own ideal image came to 'to locate a special trust in childhood' and education.[57] Part of the Protestant belief system was a kind of archetypal Puritanism which expressed itself in all sorts of taboos against such activities as card playing, dancing and especially drinking. At a more general level, as the speeches of Protestant ministers make clear, there was an ever closer identification between the nation and the church. Leading Methodists, in response to the new immigration, began to explore the possibility of church union because what was at stake, argued Nathanael Burwash, prominent Canadian theologian and educator, was 'the continuation of Canada as a Christian nation'.[58] Although the culmination of this line of thought would not take place until the 1920s when the United Church came into being, it does help us to understand the way in which Protestantism and national life were reciprocally related.

The Canadian temperance movement was strongly nationalistic in its belief that Canada could realize its true potentiality as a nation by adopting a temperate way of life. Such an accomplishment would also allow Canada to make its well-deserved mark in the world and gain the status which was its due. The pronouncements of temperance leaders were thoroughly imbued with the spirit of Canadianism as well as, incidentally, occasional expressions of impatience with Britain's inability to raise itself in this regard from the more decadent aspects of European social morality.[59]

Conclusion

One might have thought, considering all the lamentations concerning the lack of national feeling in Canada, that its traces might have been difficult to detect. But far from it. One is tempted, perhaps much too glibly, to say that Canadians expressed their nationalism by looking for it. But that might be putting the degree of national faith at too low a level of intensity. Even such a liberal and urbane journal as *Saturday Night* could rhapsodize in 1898 that 'Canada is gaining in population, her name is being heard amongst the peoples of the earth, and the grandeur and glory which comes to a newly awakened people is ours'. It went on to say that Canadians had greater faith in themselves as well as better appreciation of the traditions which bound them to the British Empire. It was a time for rejoicing since 'Canada stands more than ever before pre-eminent amongst the countries of the world, as the greatest, most self-contained and attractive spot upon which the sun shines and over which the British flag flies.'[60]

Canadian nationalism was much affected by the proximity to the United States and to the belief that the Republic had found the means to assimilate a heterogeneous set of newcomers and their children into Americans. Educators there assumed that this process would basically occur within a time-span of one generation,[61] and some of this optimism was absorbed by Canadian experts. There is no doubt that Canadians, like Americans, saw the little red schoolhouse as the ultimate agency of ethnic change. In Winnipeg the assumptions and policies of the charter group derived from what they perceived was happening in American cities.[62] When it came to celebrations of nationalism, the influence upon Canadians of the 'Glorious Fourth' was also evident, in the desire to manifest the love of country more openly. And while perhaps the process of the nationalizing of the Church, which also took place in the United States,[63] did not proceed to the same extent in Canada, there were, nevertheless, marked similarities in their outlook. Finally, as we have seen, Canadian women and mothers were not at all lacking in nationalistic fervour. Thus, when one looks at those matters having to do with school, home, community and church, one is viewing a formidable array of institutions which were concerned with the question of national feeling.

In Canada the difficulty of 'Canadianizing' the population was undoubtedly increased by the difficulties of explaining to a non-Anglo-Saxon how the dual loyalties to country and Empire were reconciled. The process must have taken on all the complexity of explaining the Holy Trinity to an untutored heathen. By any objective diagnostic test, Canadians were hopelessly schizophrenic. George Grant, in *Lament for a Nation*, proclaimed his own typicality:

> Growing up in Ontario, the generation of the 1920's took it for granted that they belonged to a nation. The character of the country was self-evident. To say it was British was not to deny it was North American. To be a Canadian was to be a unique species of North American. Such alternatives as F. H. Underhill's – 'Stop being British if you want to be a nationalist' – seemed obviously ridiculous.[64]

Grant also represented an increasingly bitter body of opinion by the 1950s and 1960s which regarded Liberalism as always having been quite indistinguishable from continentalism and as an organized conspiracy against the true British nature of Canada. Yet, as has been argued here, a more accurate explanation is that the tenets of a territorial nationalism had been articulated at least since the Charlottetown conference of 1864. Often, it is true that nationalism was part of a Canadian duality of outlook, but it also could and did breathe a life of its own.

Notes

1. Margaret E. Prang, 'Nationalism in Canada's First Century', The Canadian Historical Association, *Historical Papers 1968*, 118–19.
2. W. H. Heick (ed.), *A. R. M. Lower* (Vancouver, 1985), p.166.
3. Benedict Anderson, *Imagined Communities: Reflections on the Origin and Spread of Nationalism* (London, 1983), ch. 6.
4. Ibid. pp.15–16, 46–9.
5. Eric Hobsbawm and Terence Ranger (eds.), *The Invention of Tradition* (Cambridge, 1984), pp.1, 271, 279–80.
6. E. J. Hobsbawm, *Nations and Nationalism since 1780* (Cambridge, 1990), pp.89–91.
7. Ernest Gellner, *Nations and Nationalism* (Oxford, 1983), p.57.
8. *Telegram* (Toronto), 24 October 1903; as quoted in John C. Kendall, 'A Canadian Construction of Reality: Northern Images of the United States', *The American Review of Canadian Studies*, iv (1974), 24–5.
9. S. F. Wise and R. C. Brown, *Canada Views the United States: Nineteenth-Century Political Attitudes* (Seattle, 1967), ch.3; Carl Berger, *The Sense of Power: Studies in the Ideas of Canadian Imperialism* (Toronto, 1970), ch.6.
10. *The Morning Freeman* (Saint John), 10 July 1875.
11. Quoted in R. Nye, *This Almost Chosen People: Essays in the History of American Ideas* (East Lansing, Mich., 1966), p.66.
12. Michael Burgess, 'Canadian Imperialism as Nationalism: The Legacy and Significance of the Imperial Federation Movement in Canada', unpublished paper given at the Centre of Canadian Studies, University of Edinburgh, 3–6 May 1990. A newspaper sketch of a Methodist minister in New Brunswick, Robert Wilson, supports this line of argument. It noted that he was 'a Highlander by birth [and] he has been an enthusiastic advocate of what some people call "the Annexation Antidote" – imperial federation'. *Progress* (Saint John), 30 June 1888.
13. Ruth Compton Brouwer, 'Moral Nationalism in Victorian Canada: The Case of Agnes Machar', *Journal of Canadian Studies*, xx (1985–6), 97.
14. R. G. Moyles and Doug Owram, *Imperial Dreams and Colonial Realities: British Views of Canada, 1880–1914* (Toronto, 1988), pp.213–14.
15. Linda Colley, *Britons: Forging the Nation 1707–1837* (London, 1992), p.145.
16. J. H. Grainger, *Patriotisms: Britain 1900–1939* (London, 1986), pp.20–1.
17. Joseph Levitt, *A Vision beyond Reach: A Century of Images of Canadian Destiny* (Ottawa, n.d.) pp.154, 181.
18. *Saint John Globe*, 24 June 1867.
19. *The New Dominion* (Saint John), 20 June 1868.
20. Charles Gordon, *Postscript to Adventure: The Autobiography of Ralph Connor* (Toronto 1975), p.22.
21. Levitt, op. cit.

[22] Harvey J. Graff, *The Literacy Myth: Literacy and Social Structure in the Nineteenth-Century City* (London, 1979), pp.22ff.

[23] R. D. Gidney, 'Upper Canadian Public Opinion and Common School Improvements in the 1830s', *Histoire Sociale/Social History*, v (1972).

[24] Robert J. Carney, 'Going to School in Upper Canada', in E. Brian Titley (ed.), *Canadian Education: Historical Themes and Contemporary Issues* (Calgary, 1990), p.33.

[25] Graff, op. cit., pp.43ff.

[26] J. H. Gray, *R. B. Bennett: The Calgary Years* (Toronto, 1991), p.9.

[27] Katherine F. C. MacNaughton, *The Development of the Theory and Practice of Education in New Brunswick 1784–1900* (Fredericton, 1947), pp.176–7.

[28] *The Daily Sun* (Saint John), 27 June 1890.

[29] John Coldwell Adams, *Sir Charles God Damn: The Life of Sir Charles G. D. Roberts* (Toronto, 1986), pp.59–60.

[30] R. N. Berard, 'Moral Education in Nova Scotia, 1880–1920', *Acadiensis*, xiv (1984).

[31] See chapters by Nancy Sheehan, H. Van Brummeler and Morris Mott, in Nancy M Sheehan, J. Donald Wilson and Davis C. Jones (eds.), *Schools in the West: Essays in Canadian Educational History* (Calgary, 1986).

[32] Robert M. Stamp, *The Schools of Ontario, 1876–1976* (Toronto, 1982), pp.92–3.

[33] Paul T. Phillips, *Britain's Past in Canada: The Teaching and Writing of British History* (Vancouver, 1989), ch. 1.

[34] Morris Mott, in Sheehan et. al. (eds.), op. cit.

[35] Brian Titley, 'Religion, Culture and Power: The School Question in Manitoba', in Titley, op. cit., pp.56, 76.

[36] Alan F. J. Artibise, *Winnipeg: A Social History of Urban Growth 1874–1914* (Montreal, 1975), p.205.

[37] National Archives of Canada, F. J. Ney Papers.

[38] Desmond Morton, *Canada and War* (Toronto, 1981), p.49.

[39] B. Anne Wood, *Idealism Transformed: The Making of a Progressive Educator* (Kingston and Montreal, 1985), pp.128–38.

[40] See, for example: P. J. Rich, *Elixir of Empire: The English Public Schools, Ritualism, Freemasonry, and Imperialism* (London, 1989) and J. A. Mangan, *The Games Ethic and Imperialism: Aspects of the Diffusion of an Ideal* (Harmondsworth, 1986).

[41] *Manitoba Free Press*, 13 October 1909.

[42] Patrick A. Dunae, 'Education, Emigration and Empire: The Colonial College, 1887–1905', in J. A. Mangan, *Benefits Bestowed? Education and British Imperialism* (Manchester, 1988), pp.193–210.

[43] Douglas Cole, 'The Intellectual and Imaginative Development of British Columbia', *Journal of Canadian Studies*, xxiv (1989), 72–3.

[44] Jean Barman, *Growing up British in British Columbia: Boys in Private Schools* (Vancouver, 1984), p.92.

[45] Terry Cook, 'George Parkin and the Concept of Britannic Idealism', *Journal of Canadian Studies*, x (1975), 20.

[46] J. A. Mangan, 'Discipline in the Dominion: The "Canuck" and the Cult of Manliness' in Mangan, *The Games Ethic and Imperialism*, pp.142–67.

[47] B. J. Grant, *Fit To Print* (Fredericton, 1987), pp.152–3.

[48] James Sturgis, 'Dominion and National Identity in New Brunswick, 1867–1891', unpublished paper given at the Atlantic Canada Studies Conference, St John's, Newfoundland, 22 May 1992.

[49] Robert M. Stamp, 'Empire Day in the Schools of Ontario: The Training of Young Imperialists', *Journal of Canadian Studies*, viii (1973), 32–42.

[50] Neil Sutherland, *Children in English-Canadian Society: Framing the Twentieth-Century Consensus* (Toronto, 1976), pp.17–18, 27–8.

[51] R. Cook and W. Mitchison (eds.), *The Proper Sphere: Woman's Place in Canadian Society* (Toronto, 1976), p.229.

[52] R. C. Brown and R. Cook, *Canada 1896–1921* (Toronto, 1974), pp.42–3.

[53] Carol Lee Bacchi, *Liberation Deferred? The Ideas of the English-Canadian Suffragists, 1877–1918* (Toronto, 1983), ch. 7.

[54] J. H. Thompson with Allen Seager, *Canada 1922–1939* (Toronto, 1985), pp.6–7.

[55] Ross McCormack. 'Cloth Caps and Jobs: The Ethnicity of English Immigrants in Canada 1900–1914', in J. Dahlie and Tissa Fernando (eds.), *Ethnicity, Power and Politics in Canada* (Toronto, 1981), pp.42–3.

[56] William Westfall, *Two Worlds: The Protestant Culture of Nineteenth Century Ontario* (Kingston and Montreal, 1989).

[57] Neil Semple, '"The Nurture and Admonition of the Lord": Nineteenth-Century Canadian Methodism's Response to "Childhood"', *Histoire Sociale/Social History*, xiv (1981), 164.

[58] Marguerite Van Die, *An Evangelical Mind: Nathanael Burwash and the Methodist Tradition in Canada, 1839–1918* (Kingston and Montreal, 1989), pp.143–5.

[59] James Sturgis, 'Beer under Pressure: The Origins of Prohibition in Canada', *Bulletin of Canadian Studies*, viii (1984), 83–100.

[60] *Saturday Night* (Toronto), 2 July 1898.

[61] B. J. Weiss (ed.), *American Education and the European Immigrant: 1840–1940* (Urbana, 1982), p.xxii.

[62] Artibise, op. cit., p.202.

[63] R. T. Handy, *A Christian America* (Oxford, 1984), p.97.

[64] George Grant, *Lament for a Nation: The Defeat of Canadian Nationalism* (Ottawa, 1982), p.3.

6

Canada and the Allied War Economy, 1914–1919

H. R. C. WRIGHT

Although trying to be careful about language, I find it convenient to use the concept 'Pax Britannica' in the sense expounded by A. H. Imlah in 1958 (*Economic Elements in the Pax Britannica*). The term was not used in that way in 1914–1919. It was then used in a more natural analogy to the Pax Romana, to refer to the order and good government maintained in India, Egypt and so on under direct or indirect British rule; as a synonym in fact for Britain's share of the White Man's Burden. This was of course no mean achievement in itself, as we can see by comparing Somaliland then and now. I use the term Pax Britannica in Imlah's sense, however, because I believe that it encapsulates part of the collective wisdom in the British Empire, common sense so obvious that it did not need a special name or systematic exposition. The Royal Navy protected the Empire and the whole network of international trade centred in London. This system maintained a tolerable degree of peace and order in the world, which might otherwise be disturbed by conflicts in continental Europe. The balance of power in Europe might be uneasy, but so long as Britain's supremacy at sea was unchallenged, the continental powers could be left to balance each other. Britain was not a world policeman.

The Pax Britannica depended on the gold standard, on Britain's adherence to free trade, on the free flow of funds through the City of London for the clearances of multilateral trade and for investment throughout the world, and on the protection of the freedom of the seas for all in time of peace by the Royal Navy. But was Joseph Chamberlain's desire for an imperial trade bloc within the world economy compatible with the Pax Britannica? Yes, just as Canada could adopt moderate protectionism within the Empire, so the British, French, German and other empires should be able, in moderation, to pursue their own economic aims while still benefiting peaceably from participating in a world economy of mainly open doors. The system could continue so long as the other empires wanted peace and trusted the British navy to maintain the freedom of the seas for all in time of peace. Fears of blockade by the British navy in time of war helped to maintain the system.

Canadian Confederation suited imperial policy in 1867 and assured Canada's role in the Empire, not to share the burden outside North America, but certainly to sustain the Pax Britannica. The year 1867 also saw the *Ausgleich*, which created the Dual Monarchy and started the reorganization of the Habsburg Empire to meet the needs of a plural society.[1] It had some success before 1914, as we can see by comparing Bosnia then and now. For maintaining order and good government in a divided and potentially disorderly territory there is evidently much to be said for a non-democratic, dynastic or hierarchic authority, such as the Habsburgs or the Ontario establishment.

The Reform Act of 1867 advanced democracy in Britain and led to Disraeli's discovery of the electoral appeal of an imperialist jingoism, mainly concerned with the prestige of acquiring colonies in competition with the French and German Empires. It was assumed, arrogantly, that if more of the world were under orderly, enlightened British government, it would be all the better for the world and for the Pax Britannica. But the noises of popular imperialism and the scramble for Africa did not promote the confidence in international stability which the Pax Britannica required.

The Reform Act of 1867 also led to Gladstone's discovery, in the Midlothian campaign, that sentimental humanitarian emotions in foreign causes could win votes for policies which caused trouble and could not be sustained. The volatility of democratic public opinion, the South African War and the rise of new naval powers, including Germany, convinced Milner, his Kindergarten, and others, that the Pax Britannica was fragile and not in itself a guarantee of permanent peace. They started the Round Table movement to strengthen and unify the British Empire as the corner-stone for whatever new arrangements and institutions might maintain international peace in the twentieth century.

The long debate which started in 1909 about a Canadian contribution to imperial naval defence made it clear to Canadian politicians and business men that the German challenge to Britain's naval supremacy was a threat to the Pax Britannica. The matter was discussed as an emergency, and in this period the Round Table became active in Canada, bringing its own sense of urgency. But the Canadians, accustomed to take the Royal Navy for granted as Britain's responsibility, squabbled about the form of naval effort appropriate to Canada's status, and the debate did not lead to any action by Canada. Some Canadians suspected that the British Liberal government was using scare tactics to get contributions from the dominions which would release funds in the British budget for extravagant social reforms; while many British Liberals, including Churchill and Lloyd George, considered that the popular 'We want Eight' campaign in Britain in 1909, for more dreadnoughts sooner, was inspired by the Tories in order to obstruct the Liberal programme.[2]

The naval debate at any rate revealed a wide consensus in Canada, based on assumptions which had been mostly unexpressed because they were taken for granted and seemed obvious, that the Empire stood for the Pax Britannica. This explains Laurier's qualified support of the Empire. Other aspects did not appeal to him, but the Pax Britannica had maintained order in the world, and that was very much in the interests of Canada as an open economy, as well as of the civilized world.[3] Within that world, Canada's main and sufficient contribution had been the orderly government and development of her own plural society. In a genuine emergency other responsibilities had to be undertaken. There is thus continuity from Canada's action in the First World War to her role now in working towards a new world order under the auspices of the United Nations. In 1914 Canada joined a war in which Britain and France were allies, so that it could be regarded as an opportunity to assert a special Canadian nationalism. But Canada came in as part of the British Empire, with appropriate flag-waving. The public jingoism partly expressed sentimental loyalties, but also emotions which arose from internal Canadian tensions. The common-sense understanding of the role of the Empire, however, by most Canadian leaders preserved Canadian unity as a belligerent. The majority were willing, on the whole, with or without conviction, to follow the judgement of the élite.

Obviously the first duty of the civilized minority in the world is to conserve their civilization as a living organism. The stability, continuity and growth of a civilization depend on the common sense accumulated from past experience, on collective memory or collective consciousness, as explained in chapter II of Hayek's *The Constitution of Liberty* (1960). Post-modern educationists have been busy since 1960 in trying to destroy the collective memory, the sense of historical experience, and 'to sickly o'er the native hue resolution with the pale cast of thought'. They seem to have had some success in destroying the common-sense element in collective consciousness, and thereby increasingly to have released the hatreds, envy and disruptive emotions which have older and, perhaps, deeper roots.

Given what we now know about human origins, any civilization is a great and surprising achievement, and the continuity and progress of our own has been wonderful. It is therefore most useful for historians to understand and explain what has been achieved, and to give credit to the achievers, instead of dwelling always on their shortcomings. We shall learn most from the history of the Borden government by viewing it sympathetically.

In Hayek's words,

> though there is a presumption that any established social standard contributes in some way to the preservation of civilization, our only way of confirming this is to ascertain whether it continues to prove itself in competition with other standards observed by other individuals or groups.[4]

In an age when God and Karl Marx are dead, that is the best moral guide we have as an enduring verity. By that test Thomas White, the minister of finance who had a major responsibility for Canada's contribution to the Allied war economy, deserved well of his country.

B. C. Brown and G. R. Cook summed up the Borden government's handling of the war economy rather patronizingly:

> A later generation might judge this to be innocent, simple, and decidedly amateurish. The actors themselves found their commitment real enough, their work often exciting, sometimes frightening in its implications. Some could even see a certain irony in what had taken place. It had, after all, been done in the name of preserving 'civilization' – a civilization that was rooted in the assumed continuance of a *laissez-faire* style of economic life in pre-war Canada. In the attempt to preserve that way of life, the government of Canada had changed it almost beyond recognition.[5]

White started the war with the established social standards and common sense of an experienced Toronto man of business. In the light of wartime experience he modified but did not abandon his conservative principles.

White had been managing director of the National Trust Company, which had done business for the Canadian Northern Railway. Montreal and Toronto were rife with malicious rumours, and in June 1914 Borden was warned in a private letter that White was generally regarded 'as the advocate of Mackenzie and Mann in the Cabinet'.[6] William Mackenzie and Joseph Mann had made enemies by their aggressive tactics in obtaining public federal and provincial funds for their railway and in keeping control in their own hands. Michael Bliss, having studied the archives, showed in 1978 that White in fact took a hard line in Cabinet towards Canadian Northern,[7] but in 1981 Tom Naylor, without citing any evidence, permitted himself the innuendo that White was 'not altogether ingenuous' in his policy statements, since he did not declare his interest in bailing out the Canadian Bank of Commerce, which was the main creditor of Canadian Northern.[8] No doubt Naylor considered it politically correct to assume that any business man who goes into politics will continue to pursue business interests.

The New Penguin Dictionary of Quotations suggests that Winston Churchill proposed 'Business as Usual' as a maxim for wartime Britain. This is misleading. In mid-August 1914 the frequent calls for 'business as usual' in the industrial centres were cited to show that the German government was mistaken in counting on the unrest of the British working class as one of its advantages in the war; and they served as a justification for continuing the programme of professional football matches. A notice was reported on a draftsman's shop window in Glasgow, 'Business as usual during alterations of the map', and another on a shop window in London, 'The Motto of Patriotism: Business as Usual, but please pay cash'. There was correspondence in *The Times* about whether the motto was patriotic, an argument which is still being reiterated on the same lines by historians.[9] As Churchill expressed it in his Guildhall speech of 9 November 1914, 'The British people have taken to themselves the motto "Business carried on as usual, during alterations on the map of Europe".' His main point was to defend the navy after the German bombardment of Yarmouth on 3 November and other minor setbacks, by showing that the navy was successfully shielding 'business as usual' in Britain and much of the world, in fortunate contrast to the situation in France.[10] The slogan was no doubt first adopted to express stoical optimism and did not signify an unwillingness to face facts or to make sacrifices in an illusory expectation that the war would be short. Nor was it an excuse for profiteering. Profiteering came later, as a result of unusual conditions created by government actions necessary for the war.

British and Canadian politicians knew that the course of the war was uncertain and were willing to impose sacrifices, and anxious to accelerate the war effort when they usefully could. They used the slogan 'business as usual' when it suited public policy. Enthusiasts like Sam Hughes, the Canadian minister of militia, who felt that their own particular service was all-important, could cause much waste and damage in the hurry of war, so the steadying influence of 'business as usual' had a natural appeal to a finance minister. White did not hope that Toronto's comfortable business world could continue unshaken. He felt that the war was a calamity for the world he knew and would call for a great effort from Canada. He did not altogether share the belief of popular economists that the war would be short because no nation could stand the financial strain for very long, but he had a touching faith in the financial strength of the City of London to see the Empire through any process of attrition.

Bonar Law, in the British House of Commons on 11 November 1914, cited Napoleon's dictum 'Finance is the state' and said that Napoleon had been taught that lesson painfully, because Britain was an island with command of the seas, so that her normal business could continue in wartime. Actually, Napoleon had drawn comfort from the vicissitudes of the pound sterling after the suspension of cash payments by the Bank of England in 1797, and in the new Great War of 1914–18 the British Treasury was determined to do better. As a support for business confidence in London, and especially for foreign confidence in London as a financial centre and hence, it was believed, in Britain's ability to win a long war, Britain struggled to remain officially on the gold standard until 1919. White, on the other hand, suspended the convertibility of Dominion notes immediately on the outbreak of war. In the Canadian system this was necessary to enable the chartered banks in time of panic to provide credit for business as usual; but for the sake of confidence he was careful to hoard gold so far as possible.

White was aware of social discontent as a threat to his civilization in the troubled world before 1914, even in Canada. Canada was in depression in 1914. The outbreak of war interrupted some trades and created uncertainty, so that unemployment worsened and in

1915 prices and wages remained depressed.[11] In order to relieve unemployment White's policy was to speed up public works which had already started or for which contracts had been completed, but new works were suspended even when tenders had been invited, since only strictly necessary increases in government expenditure could be justified when revenues were falling.[12] When the war started, White foresaw its growing costs and decided that, apart from a small increase in some import duties, Canada's contribution must be financed by borrowing. He preferred to borrow all he could in London, for expenses in Canada as well as overseas, in order to relieve Canadian unemployment as much as possible while averting a fall in the Canadian exchange rate and 'the dreaded necessity of exporting gold'.[13] But he was careful to time his borrowings in London so as not to disturb the operations of the British Treasury.

For White, business as usual implied ethics as usual. The war should not be an excuse for not paying debts. He took power to declare moratoria in Canada, but was determined to use it only as a last resort. The Canadian government did not take advantage of the British moratorium in respect to its own debts in London. White was a little regretful about this, since it conflicted with his desire to get funds out of London, but he hoped that he was maintaining Canada's creditworthy reputation and prospects for future loans.

White's attachment to the London market was, as he admitted, partly sentimental, but when in the summer of 1915 the sterling exchange rate in New York became a major worry for the Empire, and the British government became unwilling to finance expenditure in Canada, he decided to borrow in America. Tactfully he borrowed in New York, not for war purposes but for public works in Canada. Thus he released Canadian funds for war purposes.[14]

A comparison of British and German experience in both world wars suggests that reliance on private enterprise in the market is the most efficient way of obtaining war supplies, with the introduction of controls and government enterprises only when they are seen to be necessary. Canada was naturally slow in developing procedures for determining prices in government contracts when the extent of buying by the Canadian, Imperial and Allied governments began quickly to distort some markets. The need for special procedures and controls became obvious first in Britain, and Canada was able to take advantage of British experience. When controls were needed in Canada, for instance in the grain trade in 1917, the aim was to prevent abuses of market power, but to allow prices which would encourage production and discourage consumption in Canada, and to ensure a smooth flow of supply to Canada's allies.[15]

White disliked direct taxation, because it discouraged enterprise, especially in a new country like Canada where capital was scarce, and on constitutional grounds he preferred to leave direct taxation to the provinces. While the Canadian economy remained depressed he refrained from imposing direct taxes even in wartime. He wished to encourage private enterprise to provide employment and respond to the special demands of war. In order not to crowd out private enterprise, he refrained as long as possible from long-term borrowing in Canada.[16]

Brown and Cook remark that White's pronouncements about monetary policy 'revealed more about the lack of economic sophistication in the war-time Treasury Department' than about the true effects of its policies.[17] But White knew what he was doing, although he did not explain it in the language of subsequent macro-economic theory. It is unlikely that he could have managed better for the advice of Seven Wise Men.

Admittedly he sometimes used simplified language and specious arguments which would appeal to his audience, as when he justified borrowing by saying that since the war was being fought for the benefit of future generations, it was right that they should bear part of the cost.[18] However, he was quite capable, if he had been challenged, of explaining the element of truth in such language. He well knew that internal loans affected only the internal distribution of income in Canada, while borrowing from abroad imposed a real future burden on Canadian resources. He also knew that when Canada supplied goods to Britain and the Allies on credit, she was 'paying for the war' out of her current production. He did not think it necessary to spell out these obvious facts.

The world-wide upward trend in prices after 1895 was particularly strong in Canada during the wheat boom. In 1910 it was clear that the trend had resumed after a pause due to the American crisis of 1907, and the cost of living became a subject of lively debate, and a handy focus for political agitation in Ontario. In the western provinces the desire for paper money and high agricultural prices prevailed, which was typical of North American frontier communities. In 1912 respectable opinion in Ontario became alarmed, and an approach was made to A. D. White, a veteran controversialist in the United

States. He had originally been invited as an expert in 1876 to address meetings in Washington and New York on the *assignats* in revolutionary France, in the campaign against 'the greenback craze'. His work was then published as a book, *Fiat Money Inflation in France*, and later he agreed to its use for various pamphlets against the recurrent agitations for the free minting of silver.[19] Informed that there was a similar 'crisis' in Canada in 1912, he revised his work, and a new edition was printed in Toronto for private circulation in 1914. It caused some discussion. Thomas White referred often during the war to the dangers of 'fiat money'.

Thomas White knew well that an increase in money supply would in due course lead to rising prices. So long as bank credit was being provided for legitimate business on good security, and the necessary bank reserves were being supplied by loans of inconvertible Dominion notes on good securities, he considered that the rise in prices was due to market forces, and not to 'currency inflation'. White used the term 'inflation' to mean currency inflation in the form of fiat money, an unlimited issue of paper money to finance whatever the government might judge necessary or desirable. The limit at which Dominion notes would become 'fiat money' and 'inflation' would begin was a matter for discretion, to be judged only afterwards, i.e. by the extent to which prices in fact rose. White was forced by government decisions to take some risks, but was firm that the only sound practice was to make previous financial provision for most new commitments: 'A contrary policy can only lead to fiat money and the destruction of national credit, upon which more than anything else we must rely for the long haul of this war.' In London he was strongly praised by *The Times* on 17 October 1914 for having proved himself in the crisis of war to be deaf to the arguments of Canada's 'soft money theorists'. However he knew that in extremity a paper inflation based on unlimited Dominion notes might be the only way of continuing the war.[20]

White knew that war production must lead to pressure of demand on prices, and in due course on wages, and he saw it happening in 1916. The necessary expansion of credit to encourage war production and maintain other business enabled employers to concede demands of organized labour which were abusive in exceeding the rise in the cost of living and in further raising costs and prices. White assumed that workers, as Canada pulled out of depression, would naturally want to enjoy their new good fortune, especially in drink and gambling, which might diminish their productivity. They should be told that this was unpatriotic, but were not likely to pay much attention. Some of White's like-minded colleagues urged him to launch an energetic savings campaign, on British lines, especially in munitions factories. Workers could never own real property, but if they were persuaded to invest in the new Canadian war loans they would have a stake in the country and become better citizens. White agreed with this as a long-term prospect, but was unenthusiastic about devoting much effort to such a campaign, since in Canadian conditions it was unlikely to achieve much for the war.[21]

White knew that the government had to allow generous profits on war contracts in 1916 to allow for expectations of rising costs. High profits were not desirable unless justified by entrepreneurial effort, but were a necessary result of an effective war economy. They were not harmful to the war effort, as high wages were, because profits were largely invested in further production, or, when investment needs were satisfied, in government war loans. It was therefore reasonable to refrain from direct taxation during the first phase of the war. In 1916, however, White introduced a Business Profits Tax, retroactive to the start of the war. Income tax followed in 1917. White regretted these measures, which reduced the availability of working capital and encouraged waste, making necessary some 'inflation of bank credit'; but he recognized that they were necessary to satisfy a natural and just popular sentiment and because the government had to use all possible methods of raising revenue.[22]

White was perhaps excessively cautious. Hoarding gold did not make economic sense while Canada was off the gold standard, though White insisted, 'I do not like the public to be in any way doubtful as to our Dominion note issue.' When Canada's export earnings had brought sterling credits, White wanted early in 1917 to convert part into gold to be earmarked for Canada at the Bank of England or in South Africa, but the British Treasury was unwilling, since it was exporting gold for war purposes and expected to ship to New York the gold it held in Ottawa against its own currency notes. White wanted to be quite sure that Canada could return to the gold standard quickly after the war, since some of his loans were repayable in gold in 1925.[23]

When the British government ran out of funds for buying munitions in Canada, the Canadian banks could help only with short-term credits. The Canadian government provided loans only within the limits set by White's fear of fiat money. In consequence, at times, in order to obtain loans in New York, Britain placed orders in the USA which could have been placed in Canada, so that Canadian capacity for war production was not fully used. When the USA entered the war, the US government introduced controls which prevented the British government from spending funds borrowed in the USA anywhere outside that country, except by special licence.[24] In September 1917, Robert Brand, representing the British Ministry of Munitions in liaison with the Imperial Munitions Board which organized its purchases in Canada, complained that White could have helped more if long ago he had put his finances on a war instead of a peace footing, for instance by restricting unnecessary imports and by a really vigorous savings campaign. Brand was impressed by the rapidity and strength of the war effort in the USA. He was told that White was unwilling to sacrifice customs revenue and to have the money spent on imports circulating in Canada: it would be difficult to draw it into war loans even to the extent of the lost customs revenue, and some Canadian resources would be diverted from the war effort into producing goods for the home market.[25]

In order to finance more war production, White could have raised domestic war loans and imposed direct taxes sooner than he did without discouraging private enterprise. He persistently under-estimated the actual and potential availability of savings in Canada. When he started borrowing from the Canadian public, the funds were needed to finance Canadian and British purchases of muni-tions, and so they fed the profits of private war production and the general rise in prices. White then had to borrow the savings of the profiteers, and future taxpayers would have to finance the debt. The rise in the cost of living, along with the increased taxes, was part of the sacrifice by which the Canadian people bore the material cost of the war and provided the profits. No doubt some of the war contracts were corrupt and wasteful, and some profits unjustifiable.[26] That was why, in the Round Table movement, supporters of the market system, while believing it to be the best starting-point for a war economy, desired, for moral reasons, to reinforce the Pax Britannica by a wider international organization and consensus, to ensure permanent peace.

Even in 1917 the rise in prices in Canada was moderate in comparison with other belligerents. A little more credit inflation would not have been a disaster, despite the sensitivity of central and eastern Canada to the cost of living, and of the West to the relation between the prices received by the farmer and those he had to pay for manufactured goods. In February 1917 Brand tried to collect evidence for a comparison between the British and the Canadian per capita contribution to the Allied war economy, in the hope of convincing White that he ought to finance a fuller use of Canadian resources, even if it had to be by issuing more Dominion notes.[27] But so long as Britain's performance could ward off any threat of imminent catastrophe, White was willing, in the cause of financial rectitude, to threaten a reduction in Canada's contribution, if his long-term loans in Canada were not successful: 'Unless I can count upon the continued co-operation of financial investment institutions it will be impossible for Canada to do her share in this war.'[28]

Thomas White's official writings and his *The Story of Canada's War Finance* (1921) were mainly in defence of financial rectitude. It is difficult to guess his underlying thoughts and perceptions. I have tended to rely on *The Round Table*. It is true that the Round Table movement was a propagandist organization. It was devoted to promoting imperial unity, and Canada was the main target. Its leaders believed that for a worthwhile closer union of the Empire the initiative must come from the dominions, so they used a Socratic method to draw out favourable Canadian élite opinions, and then repeated them until they stuck and began to trickle down to the people. Lionel Curtis, a true doctrinaire in his own writings, stressed that *The Round Table* must collect and express opinions which were not partisan, and which ought never to be matters of party politics because they were so obvious that they should be tacitly assumed in political controversy. Thus it seems that *The Round Table*'s published views were thought likely to be acceptable to élite opinion in Canada, and especially in Ontario. Robert Brand was a frequent contributor. Thomas White was recruited to the movement as a specimen of respected Canadian opinion on whom Round Table ideas could be tried out. He joined in 1909, but withdrew in 1911 when he became minister of finance.[29]

In 1909–14 the expressed long-term aim of *The Round Table* was a world order in which diverse peoples could live in peace, harmony and respect for established institutions. The British Empire could and should set an example, as a commonwealth in which all communities would be prepared for self-government under imperial trusteeship. It was noted with regret that Canada showed no interest in sharing this responsibility outside her own territory. But Canadians were becoming interested in improving imperial consultation and organization for defence. This might lead to imperial experience which would prove useful when the world began to feel the need for an international authority powerful enough to maintain order, distant though that time might be.

In 1914 *The Round Table* took the view that German (and Hungarian) militarism was a deadly threat not only to the British Empire but also to the idea of a world of self-governing peoples living in harmony alongside each other and of a concert of friendly, satisfied powers capable of preventing acts of aggression which threatened world peace. The old balance-of-power diplomacy must be superseded.

In 1918 the post-modern world began when President Wilson's Fourteen Points set off a new phenomenon, a wave of world opinion which imposed a kind of vocabulary of political correctness on Allied politicians. It was of course not a *wholly* new phenomenon. The anti-British mood in some parts of the world during the South African War was rather similar. In 1918 the panacea was democratic self-determination. Self-government was held to be more desirable than good government, although it was conceded that existing democratic colonial powers might have some discretion in applying the principle of trusteeship.[30] *The Round Table* adjusted itself to this mood, but consistently with its established beliefs. The Allies and Associated Powers must keep up after victory the spirit of unity and sacrifice. They must remain adequately armed, but avoid any arms race by setting up a world alliance with a common will to act as a concert instead of relying on a balance of power in Europe to keep the peace. The peace settlement should be magnanimous and enforceable.

After the Russian Revolutions the pursuit of social harmony seemed as urgent to *The Round Table* as that of international harmony. Cobden's doctrine of *laissez-faire* and premature abandonment of imperial trusteeship (the White Man's Burden) was seen to be as dangerous as German militarism. The selfish materialism of Cobdenite entrepreneurs shared with the German militarists the belief that might is right and led to the abuse of power by corporate business. The power of the state must be used to improve labour relations and ensure respect for the rights of trade unions, and the role of the state must be expanded to increase social welfare. When it came to practical questions of social policy, there was of course no consensus among members of the movement or sympathizers such as Borden and White.[31]

The mood changed again in 1919. The Allied and Associated peoples were in a hurry to enjoy their peace dividends, and individuals and groups were in a hurry to protect their material interests in a newly competitive situation by traditional methods. The governments were in a hurry to satisfy the popular demand for demobilization. It was proper to express support for the League of Nations, and *The Round Table* tried to do so. In the absence of an international community of ideas, an elaborate international institution could not achieve much, but since it was being created by an Allied agreement it was necessary to make the best of it. It must not attempt too much. It should offer services on the lines of those which had been attempted at the Hague for nations willing to use them. This would at least be a useful educative function. It should try to reserve effectual forces for meeting really dangerous aggressions, or for occasions when intervention was supported by a concert of great powers and a surge of world opinion.

The Allies and Associated Powers threw away the fruits of their victory. Canada was too concerned about her international status to exert the beneficial influence she might have had on the imperial government at that crucial time. She was, however, concerned about the continuance of good relations between the Empire and the USA and may consequently have influenced the British decision not to renew the Japanese alliance. Borden shared the Round Table view of the League of Nations and believed that unless sanctions could be made to work, 'the existing social order cannot and will not continue'; but in practice he was willing to participate in make-believe at Geneva in order to assert Canada's diplomatic status, while carefully avoiding new commitments which might involve Canada in wars over foreign territorial disputes.[32] White recognized that Canada, like the USA, had benefited from the war, and ought therefore to help to repair the damage in Europe, but in 1919 he seems to have been in a state of nervous exhaustion and to have taken no practical initiative.[33] And Canada, feeling no immediate external threat and having confidence in the Empire and the League of Nations, concentrated again on her internal politics, while sharing the prevailing sentiments of world opinion. White could withdraw from politics. Within the limits he had set himself, he had worked devotedly to provide finance for the Allied war effort. He commented later, as a poet, on the outcome.

'Collective Security', 1941
(on the League of Nations Palace in Geneva)

Lord, Thou whose mercy stoops to spare
The smoking flax and bruised reed,
Whose justice sure, with equal care
Regards the heart beyond the deed,
Forgive the folly, sloth and pride,
As we in blood and tears atone,
Whereby for safety we relied
Upon an idol made of stone,
Relied not on our own array
Of native strength beneath Thy wing,
Our sword and strength in ancient day,
But on a futile, strengthless thing
Of graven stone, with feet of clay
And semblance only unto life
And deep ingrained with foul decay
And seeds of envy, hate and strife.
Conceived in days of dire distress
At war's dread sacrifice of youth,
We deemed it wrought for righteousness,
No image, but the living truth.
Thou knowst who led our steps aside
From altars of Thy worship true –
The learned, in learning's erring pride,
The wise who nought of wisdom knew,
The statesmen who, in fateful hour,
When danger loomed on land and sea,
Like builders of the Babel Tower
Placed faith in stone and not in Thee.
Teach nations they seek peace in vain
In trustless word and faithless pact.
Her home is in the hearts of men
With strength to do and will to act –
To act with justice in Thy sight
And mercy hallowed by Thy grace
To spurn the wrong, uphold the right
And humbly walk before Thy face.[34]

Notes

This chapter combines two papers with the same title delivered at the Conference of the British Association for Canadian Studies in March 1993 and at the CSWG Day School in May 1993. Its starting-point was work in 1981 in the National Archives of Canada in Ottawa (NAC), which was supported by the Social Sciences and Humanities Research Council of Canada.

1 I. Deak, *Beyond Nationalism: A Social and Political History of the Habsburg Officer Corps 1848–1918* (Oxford, 1990), pp.54–60, 199–205.
2 Rhodri Williams, *Defending the Empire: The Conservative Party and British Defence Policy 1899–1915* (New Haven, 1991), p.157.
3 O. D. Skelton, *Life and Letters of Sir Wilfrid Laurier* (Oxford, 1922), II, pp.321–2.
4 F. A. Hayek, *The Constitution of Liberty* (London, 1960), p.36.
5 R. C. Brown and G. R. Cook, *Canada 1896–1921* (Toronto, 1974) pp.248–9.
6 T. Chase Casgrain to Borden, 20 June 1914, NAC MG27 II D18, vol.11, File 44.
7 M. Bliss, *A Canadian Millionaire: The Life and Business Times of Sir Joseph Flavelle Bart. 1858–1939* (Toronto, 1978), p.224.
8 R. T. Naylor, 'The Canadian State, the Accumulation of Capital, and the Great War', *Journal of Canadian Studies*, xvi (1981), 36 and 46.
9 *The Times*, 20–7 August 1914.
10 *The Times*, 10 November 1914.
11 J. J. Deutsch, 'War Finance and the Canadian Economy 1914–20', *The Canadian Journal of Economics and Political Science*, vi (1940), 542.
12 White to Borden, 3 August 1914, NAC MG27 II D18, vol.2.
13 White to Perley, 26 and 31 October 1914, NAC MG27 II D18, vol.2; White to Brand, 2 November 1915, NAC Brand Papers (microfilm) Reel 831.
14 White to Perley, 16 November 1914, NAC MG27 II D18, vol.2.
15 Brown and Cook, *Canada 1896–1921*, p.238.
16 W. T. White, *The Story of Canada's War Finance 1914–18* (Toronto, 1921), pp.11–19.
17 Brown and Cook, *Canada 1896–1921*, p.233.
18 White, 31 March 1916, Brand Papers Reel 831; Brown and Cook, *Canada 1896–1921*, p.230.
19 Introduction by G. L. Burr to reprint of *Fiat Money* (Cornell, 1933).
20 White to Irish, 4 December 1915, NAC MG27 II D18, vol.3 File 12a; White to Flavelle, 15 December 1916, Brand Papers Reel 830.
21 Flavelle to Brand, 19 September 1916, Brand Papers Reel 830.
22 White, *The Story*, p.33.
23 Bradbury to White, 6 February 1917, NAC MG27 D18, vol.3 File 11a; White to F. Williams Taylor, 9 February 1916, NAC MG27 D18, vol.3 File 13.

24 Brand memorandum, 6 June 1919, Brand Papers Reel 831; Naylor, 'The Canadian State', 37.
25 Brand to Flavelle, 6 September and Flavelle to Brand, 11 September 1917, Brand Papers Reel 831.
26 Naylor, 'The Canadian State', 35–6.
27 Brand to Bradbury, 12 February 1917, Brand Papers Reel 831.
28 White to Walker, 16 January 1916, NAC MG27 D18, vol.3 File 13.
29 J. E. Kendle, *The Round Table Movement and Imperial Union* (Toronto, 1975), pp.99–103.
30 Cf. H. R. C. Wright, 'Adolph Wagner and the Plural Society', *The South African Journal of Economics*, lxi (1993), 59–66.
31 C. Quigly, 'The Round Table Groups in Canada 1908–38', *Canadian Historical Review*, xliii (1962), 204–21.
32 R. C. Brown, *Robert Laird Borden* (Toronto, 1980), II, pp.146, 155.
33 Flavelle to Brand, 9 July 1919, Brand Papers Reel 830.
34 Sir Thomas White, *The Battle of Britain and Other Poems* (privately printed, Montreal, 1945), pp.5–9.

7

Partners and Rivals: Britain, Canada, the United States and the Impact of the First World War

KEITH ROBBINS

There is a saying, normally used in another context, that 'Two's company, three's a crowd' and it accurately pin-points the difficulty in talking about a triangular relationship. There is certainly nothing straightforward about it. How is the 'North Atlantic Triangle' to be characterized in the early years of the twentieth century? Historians have in the past very frequently written what purport to be studies of bilateral relationships – Anglo-German, Franco-Russian or whatever – even though they know that the character of these bilateral relationships is frequently influenced or even determined by the attitudes and actions of other players in the international game. Few bilateral relationships are in fact ever discrete and self-contained, though it has been frequently convenient and 'manageable' to write about them as though they were. In purporting to talk about a triangle, however, we are from the outset wrestling with three elements avowedly in relationship with each other. In the case of the 'North Atlantic Triangle' – a term, as we all know now, of considerable antiquity itself – we are dealing in each case with three bilateral relationships: the United States with Canada and with Britain, the United Kingdom with Canada and the United States, Canada with the United States and Britain.[1] Nineteenth-century Christian missionaries in India were helped, in their exposition of the doctrine of the Trinity by the coincidental arrival of the English game of cricket. Three stumps, when linked together by bails, became a wicket. There was only one wicket. It might be argued that the same analogy will help us with the three-sided relationship before us. The quality of each country's bilateral relationships was affected by the knowledge of the existence of a third leg. The whole, it might be suggested, was made up of the three elements. The 'North Atlantic Triangle' pointed to something beyond three sets of bilateral relationships but it was not altogether clear what that 'something' was. So, at least, it might have seemed to those contemporaries for whom these impinging bilateral relationships were of profound importance for all parties in the kind of twentieth-century world that they thought was emerging.

It is trite but nevertheless true to say that the North Atlantic Triangle concept was one based upon the patterns of contact made possible by a particular stretch of ocean. This was still a sea age, and the connections each had with the other were limited by this fact. The United States and Canada shared a land boundary and together constituted, from a certain British perspective, 'North America'. The North Atlantic could be perceived as 'the great divide' or as the ocean that united peoples on both its edges who shared assumptions and aspirations. It was not, of course, the kind of 'North Atlantic' of a subsequent era – which was to embrace such quintessentially oceanic states as Turkey! With the exception of the Danish dependencies of Greenland and Iceland and French islands of St Pierre and Miquelon, the North Atlantic was the area in which the rich ambiguities of the three countries in their relationships with each other were played out, uncomplicated by the presence of any other substantial actor.

It is of some significance, in these circumstances, which country from the three we choose to talk about. I mean no discourtesy if I start with Britain. Arguably, at the turn of the century, Britain remained the most important and potent of the three countries with which we are concerned. Britain still stood at the centre of the vast and complex network of imperial relationships. In a literal sense, Britain was a world power in a conspicuous fashion which placed it in a different category from either the United States or Canada. It is true that in the Caribbean and the Philippines 'Manifest Destiny' had evidently stirred the United States into external activity which might presage even more dramatic ambition. If so, that day had not yet arrived. In any event, after the flickering possibility of conflict concerning Venezuela and British Guiana in 1895, Anglo-US relations seemed to have settled down. Historians like Alec and Charles Campbell and the late Kenneth Bourne have charted the way in which the major issues between the two countries were settled between 1898 and 1905.[2] We can speak confidently of a growing *rapprochement* between the two countries. To some extent, we can talk about the attraction of the notion of 'Anglo-Saxon' hegemony.

We can, of course, argue all day about the extent to which in these years Britain was indeed the 'weary titan' weighed down by its massive responsibilities and was seeking a partner. Suffice it to say that at the very least it was desirable to improve the relationship between Washington and London at a time when the European picture appeared unstable, even menacing. The notion of British military involvement in North America was fading from the scene, if it had not already faded. Yet, as the abortive negotiations for an Anglo-American arbitration treaty and the conflicts over dollar diplomacy were to show in the years before 1914, it would be misleading to suppose that all the historical myths and legends which stood between Britain and a country composed in part of Britain's former colonies had been swept away. In any case, at the level of diplomacy, it could not be altogether supposed that the United States knew what was what in the world of civilized intercourse between states. Lord Hardinge of Penshurst, guardian of 'Old Diplomacy', had been good enough to draw attention to this point when he declined appointment to Washington. Lord Bryce would do that kind of job much better. Indeed, he did. Celebrated as the author of *The American Commonwealth*, he brought to the job a hitherto unknown British expertise in the strange ways of the Americans. The success of his embassy contributed to a situation whereby in 1914, when Britain had to decide whether or not to enter the European War, that decision could be taken without any anxiety that the United States administration would take advantage of Britain's preoccupations to embark on any directly hostile action.

This improvement in Anglo-US relations, though we must not exaggerate its extent, was in part made possible by the fact that it appeared that the 'Canada question' – that is to say the defence of the dominion against the United States – was now apparently no longer likely to be an issue. That this was becoming the case, of course, had not stopped soldiers still finding it necessary to examine the options. After a thirty-eight-page memorandum, prepared for the British director of military intelligence in 1903, it was concluded that in a fight to a finish 'we should lose Canada'.[3] The Canadians would not be able to defend themselves for more than a few weeks. In the decade that followed, old questions began to be looked at from different angles. The British Admiralty, looking for cuts both at Esquimalt and Halifax, to all intents and purposes refused to consider war against the United States as a practical proposition. It has been noted that the emphasis was still on winding down Royal Navy bases. There was no notion, apparently, that thought had to be given to the importance of Halifax as a port of embarkation from Canada in the event of a European war. In general, however, the British continued to believe that the destiny of the Empire lay in their hands. They had a total global perspective which a raw collection of provinces could not be expected to have. That Canada 'thought imperially' seemed still to be shown by the contingent in the South African War but there was no disguising that the question of the financing, control and deployment of navies was a contentious issue, not only in Canada of course but also throughout the self-governing dominions. It is easy now to see in this pre-war decade the emergence of intractable problems of self-definition which previous rigidities had disguised. Forty years on from 1867, it could be said from a British perspective that Canada had at length arrived. The country had been bound together by iron rails. That invasion or absorption from the south, feared for so long, whether with justice or not, appeared to be disappearing just at the moment when it was more than ever not in Britain's interest to become involved in a struggle with the United States. By the same token, Canadian complaints that Britain was not doing enough to defend Canada, which had been stock-in-trade, lost their force. But this newly developing situation brought with it further ambiguities.

At one level, Canada was indubitably the 'Senior Dominion'. At least in Ontario and among newly arriving British immigrants, the Britishness of Canada was indisputable. Even Wilfrid Laurier had been prepared to take a knighthood and revel in Britishness – at least when in London. Britain and Canada 'belonged' to each other in a way that the United States and Britain could not 'belong' to each other. Of course, there could be endless debate about what that 'belongingness' entailed and whether or not its logical outcome (not only for Canada of course) was some kind of imperial federation. Thus there was ample scope for stressing the special nature of the ties between Canada and the mother country. Admittedly, it was awkward but incontrovertible that the United Kingdom was not the mother country of all Canadians. To stress the Britishness of Canada might serve to maintain the country's unity against the corrosive influences from the south. It did nothing to advance the deeper issue of what Canadian identity might conceivably be. And, it had to be admitted that the United States had to be cultivated as much as it was feared. Although it was sometimes convenient for Canadians to blame the ineptitude of the British Embassy in Washington for its handling of issues relating to Canada, it was supposed that it could only be a matter of time before at least the formal dealings between the constituents of the triangle were handled on a basis of equality.

One could not avoid the fact that both countries shared the North American continent. Canadians used dollars (their own kind), not pounds. It was the case, however, that between 1900 and 1914 70 per cent of the capital which Canada imported came from Britain. Putting it crudely, it seemed that the Canadian government preferred 'informal economic control from London to political control by the United States'. It had been a British interest that the Dominion of Canada should survive. However, arguably, a united Canada was not possible without protection – but the effects of this protection were felt on the rapidly declining British share of Canadian imports. In January 1912 the Anglo-Canadian business community established in London a Canadian Chamber of Commerce, but it was formed at a time of some anxiety about the future economic development of Canada. The investment boom (perhaps in part motivated by the desire to escape the attentions of Mr Lloyd George) was giving rise to anxiety. How could one distinguish between good and bad Canadian investments? The collapse of the western Canada real-estate market and ensuing railway problems brought the boom to an end. In the long run, one scholar writes, this pre-war boom 'failed to change the British perception of Canada as being the poor cousin of the United States'.[4] The 'boosters', both official and unofficial, were promoting an exaggerated image of Canada which could not be sustained. It was against these harsh realities that the glowing words about the future of Britain and Canada uttered by Earl Grey at the close of his seven-year term as governor-general have to be measured.[5]

Of course, we cannot tell how these relationships would have evolved if war had not broken out in the summer of 1914. In the short term, its advent strengthened certain tendencies and weakened others in a way which might not easily have otherwise been predicted.

At one level, the fact that Canada was at war alongside the United

Kingdom, and the United States was neutral, served to strengthen the imperial Atlantic partnership. We should perhaps beware of too glib an assertion that the British and Canadian people were 'as one'. A. L. Smith, Master of Balliol, lecturing in 1915 told of an able man of his acquaintance who confessed his surprise 'at finding that Canadians and Australians spoke, dressed, even ate and drank so like ourselves'.[6] Of course, it was an immense psychological reversal from several hundred years in which British forces had been a significant factor in the shaping of North America. Now it was Canada which was to play its part, modest perhaps, in shaping the future of Europe. I think I am right in suggesting that some 65 per cent of initial volunteers in Canada had in fact been born in the British Isles. It is not surprising that *habitants* of Quebec did not feel the same enthusiasm. France of the Third Republic and the separation of Church and state was not a particularly attractive cause around which a bipartisan participation in the war could be forged. Enlistments from Quebec fell considerably behind those from other provinces. The Canadian army was perceived as an instrument of Anglicization. A host of issues emerged which, though small in themselves, all contributed to an increasing fissure on linguistic lines. Thus, although it was possible to be with *Canada in Flanders* in the no doubt delightful company of Sir Max Aitken, the emphasis on a 'British imperial' struggle divided rather than united Canada at home.[7] There are, of course, many other ramifications of the war in Canada but I will not linger over them here. And, as is well known, Canadian troops from the very outset had shown a disinclination to be treated as prairie cousins. The first Canadian division had formed part of a British army corps, but by August 1916 there were four Canadian divisions and these were united to form a separate Canadian corps with its own staff, commanded as from 1917 by a Canadian, Sir Arthur Currie. The 60,000 or so Canadians who died certainly died for 'King and Country' – but whose country?

The bitterness of the conscription campaign showed that there were indeed two nations back home in Canada. At the level of high politics, Borden sought simultaneously to show London that Canada was a loyal partner and to advance, at every turn, any issue which had a specifically Canadian dimension. Like other wartime dominion leaders, however, he was pulled in contrary directions. On the one hand, there was the anxiety to be treated as an equal and to be fully informed – the Imperial War Cabinet was the forum, or was it? On the other hand, to accept full information and participation implies at least some willingness to share responsibility. If the latter, there was the grave risk that Borden (or Hughes) would run ahead of what their domestic publics would be prepared to tolerate. If it is indeed the case not only that nations make wars but wars make nations, we may plausibly argue that the Canada that emerged from the war was a very different society from the one which entered it. The dispute about the form of signature to be adopted within the British Empire when it came to the signing of the Treaty of Versailles was entirely predictable. In turn, through the immediate post-war Imperial Conferences, the issues of diplomatic representation, halibut fisheries and other tasty matters were pursued with vigour. Throw in the Chanak crisis, and there was much room for debate about whether there could be a common foreign policy of the Empire in any sense. Philip Wigley's book explores these matters in great detail.[8] It is not my purpose either to take us through the 1926 Imperial Conference, the Statute of Westminster and beyond to follow the full course of the British–Canadian part of the North Atlantic Triangle. The impact of the war meant that Canada was more Canadian than formerly, yet it remained in an important sense British.

Of course, in the eyes of the British political élite, the Canadian response to the war in 1914 was immeasurably superior and more perceptive morally than that of the United States. We should not underestimate the scorn and contempt felt in many circles for the neutrality decided upon in Washington. How could an American administration not see the great issues that were at stake? I have to generalize, but there were many prepared to push relations with Washington almost to the point of breakdown. Although the mother of the first lord of the Admiralty had sponsored something called the *Anglo-Saxon Review* dedicated, in pre-war days to amity across the Atlantic, there were not many admirals who shared these sentiments in wartime.[9] It was possible for commercial minds to read into American conduct a lofty concern to capture British trade in third markets, notably Latin America, which the British were temporarily unable to supply. It was possible for naval minds to discern in their American counterparts a desire, longer-term, to ensure that Britannia did not rule the waves. Much of this response was a confused and bitter reaction to anxious public circumstances and to private loss. Someone had to be blamed somewhere. As the war continued, it also became clear that the financial balance across the

Atlantic was beginning to shift. If it continued, the glorious days of the City of London at the hub of the international financial system might be numbered. Of course, amid these fevered alarms and anxieties, there remained some stiff upper lips. Those of Sir Edward Grey normally came into this category. The last thing he wanted was for excited admirals to push their interpretation of 'freedom of the seas' to its limits. If the Americans could not be with Britain in the hour of need, they could at least be prevented from being against her. He bent his best efforts to this end in his diplomatic exchanges with Washington during his final years as foreign secretary up to the end of 1916. He showed a more restrained enthusiasm for the British Empire – though commonly thought of as a Liberal Imperialist – than his cousin, the former governor-general. He saw no merit in antagonizing the Americans by gratuitously contrasting their behaviour with that of the Canadians.[10]

Of course, after 1917, the picture changed again. The entry of the United States was a welcome sign that the Allies would not in the end be defeated. The British diplomatic task was now arguably that of preventing the late entrant from walking away with the prize of victory. Wilson was no less circumspect in his insistence that in his new partnership with the belligerents the United States was an 'associated state' rather than an ally. He had no wish to sully his hands with any of the notorious 'secret treaties' concluded by his new associates whose imperialist tendencies he deemed to be insatiable. In short, Britain and the United States were both partners and rivals, the emphasis upon one or other being appropriate at particular times or in particular connections. Lloyd George, no less than Churchill in another war, had not become the king's first minister to preside over the liquidation of the British Empire. It was not clear what all this talk of a League of Nations meant, but it was probably wise to go along with it for the time being. In the final stages of the war the most difficult calculation to make was how far the entry of the United States into the war betokened a lasting interest in and commitment to whatever peace settlement might eventually be negotiated in Germany. Was that North Atlantic Triangle which functioned, not without hiccups, from 1917 through to the end of the war, the permanent reality within which all future British and British/ imperial policy would have to be fashioned? Or was it a temporary phenomenon which would require the reconstruction of an imperial grand strategy or, God forbid, some lasting European commitment to France? In the event, although Sir Edward Grey was dispatched on an outing to Washington, he was not able to put Humpty Dumpty together again. The close alignment of 1917–19 would not last.

My unsurprising conclusion is that the impact of the First World War did not point inexorably to one future. To an extent, it appeared that the three partners in the triangle had all come to perceive a common vision of the issues allegedly at stake and to fashion political rhetoric which could give some substance to the notion in France that 'la paix des Anglo-Saxons' had been imposed. It is not to dismiss this rhetoric to suggest that the meeting of minds was not as lasting and as deep as it appeared to some enthusiastic contemporaries. Although Canada appeared glad to have shared in a common victory, there was no desire, as there was in Australia or South Africa, to take on an imperial role – or perhaps it was simply there were no offending German colonies close at hand. Even more fundamentally, while in 1914 Britain still owned three-quarters of all the foreign investment in Canada and the United States one-fifth, by 1930 the British share had fallen to one-third and the American had risen to two-thirds. Indeed, during the war itself, when Canada's exports to Britain rose sharply and Britain's exports to Canada fell, it could be said that it was Canada that was exporting capital to Britain – a reversal of the customary expectation. Of course, the growing presence of the United States in financial terms could lead Canadian Americophobes to become Anglophiles, at least temporarily. The ultimate direction in which the triangle would tilt was obscure.

When he addressed the Canadian Club in Ottawa in October 1908 Lord Milner declared that the last thing which the thought of the Empire inspired in him was a desire to boast – to wave a flag or to shout 'Rule Britannia'. He was much more inclined to go into a corner by himself and pray.[11] The history of the North Atlantic Triangle in the first quarter of the century was to provide him, and others, with many opportunities for quiet devotion. They could not have been certain that their prayers were answered in the way they desired.

Notes

[1] J. B. Brebner, *North American Triangle: The Interplay of Canada, the United States and Britain* (Toronto and New Haven, 1945).

2 A. E. Campbell, *Great Britain and the United States: 1895–1903* (London, 1960); B. Perkins, *The Great Rapprochment: England and the United States, 1895–1914* (New York, 1968); K. Bourne, *Britain and the Balance of Power in North America, 1815–1908* (London, 1967).

3 R. A. Preston, *Canada and 'Imperial Defense'* (Durham, NC, 1967).

4 J. F. Gilpin, *The Poor Relation has Come into Her Fortune: The British Investment Boom in Canada 1905–1915* (London, 1992).

5 H. Begbie, *Albert, 4th Earl Grey: A Last Word* (London, 1917), pp.123–5. For a Canadian perspective which matches that of Grey, see G. T. Denison, *The Struggle for Imperial Unity: Recollections and Experiences* (London, 1909).

6 *The Empire and the Future* (London, 1916), p.29.

7 M. Aitken, *Canada in Flanders* (London, 1916).

8 P. Wigley, *Canada and the Transition to Commonwealth: British-Canadian Relations, 1917–1926* (Cambridge, 1977).

9 K. Robbins, *Churchill* (London, 1992), pp.30–1.

10 K. Robbins, *Sir Edward Grey* (London, 1971); idem, *Politicians, Diplomacy and War in Modern British History* (London, 1994), pp.165–73.

11 Lord Milner, *The Nation and the Empire* (London, 1913), p.330.

8

The Political Economy of the North Atlantic Triangle in the 1930s

TIM ROOTH

It has become increasingly common to analyse international economic relationships in terms of the presence or absence of a hegemonic power.[1] During the past 150 years an open international system has been associated with the leadership of a dominant economic power, a role performed by the United Kingdom in the second half of the nineteenth century and by the United States in the quarter-century or so after the Second World War. By contrast, when economic power has been more evenly distributed, the international economy has tended towards closure, protectionism has flourished and regional or imperial trading arrangements have become more entrenched. The 1930s were, of course, just such a period of closure, but this was also a transitional decade, with the UK adopting protection and with attitudes in the USA undergoing something of a sea change. The trade policies of its two major trading partners were of profound interest to the third member of the North Atlantic Triangle, Canada, a country that has tended to identify prosperity and relative autonomy with a liberal and multilateral economy.

In this chapter it is proposed to outline the major changes in the North Atlantic Triangle in the 1930s, first tracing the shifting economic relationships during a decade of slump and economic nationalism, and then focusing on two sets of negotiations, the World Economic and Monetary Conference of 1933 and the triangular trade negotiations of 1937–8.

The world slump gave powerful impetus to the erection of trade barriers. Theorists of hegemonic trade policy suggest that there is often a lag between a country's relative economic standing and its adoption of the appropriate commercial regime.[2] The USA, which possessed unquestionably the most powerful economy by the 1920s, responded to the slump by a huge hoist of tariffs in 1930 (Hawley-Smoot) and a further rise in 1932 under the Revenue Act. The UK, a second-level power by the 1920s, although introducing a few tariffs, had more or less stayed true to what was essentially still a free-trade policy at the end of the decade. However, a protectionist constituency existed, and although internationalism appeared to have triumphed when the decision was made in 1925 to return to the gold standard, this proved a pyrrhic victory, the costs of an overvalued exchange rate helping to erode support for free trade even before the onset of the slump.[3] The depression gave the final decisive thrust to the adoption of protection, the British government introducing the full panoply of tariffs and imperial preference during 1931–2. The other symbol of Britain's nineteenth-century international economic leadership, the gold standard, had been abandoned in the wake of the European financial crisis of 1931. Britain's departure from the gold standard and subsequent adoption of protection had a major impact on international economic relations in the 1930s. In part this was because of the direct influence on trade flows, but these actions were also important because they affected perceptions of events and therefore policy. British policy was one of several forces serving to realign the North Atlantic Triangle.

I

Until the onset of the slump in 1929 the North Atlantic Triangle had worked with a minimum of friction. It had provided the Canadian economy with a vital stimulus. Wheat shipments to Europe held up so well that by the late 1920s they had reached more than three times their 1911–13 level. But the main thrust to Canadian prosperity had come from supplying the raw-material needs of the great American upswing of the 1920s: timber exports had been stimulated by the construction boom, and the expansion of the automobile industry, electrical products and other consumer durables, along with the voracious demands for newsprint, encouraged a new generation of staples – pulp, paper, hydro-electricity, non-ferrous metals – and had concentrated the benefits in central Canada and British Columbia. The intensity of the boom was magnified by the inflow of US funds to develop resources and to finance branch plants. Multilateralism oiled the system of international payments. Although Canadian exports to the USA boomed, they were outpaced by

Canada's demand for American imports, and it seems likely that when investment income and shipping services are taken into account, Canada also ran a payments deficit with the UK. This was covered by the inflow of capital from the USA. Britain too was in deficit with the USA, but paid for this with some dollars from Canada and, more importantly, through the surpluses Britain ran with its Asian empire, countries which in turn found lucrative export outlets for their tin, rubber and jute in the USA.

The slump that the Wall Street crash heralded in the autumn of 1929 crippled the North American economy and was a powerful force in the spread of the international depression. Since the USA was the epicentre of the world depression, Canada paid dearly for its heavy reliance on sales south of the border, exports falling from $515 million in 1929 to only $165 million in 1932. The main reason was the collapse of American production and incomes, but the great wall of tariffs extended in 1930 and again in 1932 not only aggravated the damage but caused huge resentment in Canada and led to a series of retaliatory measures. The slump and trade barriers contributed to a distancing between the two North American nations, all the more so as capital flows from the USA fell away sharply. Under Bennett's premiership, the Canadians were enthusiastic participants in tariff and preference-building. Suffering grievously from the loss of the US market and from the collapse of world commodity prices, the Canadian government sought redress in the British market. Newly protectionist Britain was able to respond – indeed it had little realistic option but to respond – and in the summer of 1932, at the end of the Ottawa Conference, a network of imperial commercial agreements were signed.

The revolution in British commercial policy certainly paved the way for Canadian exports, and the UK market provided some offset to the heavy losses Canadians were suffering south of the border. Measured by UK statistics, British imports from Canada rose from £31 million in 1931 to an average of £76 million in 1936-8 (in 1928–30 imports from Canada had averaged £45 million). This was all the more remarkable because it was achieved in the face of a fall in price levels and, more importantly, a major decline in sales of wheat. Canada moved from ninth to second in a league table of suppliers of the British market. By no means all of this was due to preferences, but it was a welcome boost for exports and relieved the Canadian balance of payments. Before the depression the inflow of

Table 1   Percentage distribution of Canadian exports

	UK	USA
1928	32·8 (22·6)	36·9
1929	24·8 (23·3)	43·7
1933	39·4 (28·9)	32·3
1937	39·8 (39·0)	36·8
1938	40·2 (39·4)	32·9

The figures in brackets refer to exports adjusted to take account of the over-recording of wheat shipments to the UK discussed in J. Stovel, *Canada in the World Economy* (Cambridge, Mass., 1967), pp.326–7. Official statistics exaggerate sales to the UK because all exports of grain shipped in bond to the USA were classified as going to Britain, and even those recorded as going direct to the UK may well have been re-exported or diverted *en route*. *Source*: M. C. Urquhart and K. A. C. Buckley, *Historical Statistics of Canada* (Toronto, 1965), F348–56.

investment funds from the USA had enabled Canada to balance its international accounts. When in the 1930s these ceased, Canada was forced to reduce the trade deficit with its neighbour. This still left dollars to be found, but crucially, Canada was able to turn the deficit with the UK into a surplus, and therefore pay the USA.

In economic terms Canada thus drew nearer to the UK in the 1930s, and, as table 1 shows, Britain overtook the USA as the principal export outlet. But this was not done unreservedly by the Canadians. Far from it, for although Prime Minister R. B. Bennett had described the Empire as 'an economic unit [that] can face foursquare every storm that blows', this was manifest nonsense, and it was nonsense above all for Canada. Britain may have overhauled the USA as Canada's principal export market, but, locked into a North American economy, Canada was critically dependent for any semblance of prosperity on the reopening of the American market, particularly for pulp, paper and timber. Therefore the Canadian dollar was not linked to sterling, and Canada rejected faint overtures to join the sterling area.

British protectionism, the Ottawa agreements and the subsequent trade pacts with other dependent suppliers were doubly damaging to US trade, for while the British market was being closed to American exports, and imports switched to other suppliers, London sought reciprocal privileges in return for preferential access to the UK market. The Americans were forced to stand helplessly by. The decline in US

Table 2   UK imports from Canada and the USA

	Canada		USA	
	£ million	*Percent of imports*	*£ million*	*Percent of imports*
1928	54	5·0	178	16·5
1929	44	3·9	184	16·6
1930	36	3·7	144	15·0
1931	31	3·9	98	12·2
1932	40	6·2	79	12·1
1933	44	7·0	71	11·4
1934	48	7·4	77	11·8
1935	53	7·5	81	11·6
1936	71	9·0	87	11·1
1937	84	8·8	106	11·1
1938	73	8·5	112	13·0
1939	78	9·2	114	13·5

Source: UK *Annual Statement of Trade* (various years).

exports to Canada and the UK was precipitous: by 1932 sales to Britain stood at $288 million, only one-third of their 1929 level of $848 million, and losses in Canada were even more disastrous.[4] Although not the full story, protection and imperial preference played a part in the Americans losing their share of both markets. But the irony was that despite discrimination and the collapse of sales to Britain, the British market had emerged as the most important destination for US exports. This was to add piquancy to Anglo-American relations for the rest of the decade.

II

British protection and imperial preference signified a rejection of economic internationalism. The absence of international leadership was clearly evident in the fiasco of the World Economic Conference held in London in the summer of 1933. Where once there was a tendency to blame the USA, and in particular Roosevelt, for wrecking the conference, a revisionist literature stresses either Britain's contribution to failure or the more intractable domestic problems of each of the major participants that precluded international solutions.[5] It is probable that no single country could have taken action to secure an outcome from the conference that would have achieved much for international recovery. Yet there might have existed a basis for common action by the USA, Britain, Canada and other dominions. But while these countries all regarded an increase in world prices as essential for economic recovery, the gold-bloc countries,[6] several with the great inflations of the early 1920s fresh in their collective memories, were sceptical; while they paid lip-service to the idea, their methods of achieving it, through the restoration of business confidence in the wake of a return to the international gold standard, were extremely nebulous, and the main thrust of their policies was directed towards the stabilization of currencies.

While the gold-bloc countries were at least consistent in their position, the UK and the USA were never able to act in concert. Similarities of interpretation were obscured by tension over war debts and, even more importantly, by a sharp switch in their respective stances towards currency stabilization. In the early stages of preparation for the conference the US government tended to argue for stabilization of currencies as a prerequisite to international accord, placing itself in alliance with the gold bloc and leaving the UK isolated in its refusal to countenance fixing a value for sterling. By the time the conference was held in the summer of 1933 the positions had been reversed. By then the USA had also left the gold standard and it was the Americans who were isolated: Britain had now joined forces with the gold bloc in pressuring the Americans to fix a value for the dollar. Roosevelt's refusal to do so scuppered whatever slender chances the conference had of achieving useful results.

The underlying purpose of the WEC has been traced back by Ian Drummond to a desire on the part of the American and British governments to raise world commodity prices through joint action on monetary expansion.[7] The proximate origins can be found in a League of Nations conference held in Lausanne in July 1932. Because it was a League conference, and because war debts and reparations featured prominently on the agenda, the USA had not been present. Aware of impending Anglo-American discussions on world commodity prices, and of the restricted nature of their agenda, the Lausanne delegates agreed that the League should convene a world economic and financial conference and that the USA should be asked to attend.

Why were prices so important, and what was thought to have caused their spectacular decline? In the domestic economy, it was argued, the tendency for prices to fall faster than money wages had increased the level of real wages, encouraged firms to shed labour, and, by reducing profits, to cut investment. At an international level the collapse of primary-product prices was one of the most striking characteristics of the depression. The deflationary process crippled purchasing power, dangerously impaired the ability of borrowers to maintain debt servicing and, because of balance-of-payments problems, encouraged the paraphernalia of exchange controls and quotas that were paralysing international trade. Uncertainty and lack of confidence had led to a virtual cessation of capital exports. These views were propagated vigorously by Sir Henry Strackosch, financier, chairman of *The Economist* and indefatigible conference delegate. He was an able and energetic advocate of the absolute necessity for a rise in world price levels. He had been an influential member of the League of Nations Gold Delegation, and a key figure in the production of a minority report. Such a viewpoint gained greater authority through its support from the Swedish economist Gustav Cassel, another member of the Gold Delegation and one of the most influential economists of his generation.[8]

Yet in terms of economic policy, the USA and the gold-bloc countries wanted Britain to stabilize the pound, and best of all to return to the gold standard. London, however, held that it was out of the question for the UK to return to gold without fundamental changes in world monetary arrangements. These included a settlement of war debts, which remained as a major source of friction between Paris and London on the one hand and Washington on the other. A pronounced sense of grievance, even of injustice, permeated British and French attitudes to the debts, but hostility to them was further stoked by the pressure they placed on the budget and the balance of payments (they absorbed 12 per cent of Britain's 1932 export earnings), and an awareness of their contribution to the breakdown of the world monetary system. The UK government also wanted the gold-glut countries, France and USA, to initiate expansionary monetary policies, to agree to a redistribution of gold and to reduce tariffs as well.[9] All in all, it was a package that stood no chance whatever of acceptance. London and Washington might have wanted a rise in world prices, but during the winter of 1932–3 failure to achieve any accord on this was a consequence of the primacy given to the achievement of currency stabilization: the Americans wanted Britain back on the gold standard, and the gold-bloc countries of Europe also saw this as a pre-condition to a broader understanding.

The total configuration of the conference and of national align-ments was transformed by the American decision to leave the gold standard and let the dollar depreciate. This was announced in April 1933 while the British delegation, headed by Ramsay MacDonald, was travelling on the SS *Berengaria* to New York. Although the prime minister rejected the advice of the government's chief economic adviser, Sir Frederick Leith-Ross, to return home on the next avail-able ship, there is no mistaking the anger felt by the British govern-ment. An appreciation of the new situation by the Treasury was wired to the prime minister. Treasury officials stressed the almost gratuitous nature of America's departure from the gold standard, 'when invulnerable to outside action and when still possessing favour-able trade balance'. It was totally unlike Britain's enforced departure from gold in 1931, and it was the first time in history, they asserted, when a currency had been allowed to go under circumstances when it could easily have been held; 'on top of its high tariffs, sudden withdrawal of creditors from Europe and demands for war debts, America now throws a new source of confusion into the world.'[10]

There was a line of consistency in Roosevelt's decision to leave the gold standard and allow the dollar to depreciate. The administra-tion was under strong pressure to raise prices. Farmers, the silver lobby, forcefully led by Key Pittman, senator from Nevada and chair-man of the Senate Foreign Relations Committee, academic economists as reputable as Irving Fisher, and influential sections of the business community, including bankers, who had formed the Committee for the Nation to Rebuild Prices and Purchasing Power, all campaigned for higher prices. But, as Freidel emphasizes in his careful analysis, none of the pressure for inflationary policies conflicted with the predilections of Roosevelt himself.[11] True, he might quibble about the means, showing little enthusiasm for the restorative properties of silver revaluation, but he was convinced of the need for price rises. The objective of mild inflation also influenced the welter of otherwise often contradictory policies that comprised the New Deal, lending it at least one element of consistency. This was reflected in a joint statement made by MacDonald and Roosevelt at the end of their talks in April: 'the necessity for an increase in the general level of commodity prices was recognised as primary and fundamental'.[12] This was one factor in Roosevelt's decision. It was given urgency because the administration became anxious that gold losses in March

and April 1933 would lead to a tightening of domestic credit conditions, reinforcing what they feared might be the deflationary
consequences of federal government measures aimed at cutting the
budget deficit. Paradoxically, leaving gold also allowed Roosevelt to
head off pressure from Congress for more extreme inflationary
measures. There was an international strand too. James Warburg,
the 'shimmering bright' young banker who advised Roosevelt,[13]
thought the dollar was too high, and that because of the strength of
the balance of payments administrative action was needed to draw
it down and thereby to restore American competitiveness. On 15
March Warburg had advocated the establishment of a stabilization
fund, modelled on the British exchange equalization account, which
by buying and selling dollars could be used to force the dollar down.
It would, moreover, give the Americans greater bargaining leverage
on negotiations with Britain. The banker used the imagery of the
West:

> Irrespective of whether we ever use the fund, it is a very much healthier
> way for us to sit down at the table with the British if we have a gun on
> our hip so long as we know that they are coming with a gun on their hip.
> It is very much easier to suggest that we both unbuckle our belts and lay
> the guns on the table than for us to make the suggestion to the British if
> they know and we know that we have no gun.[14]

Letting the dollar depreciate therefore held out the hope of remov-
ing the threat of deflation posed by gold outflows, freeing the
administration from international constraints on the New Deal
programme, restoring America's diminished competitiveness on world
markets and, while helping to reverse price movements, appeasing
Congress and meeting Roosevelt's own objectives of moderate inflation.

With the devalued dollar now threatening to underbid sterling,
London rediscovered an interest in discussing stabilization – the
stabilization of the dollar, and this became the central issue of the
conference. As Feis has suggested about the early emphasis on fixing a value for the pound,

> [t]his was the start of a slide into a strategy for the conference which
> caused all the other measures which had figured in the original cor-
> respondence to pivot around a stabilisation accord. It was not foreseen
> that the demand for stabilisation would concentrate upon the dollar.[15]

When MacDonald met Roosevelt in April he was convinced of the American desire to fix a rate for the dollar. Warburg suggested a stabilization fund to which Britain and France would contribute. The French, however, regarded stabilization as essentially a matter for Britain and the USA, while Britain worried about the extent of the devaluation the Americans were aiming to achieve. As American ideas on this evolved, and as the dollar continued its slide, British and French anxieties grew. It was agreed that talks about currencies would be held in London, although they would be fenced off from the official conference, and would take place between American, British and French government officials and central bankers. The key role of these to the conference lies partly in the weight given to currency stabilization during the preparatory talks, but also because other moves depended on resolution of the issue. Until this was settled it was virtually impossible to get any agreement on tariffs.

Tariffs interested the State Department, and particularly Secretary of State Cordell Hull who had an almost obsessive concern with trade liberalization, which he saw as an integral part of harmonious relations between nations. Charles Kindleberger states that Hull had only one formula: 'stop raising tariffs and start lowering them. It was hard to see the mechanism by which this could lead to recovery.'[16] For the most part, because everyone became weary of Hull's lengthy, rambling sermons, Feis handled the negotiations for the Americans as often as possible.[17]

By March 1933 British commercial policy was well defined, although it had changed little since the early preparations for the conference the previous October.[18] The crucial question centred on whether to retain the most-favoured-nation (m.f.n.) clause and whether to use clearing arrangements as a normal instrument of policy. There was strong domestic pressure to abandon multilateralism so as to secure maximum bargaining leverage; clearing agreements were another manifestation of the same objectives. The rejection of these arguments appears to have had no relation to the World Economic Conference or any external pressure. Preparatory British documents for the conference show little fresh thought in Whitehall, merely a justification for continuing with existing policies. London was strongly in favour of tariff liberalization provided it was done by other countries. As a late starter in the tariff game, British protection was comparatively mild. Hull's proposals for multilateralism were looked upon sceptically in Whitehall. It was argued these would

tend to involve moderate-tariff countries in making disproportionate concessions, would on past experience be difficult to achieve,
and were shot through with technical difficulties over *ad valorem*
equivalents for specific duties and the definition of 'revenue' tariffs.
The most promising route to liberalization lay through bilateral agreements precisely of the type Britain was making with the Scandina-
vians and Germany. These were defined as meeting Britain's
requirements of securing the widest and most unconditional
interpretation of the m.f.n. clause. In consequence, London looked
upon regional or group agreements for exclusive tariffs with a
jaundiced eye, permissible only in 'quite exceptional circumstances'.
Although Washington expressed its anger at the Ottawa agreements
on several occasions, protests were dismissed with the argument
that the treaties were 'a domestic affair between the British nations'.[19]
As Leith-Ross predicted, however, this question was to be raised
again when bilateral negotiations were opened with the United States
later in the decade. Quotas and similar restrictions were jointly
condemned by the UK and the USA, although they feared that France,
with quotas on more than a thousand articles, would be opposed to
their abolition, especially without any agreement to stabilize exchange
rates. But London's opposition was qualified: for was not Britain in
the process of erecting virtually identical barriers to agricultural
imports such as bacon and meat? A distinction had therefore to be
made between quotas on agricultural products and those on raw
materials and industrial goods, justified by the argument that the
structure of farming, with numerous producers, meant that price
falls often stimulated output rather than discouraged it.

Hull's suggestion of a tariff truce was pursued, however, although
in Whitehall this was done with a martyred air. The French were
doubtful, arguing with some substance that pledges given on fixing
existing tariff levels could be entirely nullified by currency movements. Stabilization of the dollar was therefore a prerequisite to any
agreement on relaxing tariffs and quotas. None the less tariff truces
were placed on the agenda, although in the event the schemes became
so hedged about with reservations and qualifications as to be virtually
worthless. A resolution was adopted by the Organizing Committee of
the conference on 12 May by which governments pledged themselves
not to introduce 'any new initiatives which might increase the many
varieties of difficulties now arresting international commerce'.[20] It also

envisaged a tariff truce to be arranged for the duration of the conference. Whitehall insisted that bacon quota schemes, already in the process of being implemented, should be exempted, as should applications for duty increases made to the Import Duties Advisory Committee by 12 May. On the same day the United States Agricultural Adjustment Act became law, allowing the administration to impose compensatory taxes on imports of commodities that were subject to processing taxes in the USA.[21] The French and Germans also made reservations which severely limited the value of the tariff truce.

The conference duly opened on 12 June. It soon settled into a process of waiting for the Americans to agree on stabilizing the dollar. The official committees of the conference became dependent on the outcome of the tripartite negotiations on exchange-rate-stabilization, talks lying outside the official framework of the conference and themselves ultimately reliant, as it transpired, on decisions made in Washington, or, more accurately, wherever President Roosevelt's sailing holiday took him.

The American delegation was a divided delegation without full authority and having to negotiate against a background of unsettled US policy. Liaison between the official delegates and the finance group, the latter reporting direct to Washington and not to the secretary of state, was poor. Hull, interested in tariff reductions and little else, was not close to Roosevelt, and alleged to MacDonald that there was no one in the delegation he could trust.[22] It included Senator Pittman, whose escapades were to provide good material for the gossip columns, Cox, an ex-presidential candidate and very able, and others there largely because of political favours or their position: 'a motley group', concluded Feis, one of the advisers, as he read the roster.[23]

Divisions in the delegation soon became public. With Hull's assent, Feis submitted to the conference secretariat a number of proposals for discussion in the field of international trade, including a suggestion of a 10 per cent cut in tariff rates. When this was published in the press on 17 June, Pittman issued a statement denying that the American delegation was sponsoring any such action. Hull, in turn, had to produce an explanation emphasizing that it was a topic for discussion, not a statement of United States policy. Pittman appears to have taken the proposal unusually hard, and Feis records an episode when shortly after these events the senator drunkenly pursued him along the corridors of Claridge's wielding a hunting knife.[24]

Tariff matters, as emphasized above, were of secondary importance: once the Americans had dropped off the gold standard, the stabilization of the dollar dominated proceedings. It assumed even greater importance because of the rapid fall of the dollar, which in itself worried the British, but also threatened a financial crisis in Europe as gold flowed out of the smaller European gold-bloc countries.[25] American stabilization was seen as essential if currency chaos in Europe was to be averted. In fact the Treasury and banking representatives had devised a scheme, based around a middle rate of $4 to the pound and to be backed by gold of up to three million ounces from each of the three central banks.[26] Agreed on 15 June, rumours of the scheme leaked, causing the dollar to rise and stocks and commodity prices to fall sharply. It appeared therefore to threaten the very objectives that Roosevelt was seeking, and it stirred up the inflationists again. As General Hugh Johnson, head of the newly formed National Recovery Administration, told Raymond Moley, 'an agreement to stabilise now on the lines your boy friends in London are suggesting would bust to hell and gone the prices we're sweating to raise.'[27]

Roosevelt refused to agree the proposals, instead sending Moley, who had the reputation of an economic nationalist, to London to see if he could work out a deal more to the liking of the president. While Moley took ship across the Atlantic the conference stalled. He arrived on 27 June as anxiety about the sustainability of the gold standard was reaching a new pitch. To calm speculation, an innocuous statement was drafted and dispatched to Roosevelt for approval. Although it committed the signatories to virtually nothing, not even a temporary stabilization, and it spoke of co-operation to calm speculation, it appears to have been misunderstood by the president as limiting his freedom of action. He elaborated his reasons in the infamous 'bombshell' message of 3 July which emphatically rejected any thought of stabilization, and in the process referred to the 'old fetishes of so-called international bankers'. It was, said Chamberlain, 'couched in language which could not fail to give deep offence to almost every other Delegation at the Conference. Its tone was arrogant and it lectured the Conference in a manner and circumstances which were hardly believable'.[28] It effectively killed the conference, although as *The Economist* remarked, it took 'an unconsciable time to die'.[29] It was kept going, more for psychological than for practical reasons, until it adjourned on 27 July. It did not reconvene.

The proximate causes of failure lay in the United States and in Roosevelt's refusal to contemplate anything that smacked of stabilization. The price jitters of mid-June when rumours of a London agreement on exchange rates hit New York had probably helped confirm Roosevelt in his determination to avoid obligations to fix the dollar. The domestic programme had to be given priority. In March and April internationalism had been nearer the foreground, but in the next two months there was a swing towards isolationism, a trend that was widely recognized. It was referred to several times in the London press, Hull emphasized to MacDonald the isolationist shift in the United States, and a State Department friend warned Feis, 'You fellows must not expect to find America the same as it was when you left.'[30] These factors were paramount. They were almost certainly encouraged by an American perception of European duplicity and fear of European entanglements. Britain had ruled the Ottawa agreements as out of contention, but had confirmed the main thrust of policy, as Norman Davis reported from London, by signing trade agreements with quotas and preferential clauses, one of the most objectionable of which was being negotiated with Argentina.[31] Behaviour over war debts fuelled American resentment. The French government refused to make its payment on 15 June, and although Britain paid $10 million, this was the equivalent of only 13 per cent of the amount due, and was paid in silver obtained cheaply from India. Feis records:

> it is probable that the default washed away the remnants of Roosevelt's tolerance for the French effort to cause us to return to the international gold standard at a fixed rate to the franc, and made him more determined not to let the British authorities ease him into an agreement about the relative pound-dollar value which might be to Britain's advantage.[32]

There was also a sense that the United States got the worst of deals when negotiating[33] with Europe. Roosevelt felt that although his message may have been rather brusque, it might none the less have given a psychological lift at home and helped dispel the view that at every conference the Americans came out the losers.

The emphasis placed on exchange-rate stability was understandable in the light of fears of a European financial crisis in the wake of devaluation of the dollar and because tariff concessions, even a truce, could quickly be undermined by depreciation of currencies. Yet even if some currency accord had been achieved, it was little guarantee that much else could be accomplished as a result: as the Swedish delegate reminded the conference, trade restrictions were a consequence as much as a cause of the depression, and although exchange rates had been stable prior to September 1931, this had not prevented the erection and extension of trade barriers.[34] The best hopes of contributing to international recovery had lain in the schemes that had been advanced earlier. The International Labour Organization had advocated extensive public works schemes, but although the Americans expressed some interest, few other delegates did, and the British Treasury was well rehearsed in arguments against such projects (although it had no objection to schemes elsewhere, especially in France and the gold-bloc countries).[35] The British proposals for international credits might have eased foreign-exchange shortages and encouraged lending, but stood slender chance of acceptance by the gold-standard countries: the inability of the United States and Britain to reach any accord over them guaranteed failure. So the conference was left with a feeble tariff truce to show for its endeavours, and that was dead by December.

The World Economic Conference was significant in a number of ways. Its failure demonstrated the lack of international leadership: there was no harmonious accord between the major participants, nor was there a dominant power possessing both the vision of what needed doing and the means of persuading other countries to implement its programme. A German official had complained before the conference that 'things are not the same as they used to be, in that England would to a certain extent lead at world economic conferences; now it is the reverse, she must be led'.[36] The Americans were preoccupied with domestic objectives and were certainly not willing to subordinate these to international aims. The failure of the conference also confirmed countries in the pursuit of protection and bilateralism. If Britain had slowed its treaty-making during the course of the conference, this probably reflected the constraints on the administrative capacity of the Board of Trade rather than any hesitations about policy.

III

American international economic policy had begun to shift, however, in 1934, with Hull, after the humiliating treatment he had received from Roosevelt during the World Economic Conference, playing a major part in this shift. Hull was a crusader, a tireless advocate of liberalizing trade, the virtues of which he would extol frequently and at length. At one level, it was in Hull's view a policy for peace. 'To me, unhampered trade dovetailed with peace; high tariffs, trade barriers and unfair economic competition with war.'[37] The removal of trade barriers, the free flow of goods and exchange, would foster economic interdependence and the peace of nations. Such an equation, which had a respectable antecedent in the ideas expressed so forcibly by Cobden and other English Liberals in the mid-nineteenth century, found in the deteriorating international situation of the 1930s continued and widespread acceptance. While there seemed little doubt that Hull held these views with genuine, fierce conviction, he none the less had, as one commentator has observed, an 'awesome faculty for transmuting American interests into universal moral principles'.[38]

The passage and implementation of the trade-agreements programme was, however, the product of various pressures. Along with events such as the establishment of an Export–Import Bank and diplomatic recognition of Soviet Russia, the trade agreements marked a commitment by the USA to a world economic role, a commitment that was to grow stronger over the next decade. In 1934 Leon Trotsky had written in *Foreign Affairs* that the power of American capitalism was such that it 'must open up ways for itself throughout the length and breadth of our entire planet'.[39] F. V. Meyer has subsequently argued that trends within the US economy created pressure for international markets: as product life shortened, and research and development costs grew ever more massive, it became imperative for corporations to maximize sales world-wide.[40] The Reciprocal Trade Agreements Act of 1934 was the turning point in American policy, the watershed between the high protectionism of the 1930 Hawley–Smoot tariff and 1932 Revenue Act duties, and the forceful American pursuit of trade liberalization in the 1940s.[41] Such trade expansionism accords with the view of how dominant economic powers behave: those with the technological and competitive edge have an interest in maximizing sales through an open multilateral economy. There may be a delay between the establishment of economic leadership, a country's recognition that it has achieved it, and consequently the adoption of the appropriate policies. Inevitably some lagging or less internationally competitive sectors of the economy will cling to protectionism, but it is notable that export interests were behind Hull's programme. The American

Automobile Manufacturers Association had backed Roosevelt in 1932 because they thought he would pursue a tariff policy designed to open up markets abroad, and he was still getting support from sections of the motor industry in 1936 on the grounds that however much they disagreed with his other policies, they approved of what he had done for foreign trade.[42] Some conservatives supported an active foreign trade programme precisely because they saw it as an alternative to increasing government regulation.

By 1934 Hull had overcome powerful opposition from industries that felt threatened by foreign competitions, from isolationists and, most strongly of all, from farmers. George Peek, director of the Agricultural Adjustment Administration, was an influential opponent of Hull within government, and there had been an epic contest between them in 1934. Once Peek had resigned in July 1935, Hull was the dominant voice on trade in the Roosevelt administration. Armed with the powers of the Reciprocal Trade Agreements Act, Hull could make an onslaught on the Ottawa system. The imperial trade agreements, embodying just about everything Hull detested in commercial policy in the 1930s, drew his special ire. Some years later he described the system as 'the greatest injury, in a commercial way, that has ever been inflicted on this country since I have been in public life'.[43] Not only had tariff barriers been raised, but, as mentioned above, American exports were being discriminated against both in their most valuable market, the UK, and in Empire countries. Furthermore, in Hull's view Britain's economic empire undermined a peaceful world order. With the object of attacking the imperial preference system, the State Department in the summer of 1934 set up the British Empire Committee. It involved a twofold strategy, first an attack via the periphery through agreements with the Dominion countries, and secondly an assault on the system by direct bilateral negotiations with Britain.

The first part of this move met with early but limited success in the form of a trade agreement with Canada announced on 11 November 1935.[44] This was achieved easily because of the desperate concern of the Canadians to regain some of their lost markets in the United States. The initiative had come from R. B. Bennett, the Conservative prime minister, but Washington held back from concluding a treaty until after the 1935 Canadian elections. American officials had discussed matters with Liberal leader Mackenzie King, and judging that a more favourable deal could be made with him, delayed concluding an agreement until after the Liberal victory. While as a result the USA almost certainly gained more from the agreement than would have been possible from Bennett, the pact none the less highlighted the limitations of the peripheral approach. It is true that the United States secured m.f.n. treatment for its exports and freedom from arbitrary customs regulations, but the Canadians corralled off the British preferential rates from m.f.n. coverage, so the Americans were frustrated in securing larger concessions on many items because the Ottawa agreements limited Canada's freedom of manoeuvre.

In pursuit of the second arm of Washington's assault on the Ottawa system, direct negotiations with London, various informal soundings were made of British officials and ministers in 1934 and 1935, but met with little positive response. The attack through the periphery had temporarily exhausted itself after the Canada–USA pact of 1935, an agreement that had in itself highlighted the trade-restricting power of the Ottawa treaties. Washington had brushed off approaches from Canberra and by 1936 found itself embroiled in a trade war with the Australians.[45] Moreover, Hull's reciprocal Trade Agreements Act was in jeopardy because of opposition from farmers. By 1936 fourteen trade treaties had been signed, practically all with primary producing countries and therefore incorporating agricultural concessions by the United States in exchange for improved access for American industrial exports. If angry farmers were to be appeased, Hull badly needed an agreement with an industrial country.[46] The UK, by a wide margin the most valuable external outlet for US farm produce, fitted the bill.

Hull therefore intensified his pressure on Britain in 1936. He twice interviewed Sir Ronald Lindsay (UK ambassador in Washington) early in the year, drawing out the political implications of restrictive trade policies and causing the ambassador to comment that not only economic recovery but 'world peace itself' would emerge from the trade-agreements programme. As the year wore on, the deteriorating international position made 'world peace itself' look increasingly fragile. Most ominously, German troops re-entered the Rhineland in March 1936, in July Austria declared itself a German state, and by September there were 40,000 Italian 'volunteers' in Spain. Direct approaches were made to Anthony Eden, who was considered sympathetic to the United States, memoranda and speeches were composed and delivered.

For the first eight months of 1936 London stalled, much as it had done in 1934 and 1935. There existed a distrust of America among the British political élite. Stanley Baldwin, during the 1931 Manchurian crisis, had remarked that 'you will get nothing out of the Americans but words. Big words, but only words', a comment on a subsequent occasion echoed by Neville Chamberlain.[47] Baldwin admitted that 'he had got to loathe the Americans so much' he hated meeting them. Chamberlain, whose distrust had been fed by what he saw as Roosevelt's torpedoing of the World Economic Conference in 1933 and by American bad faith at the Washington Naval Talks of 1934, feared being manoeuvred into an exposed position and then abandoned. Sir Robert Vansittart's attitude was similar. Head of the American Department of the Foreign Office in the late 1920s, and permanent secretary from 1930 until his removal in 1938, he was probably much more sympathetic, but even he wrote, in 1934, 'it is still necessary, and I still desire as much as ever that we should get on with this untrustworthy race . . . We shall never get very far; they will always let us down.'[48]

He was certainly outdone in his anti-Americanism by Sir Warren Fisher, whose business as permanent secretary to the Treasury and as Head of the Civil Service none of this should have been, but who was closely involved none the less. Many, including Walter Runciman and his successor as president of the Board of Trade, Oliver Stanley, felt that any serious attack on the Ottawa system must be resisted. Distrust of America was often less a distrust of Washington's intentions than scepticism over its ability to deliver in the face of strong isolationism. After all, it was reasoned, if the dictatorships were to be deterred by gestures of solidarity among the democracies, why not modify or repeal the Neutrality Laws that inhibited America giving assistance in time of war? Instead the Americans insisted on trade liberalization, and trade liberalization that was targeted at the imperial preference system. Uncertain gains from an Anglo-American accord were to be pursued at the expense of the more dependable Empire. As J. M. Troutbeck of the Foreign Office expressed it,

> it was perfectly true that we want to keep on the best possible terms with the United States Government in the present critical situation in the world. But for precisely the same reason it is imperative to keep on good terms with the Dominions. And clearly if it comes to the point, the Dominions must come before the United States.[49]

If the political gains from an accord with the USA looked uncertain at best, the economic case was even weaker. America was an important market for British producers, accounting in 1936 for 6·3 per cent of domestic exports, but it was exceeded by each of South Africa, Australia and India. The prospect of a major gain in British exports was thin: even if maximum tariff reductions of the 50 per cent allowed by US legislation were obtained, many American tariffs would stay at a high level; 'moreover, a considerable part of our export trade is in luxuries, the market for which depends more upon internal prosperity within the U.S.A. than upon anything else.'[50] There was an uncomfortable recognition that any trade arrangement might widen the trade gap rather than narrow it. While London had been able to use balance-of-payments deficits to its advantage in negotiating with trading partners in northern Europe, there was little chance of repeating this success with the USA. American dependence on the British market was too small for leverage to be exercised and the realities of political power also dictated otherwise.

What also became abundantly clear was that the Americans were not interested in a token agreement but wanted instead real concessions that would cut into the Ottawa agreements. This might entail double losses for the UK because if the dominions were to lose some of their preferential position in the British market, how were they to be compensated? Unless they were to be persuaded that political advantages were to accrue from an Anglo-American accord that would transcend any material loss, or that the general stimulus that such an agreement would give to the international economy would compensate them for the loss of privileges, the dominions needed the assurance of some tangible concessions. There was no question of the Americans offering any such compensation: the USA had no intention of paying twice for any improvement of their position in the British market. Nor was there much scope for Britain to offer the dominions offsetting advantages: most of their exports were admitted duty-free, and even if London had wanted to raise preferential margins, treaty obligations blocked such a course. This left Britain with little option but to acquiesce in the relaxation of the preferential margin British goods enjoyed in Empire markets, a move which would give the dominions greater freedom to negotiate offsetting deals with third countries.

There were other problems. US demands were likely to threaten customs receipts, a lucrative source of budgetary revenue. This became a more important consideration as discussions progressed, certainly by 1937 when both the shape of American demands had become clearer, with their emphasis on such revenue raisers as tobacco and timber, and when the rearmament programme was starting to impose strains on government finance.

In summary, the economic case for negotiation with the United States appeared very thin. An agreement would probably widen the balance-of-payments deficit, already causing considerable anxiety by 1936, reduce customs revenue and involve paying twice for any concessions in the American market. And these, moreover, looked to be modest. In principle, at least, Britain would only be able to negotiate on items for which she was the main supplier, and tariffs were likely to remain at uncomfortably high levels. All this in a market which absorbed a little over 6 per cent of UK exports, a figure dwarfed by the dominion markets from which Britain was going to accept a retreat.

From the British government's viewpoint, the case against talks was strong. None the less they started, albeit tentatively and on an exploratory basis. Informal talks reached the stage where in September 1936 the British commercial counsellor in Washington, H. O. Chalkley, agreed with American officials to exchange a list of requests by 16 November.[51] This was to be the first part of three official stages required of negotiations by the US Reciprocal Trade Agreements Act of 1934, that of 'conversations'. These were to last a year until, on 18 November 1937, both governments announced that negotiations were contemplated, the second stage in the process.

Two forces were at work to induce British participation. One was undoubtedly the pressure generated by Hull. Not content with haranguing Lindsay and other visitors, he kept up the momentum by sending memoranda and making representations through the US ambassador in London, R. W. Bingham.[52] At first Hull sought a general declaration of support for his policies of international trade liberalization. But when, after some prevarication in London, this was duly made, Hull considered the declaration inadequate both in tone and substance. To the irritation of Whitehall, he insisted it should be followed up by tangible action. On the basis of the surviving documents it is difficult to imagine that much would have happened if the initiative had been left to London. Even then, Hull's remonstrations might have led to nothing more than a rising tide of resentment in Whitehall if the deteriorating European situation had not created a second set of forces that pushed the British government towards *rapprochement* with the United States.

Lindsay had noted in February 1936 that American trade officials were starting to change their advocacy of the American programme: whereas previously they had argued that economic nationalism retarded recovery while US policy promoted it, they now emphasized the contrasting effects of these policies on world peace.[53] This was symptomatic of growing anxiety about the international situation. As tensions rose, especially in Europe, improved relations with the USA became ever more vital for Britain. When British officials first met to consider the Anglo-American conversations, by then under way, the Board of Trade's W. B. Brown opened the discussions by saying that the board 'did not attach any great commercial importance to an agreement with the United States'.[54] He was countered by Frank Ashton Gwatkin, who said that the Foreign Office 'would look upon an agreement with the United States as of major importance from the political point of view'. To lend weight to the Foreign Office case, Lindsay, prompted by Eden, produced an influential review of Anglo-American relations.[55] Asked for suggestions on how the good will of the American government and public opinion might be maintained in the event of a major crisis in Europe, Lindsay's recommendations were clear: America was generally unapproachable on major political issues, the Ambassador asserted, and was particularly so at the present moment. But the economic approach was open, and moreover, if the initiative came from the USA, it was imperative not to reject it. Furthermore,

> in the event of a major crisis in Europe, the factor which will most impede any measures which the American Government might take in favour of Great Britain will be the Middle West, and it is just the Middle West, the centre of the agricultural community, which will be directly and favourably affected by the conclusion of a commercial treaty with the United Kingdom, improving or facilitating the export of agricultural produce from the United States to Great Britain. It might even be a deciding factor in the attitude which America would take. I respectfully, but forcibly submit to you, Sir, that an American hand is being proffered to us, and it is full of gifts . . . I earnestly hope that it will be grasped.

Essentially the same message had been given to Eden by one of Roosevelt's emissaries, Norman Davis, who had stated that while a political settlement was unlikely, the United States might be persuaded to involve itself in Europe through an economic agreement: 'One could get away with murder under the name of economic appeasement in the United States today', and the administration was particularly anxious for a trade agreement with Britain.[56]

There is no need here to detail the prolonged negotiations that occurred. Several points, however, do need emphasizing. One concerns the role of Canada, which virtually throughout the proceedings attempted to smooth the way for an Anglo-American accord. Curiously, the greatest single gain that the UK made from the negotiations came as a by-product of the Canada–USA pact of 1935. This had featured a 50 per cent reduction in the duty on imports of whisky into the USA, a reduction that also applied to British exports by virtue of m.f.n. standing. The repeal of prohibition together with the duty reduction of 1935, a unilateral gesture by the United States that was anticipated to benefit sales of Scotch, did more for British exports to the USA in the 1930s than the collective and arduous labours of British negotiators over the four years from 1934 to the conclusion of the pact in November 1938. Since by 1938 the Canadians had virtually exhausted their stocks of matured whisky and were thought to be less interested in maintaining the lower rate of duty, the UK team were keen to impress on Ottawa the value of keeping the duty low. Canadian good will was essential to proceedings. American demands were frustrated by the web of obligations that Britain had incurred in the previous six years of treaty making. That as much progress as in fact was made was due in large part to the willingness of the Canadians to give up or accept reduced privileges in the British market, notably for wheat, timber and apples. True, over and above their role as honest brokers, the Canadians hoped to see in response easier access for their exports south of the border, but it would have been virtually impossible to have secured an Anglo-American accord without Canadian compliance. For its part, the UK was prepared to see some whittling away of preferences for its exports in the dominion markets. At least Britain was willing to do so in principle, but less happy when it came to specific instances, when Britain could be found hanging on tenaciously: anthracite in the Canadian market was a case in point.

The second point is that, judged on commercial criteria alone, Britain almost certainly would not have signed the treaty. More than once the Cabinet was on the verge of terminating the negotiations. In Cabinet committee, Oliver Stanley, president of the Board of Trade, argued that since 'we can neither wait for ever or pay a price out of all proportion to the benefits we are to receive', the time had come, political considerations notwithstanding, to 'make our position quite plain and insist on a definite decision by the United States Government to conclude the Agreement or to break off negotiations'. Although the committee decided to recommend accepting some US requests, it brushed aside Foreign Office views in refusing others and left it to the Cabinet to decide whether the negotiations should be broken off if the offer proved unacceptable to the Americans.[57] In Cabinet there was pressure for a strong stand, notably by Stanley but also by the chancellor, and ex-foreign secretary, John Simon, who observed that it 'was impossible to say that the treaty, as it now stood, was one which on balance would be approved by the commercial community'.[58] Yet even at this stage it was Chamberlain who stood out for further Cabinet consultation if necessary. In the event, Hull grudgingly recommended the agreement to Roosevelt, subject to a few drafting modifications, particularly over the complex timber clauses. As he informed Joseph Kennedy, the new ambassador in London, 'the present offers represent the ultimate limit to which the British are prepared to go without reopening our proposed concessions to the United Kingdom.'[59]

The final point is that the negotiations were fractious and their eventual outcome distinctly illiberal. That they proved so rancourous is not difficult to explain. One problem was the difference in negotiating tactics. The British procedure was to maximize the concessions from an unchanging list of requests. By contrast, the American practice, if blocked on one request, was to substitute another entirely fresh demand. Personality may well have contributed to the difficulties.[60] The Canada–USA discussions had been smooth, perhaps in part because of closer personal rapport, possibly helped by shared North American interests: Jack Hickerson, heading the US team, would sometimes slip off with his Canadian counterpart Norman Robertson to watch a game of baseball when the Washington Senators were playing at their home Field. As Robertson wrote, striking according to his biographer an uncharacteristic note, 'our direct negotiations with the Americans are the least of our worries right now. We can cope with them but not with God's Englishmen and the inescapable moral ascendancy over us lesser breeds.'[61] The economic backdrop to the negotiations was also distinctly unhelpful. The very sharp recession of 1937–8 was particularly severe in the USA, which anyway by most indicators had not recovered from the traumas of the earlier depression. Sterling's depreciation from the middle of 1938 increased American doubts about the value of the concessions they were getting. But the UK side felt they were benefiting little from the negotiations: American tariff barriers, even when reduced by the maximum 50 per cent, generally remained high, and liberalization on this scale was likely to do nothing to rectify the enormous American trade surplus with Britain.

For their part, the Americans found the UK unyielding, and certainly British domestic protection remained virtually unbreached. Carl Kreider's study, published in 1943, made this clear.[62] Agricultural concessions had spearheaded American demands, and while some inroads into the Ottawa system had been made, little was achieved at the expense of British farmers. Even though duties on apples and pears were reduced, they were still equivalent to roughly 15 per cent, and there was the added buffer of transatlantic freight rates. The earnings of wheat growers were buoyed up by subsidies, and bacon producers were safeguarded by a Treasury guarantee under the Bacon Industry Act. The same legislation could have been extended if the removal of the duty on lard threatened the income of the pig farmers. Whitehall had refused to lower tariffs on malting barley. By the late 1930s a system of exchequer-financed subsidies had evolved to protect agriculture, and the modest concessions made to the Americans were mainly at the expense of the Treasury rather than the British farmer.

The major American exports of machine tools, of iron and steel and of cars gained practically nothing. No guarantees were secured for machine-tool exports, many of which were subject to Board of Trade discretionary licences for tariff-free import. Although the existing tariff on cars of 25 horsepower and more was conventionalized, this was more than negated by a sharp rise in road-tax licence fees in the Finance Act of 1939 that particularly penalized larger-engined vehicles.[63] Although concessions were made on less important items, they were generally on products not manufactured on any scale in the UK, and, moreover, frequently involved tariff reclassification so as to restrict the advantage to US exporters and to prevent other countries benefiting. As Britain geared itself for war the American exports that gained most in 1939 were aircraft, machine tools and aluminium.

IV

On the face of things, the United States had been one agent in the pursuit of more liberal international economic policies, and the Anglo-American accord has been interpreted in these terms. United States influence had been discernible in the pledge forming part of the Tripartite Monetary Agreement of September 1936 to seek the relaxation and eventual abolition of quotas and exchange controls. British protection stood virtually intact at the end of 1938. The growing menace of Germany had led to consideration of more liberal measures. It had intensified Hull's campaign as well as making British policy makers more than usually solicitous of American good will. It had also stimulated some debate in Whitehall about the economic appeasement of Germany. But the eventual outcome of these responses was decidedly illiberal: the relaxation of the trade agreements had been grudging and modest, as represented in the Anglo-American treaty, while German economic appeasement had finally manifested itself in the form of abortive cartel discussions between industrialists.

By the end of the 1930s the Canadians found themselves more dependent on their two principal trading partners than before the slump, a consequence of the closure of world markets. The pattern of trade and of settlements had changed sharply during the decade. But another change had been the unprecedented amount of economic diplomacy between the three partners: this was a harbinger of the intense negotiations that were to be such a feature of the war and the post-war reconstruction years. On the other hand, British policy at the end of the decade remained firmly wedded to protection and to the retention of as many of the privileges won in earlier negotiations as possible. When the British delegation were drawn reluctantly across the Atlantic to the negotiating rooms of Washington, political necessity impelled their journey. United States policy was shifting, however, although the main emphasis of the bargaining was on the removal of barriers to US exports rather than any grand initiative in the liberalizing of international trade. Significantly, the USA gained leverage because with the deterioration of the international situation, Britain needed American friendship and good will. The treaty probably played a part in improving relations between the three countries on the eve of the European war, and it was also a portent of the way in which the Americans were to use their growing power in an attempt to re-create a more liberal and open world economic regime in the quarter-century after the war, by when their hegemony had been truly established.

Notes

[1] Stephen D. Krasner, 'State Power and the Structure of International Trade', *World Politics*, xxviii (1976); B. M. Rowland (ed.), *Balance of Power or Hegemony: The Interwar Monetary System* (New York, 1976); Robert Gilpin, *The Political Economy of International Relations* (Princeton, 1987) and Robert W. Cox, *Production, Power and World Order: Social Forces in the Making of History* (New York, 1987).

[2] Krasner, 'State Power'.

[3] Tim Rooth, 'The Political Economy of Protectionism in Britain, 1919–32', *Journal of European Economic History*, 21 (1992), 47–97.

[4] From $948 million in 1929 to $211 million in 1933.

[5] Patricia Clavin, 'The World Economic Conference 1933: The Failure of British Internationalism', *Journal of European Economic History*, 20 (1991), 489–527; B. Eichengreen, *Golden Fetters: The Gold Standard and the Great Depression, 1919–1939* (New York, 1992); Tim Rooth, *British Protectionism and the International Economy: Overseas Commercial Policy in the 1930s* (Cambridge, 1993). The rest of this chapter draws heavily on material from this last source. Also see I. M. Drummond, *The Floating Pound and the Sterling Area, 1931–1939* (Cambridge, 1981) and Kenneth Moure, *Managing the Franc Poincaré: Economic Understanding and Political Constraint in French Monetary Policy, 1928–1936* (Cambridge, 1991), ch.3.

[6] These included France, Belgium, Holland, Switzerland, Italy and Poland.

[7] Drummond, *Floating Pound*, pp.120–7.

[8] See, for example, G. Cassel, *The Crisis in the World's Monetary System*, 2nd edn (Oxford, 1932).

[9] T 172/1814, Leith-Ross, Prospects of the Economic Conference, 20 December 1932.

[10] FO 371/16604, Sir Richard Hopkins and Sir Frederick Phillips to prime minister, 19 April 1933.

[11] F. Freidel, *Franklin D. Roosevelt: Launching the New Deal* (Boston, 1973), esp. ch.19. The following three paragraphs draw heavily on this source, together with C. P. Kindleberger, *The World in Depression, 1929–1939* (1973); Herbert Feis, *1933: Characters in Crisis* (Boston, 1966), p.143; A. M. Schlesinger Jnr, *The Age of Roosevelt. 2: The Coming of the New Deal* (London, 1960).

[12] CAB 29/142, Joint statement by the prime minister and President Roosevelt, 26 April 1933.

[13] Feis, *1933*, p.152.

[14] Freidel, *Roosevelt*, p.327.

[15] Feis, *1933*, p.115.

[16] Kindleberger, *World in Depression*, p.201.

[17] Freidel, *Roosevelt*, p.384.

[18] CAB 29/142, Board of Trade memorandum, 19 October 1932 and ibid, ME(B) 5, Policy of the United Kingdom on Main Questions Raised on Agenda: Trade Restrictions and Tariff Policy, 18 May 1933.

[19] CAB 29/142, Leith-Ross, Discussions at Washington on the Programme of the World Conference, 12 May 1933.

[20] CAB 29/142, ME(B) 5.

[21] R. M. Kottman, *Reciprocity and the North Atlantic Triangle, 1932–1938* (Ithaca, 1968), pp.54–68.

[22] CAB 29/142 Pt.2, Meeting between PM and Hull, 19 June 1933.

[23] Feis, *1933*, p.174.

[24] Ibid., pp.188–9.

[25] CAB 29/142 Pt.2, Meeting between UK and US delegations, 27 June 1933.

[26] Drummond, *Floating Pound*, p.164.

[27] Quoted in Schlesinger, *The Age of Roosevelt*, p.207.

[28] CAB 29/142 Pt.1, Minutes of 19th meeting, 3 July 1933.

[29] *Economist*, 8 July 1933, cited by Feis, *1933*, p.252.

[30] For example, *Times*, 13, 15, 29 and 30 May 1933, and meeting between PM and Hull, 19 June 1933, CAB 29/142 Pt.2.

[31] L. C. Gardner, *Economic Aspects of New Deal Diplomacy* (Madison, 1964), p.28.

[32] Feis, *1933*, p.182 and Gardner, *Economic Aspects*, p.30.

[33] Kindleberger, *World in Depression*, p.231.

[34] CAB 29/142 Pt.1, Meeting of Bureau, 6 July 1933.

[35] For example, memorandum by Phillips on General Smuts's memorandum, 17 July 1933, and twenty-fifth meeting, 13 July 1933, CAB 29/142.

[36] Clavin, 'The World Economic Conference', 495.

[37] C. Hull, *The Memoirs of Cordell Hull* (London, 1948), I, p.81.

[38] B. M. Rowland, *Commercial Conflict and Foreign Policy* (New York, 1987), p.178.

[39] Quoted in Gardner, *Economic Aspects*, p.26.

[40] F. V. Meyer, *International Trade Policy* (London, 1978).

[41] David A. Lake, *Power, Protection and Free Trade: International Sources of U.S. Commercial Strategy, 1887–1939* (Ithaca and London, 1988), who emphasizes that the USA was firmly committed to protectionism, and that the 1934 Act was intended as a complement to protection, enabling the USA to reopen foreign markets for its exports. See pp.7, 184 and 207.

[42] Gardner, *Economic Aspects*, p.39.

[43] US Congress Hearings, 1940, cited Rowland, *Commercial Conflict*, p.180.

[44] This is discussed by Marc Boucher, 'The Politics of Economic Depression: Canadian–American Relations in the mid 1930s', paper presented

to the Association of Canadian Studies meeting, Montreal, 1985; Kott-man, *Reciprocity*; Ian M. Drummond and Norman Hillmer, *Negotiating Freer Trade: The United Kingdom, the United States, Canada and the Trade Agreements of 1938* (Waterloo, Ont., 1989), and for some of the background, Tim Rooth, 'Britain and Canada between Two Wars: The Economic Dimension', C. C. Eldridge (ed.), *From Rebellion to Patriation: Canada and Britain in the Nineteenth and Twentieth Centuries* (Lampeter, 1989).

45 M. Ruth Megaw, 'Australia and the Anglo-American Trade Agreement 1938', *Journal of Imperial and Commonwealth History*, 3 (1974–5), 191–211.
46 George Schatz, 'The Anglo-American Trade Agreement and Cordell Hull's Search for Peace, 1936–38', *Journal of American History*, 57 (1970), 90.
47 C. A. MacDonald, *The United States, Britain and Appeasement 1936–1939* (London, 1981), p.20.
48 Norman Rose, *Vansittart: Study of a Diplomat* (London, 1978), p.127.
49 Troutbeck, FO 371/19834, 23 November 1936, cited Rowland, *Commercial Conflict*, p.213.
50 BT 11/918, Draft instructions to UK delegates, n.d. but January 1938.
51 Drummer and Hillmer, *Negotiating Freer Trade*, p.42.
52 Ibid., pp.41–4, and Rowland, *Commercial Conflict*, pp.199–209.
53 BT 11/591, Lindsay to Eden, 5 February 1936.
54 BT 11/796, USA minutes (UK) 1/36 UK–USA Commercial Negotiations, 3 December 1936.
55 CAB 27/620, TAC (36)37, Memorandum by Eden, 7 March 1937, enclosing dispatch by Lindsay, 22 March 1937.
56 Quoted by Drummond and Hillmer, *Negotiating Freer Trade*, p.34.
57 CAB 27/619, TAC (36) seventeenth meeting, 13 October 1938.
58 CAB 23/96, CAB 49 (38), 19 October 1938.
59 Drummond and Hillmer, *Negotiating Freer Trade*, p.141.
60 See Ritchie Ovendale, *'Appeasement' and the English Speaking World: Britain, the United States, the Dominions, and the Policy of 'Appeasement', 1937–1939*, pp.199–200, for some discussion of the 'aloof and arrogant atmosphere of the British embassy in Washington'.
61 Robertson to Lester Pearson, July(?) 1938, quoted by J. L. Granatstein, *A Man of Influence: Norman Robertson and Canadian Statecraft, 1928–1968* (Ottawa, 1981).
62 C. Kreider, *Anglo-American Trade Agreement: A Study of British and American Commercial Policies, 1934–1939* (Princeton, 1943), chs.6 and 7.
63 Ibid., p.133.

9

Canada, Britain, the United States and the Policy of 'Appeasement'

RITCHIE OVENDALE

During the crisis that followed Mussolini's occupation of Abyssinia in 1935, William Lyon Mackenzie King and the Liberal Party returned to power in Canada. They remained for twenty-two years. Canadian foreign affairs were dominated by a man 'outwardly dull', but by one whose 'instincts were fixed on a world beyond the grave'. As one of his early biographers has observed:

> Haunted by death, hagridden by a sense of original sin, engulfed in the black tides of time, always hurrying to the end of a brief journey, he erected his public career to vindicate himself to himself, to his rebel grandfather, to his mother, to mankind, and to God, before he moved on.[1]

In the end it is difficult to estimate the influence of spiritualism on Mackenzie King's decisions. Mackenzie King was assisted by an effective Department of External Affairs. Initially established in June 1909 but joined by statute to the office of the prime minister in 1912, it was not until 1946 that a secretary of state for foreign affairs was appointed.[2] Dr O. D. Skelton was the permanent civil servant who, as under-secretary of state for external affairs from 1925 to 1941, led this department. He was chosen by Mackenzie King after the prime minister had heard him, as dean of the Faculty of Arts at Queen's University, Kingston, bitterly attack the concept of imperial foreign policy. Against the background of the Chanak crisis of 1922, during which the British government appealed for dominion support as the Young Turks defeated the Greek army and advanced towards the Dardanelles and Constantinople and a British contingent in the neutral zone, Mackenzie King invited Skelton to prepare the Canadian case for the 1923 Imperial Conference.

Both men objected to an imperial connection that could lead Canada into war in far-away countries. At the 1923 conference the Canadian prime minister attacked the idea of a single body deciding the foreign policy of the Empire. Mackenzie King's contention that only the Parliament of a dominion could decide whether a country was at peace or war, was accepted by the British government with the passing of the Statute of Westminster in 1931. Skelton developed the Canadian Department of External Affairs along the lines of the British Foreign Office. He recruited 'well-educated generalists' and between 1922 and 1944 30·5 per cent of recruits to the department had doctorates. But as the prime minister remained secretary of state for external affairs it was difficult for Skelton to develop an independent department. By 1936 Canada was represented in Washington, Paris and Tokyo, but usually it was telegrams from the Dominions Office in London which provided the full information and helped to form Canadian policy.[3] Canada was represented in London by its high commissioner, Vincent Massey, between 1935 and 1946. Mackenzie King did not trust Massey and regarded him as both a snob and dangerously ambitious. As high commissioner, Massey usually did not have the authority to speak for his government but was seen as a means through which information could be transferred. Massey thought that Mackenzie King was antagonistic towards Britain.[4]

As the international situation deteriorated during the 1930s, firstly with Mussolini's invasion of Abyssinia in 1935, and then with Hitler's reoccupation of the Rhineland in 1936, Canada was involved both through its membership of the League of Nations and the meetings of the high commissioners in London. Indeed during the last months of the Conservative administration under R. B. Bennett Canada appeared to take the lead in showing its willingness to help to secure a peaceful settlement and on the matter of advocating sanctions against Italy. But on 5 December the high commissioners in London learnt from Vincent Massey, who was speaking for the newly elected Liberal administration under W. L. Mackenzie King, that Canada would loyally observe any sanctions, but that there should be no repetition of an earlier incident which had given the impression that Canada was taking the lead in this matter.[5] Mackenzie King was personally elated by Neville Chamberlain's reference on 10 June 1936 to the maintenance of sanctions against Italy as being 'midsummer madness', and in a speech to the Canadian Parliament on 18

June 1936 the prime minister reflected Canadian opinion when he said that the Canadian delegation to the League Assembly would be instructed to support the discontinuance of sanctions.[6] When Hitler occupied the Rhineland, Massey was at a weekend party at Blickling, Lord Lothian's country home, where the guests included Tom Jones, Arnold Toynbee and Sir Thomas and Lady Inskip, and the general view was that it was important not to get too excited about Hitler's technical breach of treaties. In the interests of national unity Mackenzie King felt that Canada should not respond publicly to Hitler's move. With the exception of the *Winnipeg Free Press* under J. W. Dafoe, the Canadian newspapers all urged acceptance of the German reoccupation. On 17 March 1936 Ottawa did inform London that if Britain joined France in a venture to force German troops out of the Rhineland it could not expect Canada to participate, even if such an operation were authorized by the League of Nations.[7]

A section of the Canadian public tended to be anti-British and against any commitment by the government to foreign wars. The French Canadians had made their stand on this point clear during the 1914–18 war, and the following two decades had not mollified their rancour. Loring C. Christie of the Canadian Department of External Affairs wrote to Lord Lothian saying that a Canadian speaking to an Englishman could only play the role of a 'well-wisher'.[8] Public concern in Canada was increasing: there was a series of national radio talks and articles in *Macleans Magazine* on defence; the fourth study conference of the Canadian Institute of International Affairs in May 1937 took as its theme 'Canada's Defence Policy' and 'Canada and the Americans'.[9]

The parliamentary debates in 1937 revealed the Canadian government's predicament. Cabinet criticism, especially from the Middle Westerners concerned with social reform, was so severe that defence estimates were cut by 30 per cent. At the end of January the House of Commons debated a motion by the Co-operative Commonwealth Federation (the CCF), a socialist party, that Canada should be neutral in the event of war regardless of who the belligerents might be. Canada should ignore any scheme for imperial defence. This debate reflected the various attitudes in Canada. The leader of the CCF, J. S. Woodsworth, gave the isolationist viewpoint. Increased defence expenditure only foreshadowed the possibility of Canada being drawn into another European war. Over 50 per cent of the people in the Middle West were not of Anglo-Saxon origin. British entanglements were hardly their concern. Canada was in no immediate danger. The United States would counter any aggression towards Canada, if only for its own sake. In replying, Mackenzie King gave his government's stand: it would be for the Canadian Parliament to say, in any situation, whether or not Canada should remain neutral. He doubted whether any Canadian government would send troops beyond the border without parliamentary sanction. Mackenzie King also offered an analysis of the divisions in Canadian public opinion. Firstly, there were those whom he labelled the imperialist school. They considered the British Empire indivisible, and from this followed the need for a common defence and foreign policy. Secondly, some favoured the isolation of Canada. Mackenzie King felt that the vast majority fell into a third division between those two extremes, and favoured the policy that he supported. There was much talk of a North American 'mentality', and a feeling that Canadians should keep their own blood for their own country. Speakers from Quebec spoke of secession from the Commonwealth in the event of Canadian imperial or European commitments. The defence estimates had a difficult passage: at the committee stage thirteen liberals, including twelve French Canadians, voted against them. There were murmurings in the rural constituencies, and the ticklish conscription issue was brandished in the Quebec press. In the end only twenty-two members out of 245 voted against the defence estimates, but this could be attributed to party discipline, and was hardly an indication of opinion in Parliament or the country.[10]

Following the defence debate Mackenzie King accepted the invitation of President Franklin D. Roosevelt to visit Washington to discuss the European situation. The relationship of the North American leaders had been formed in October 1935 when Mackenzie King and Skelton had visited Washington, and had been renewed when the president paid a state visit to Canada in 1936. On 5 March 1937, before seeing Roosevelt, Mackenzie King spoke to the secretary of state, Cordell Hull, who was anxious to use Mackenzie King as a means of getting his views on the international situation, and particularly his concept of wider international trade including a trade agreement between Britain and the United States, across to the British government. Mackenzie King proposed to Roosevelt that he, as American president, take the lead in convening, through the League of Nations, a world conference on economic and social problems.[11]

Throughout 1936 Hull had publicly hoped for international

co-operation through trade agreements. When Walter Runciman, the president of the Board of Trade, visited Washington in January 1937 he was told that if Britain proclaimed a programme of liberal economic relations, nearly forty nations would follow and international order might be restored.[12] The State Department protested to the Foreign Office on 17 January 1937 that the trade talks in progress between Britain and Canada impeded the programme for economic disarmament, and suggested co-operation between Britain and the United States to eliminate 'these restrictions which today are stifling legitimate international trade'.[13] Runciman was told that an Anglo-American trade agreement would improve trade relations and symbolize the community of basic views and politics between the two countries. But a reduction on imperial preference rates was indispensable to successful negotiations.[14]

Following his discussions with the American leaders, Mackenzie King called on the British ambassador in Washington, Sir Ronald Lindsay, and launched into 'a diatribe . . . against sanctions . . . He said that Canada was resolved to maintain neutrality in any war at any price, and that on no account would she be dragged into any hostilities. His attitude corresponded very closely to that generally adopted in America.' In the Foreign Office Sir Robert Vansittart minuted: 'Mackenzie King seems to lose rather than to gain intelligence as he gets older. This is drivel, and dangerous drivel. I hope he will be sternly discouraged when he comes here from "thinking" on these lines.'[15]

At the Imperial Conference in London on 21 May Mackenzie King did act as a spokesman for the United States. He responded to a grim picture of the European situation drawn by Anthony Eden, in which the foreign secretary explained that *Mein Kampf* and the speeches and writings of the German leaders suggested that the main objective of Germany was the extension of German dominion to all territories where there were German populations or empty spaces to colonize. The Germans were anxious to reach an agreement with Britain. British neutrality and detachment from France would leave Germany free to pursue an expansionist policy. Eden felt that such a settlement would be immoral. German moves against Austria and Czechoslovakia were anticipated. But the more immediate danger of hostilities came from Italy rather than Germany. In the first meeting which Neville Chamberlain chaired as prime minister, Mackenzie King led the Commonwealth reply. The Canadian prime minister explained that Canada's outlook was largely shaped by its geographical position and its special relationship with the United States. The United States, in its own interests, would intervene if Canada were attacked. Roosevelt had made this explicit in private discussions. Mackenzie King explained that the only safe calculation was that if war broke out in Europe or Asia, the United States Neutrality Acts would be put into effect. He mentioned possible United States membership of the League if sanctions articles were removed. Mackenzie King drew a distinction between Congress and the administration, and impressed that Roosevelt and Hull were convinced of the value of a policy of economic appeasement. After this Mackenzie King explained Canada's position in time of war:

> There are many forces which would make for Canadian participation in a conflict in which Britain's interests were seriously at stake. There would be a strong pull of kinship, the pride in common traditions, the desire to save democratic institutions, the admiration for the stability, the fairness, the independence that characterise English public life, the feeling that a world in which Britain was weak would be a more chaotic and more dangerous world to live in. The influence of trade interests, the campaign by a part of the press, the legal anomalies of abstention, the appeal of war to adventurous spirits, would make in the same direction.
>
> On the other hand opposition to participation in war, any war, is growing. It is not believed that Canada itself is in any serious danger. It is felt that the burdens left by our participation in the last war are largely responsible for the present financial difficulties. There is wide impatience, doubtless often based upon inadequate information, with the inability of Continental Europe to settle its own disputes. The isolationist swing in the United States, its renunciation of war profits and neutral rights to keep out of war, have made a strong impression on Canadian opinion. In some sections of the country opinion is practically unanimous against any participation in either a League or a Commonwealth war. There is outspoken rejection of the theory that whenever and wherever conflict arises in Europe, Canada can be expected to send armed forces overseas to help solve the quarrels of continental countries about which Canadians know little, and which they feel, know and care less about Canada's difficulties, and particularly so if a powerful country like the United States assumes no similar obligation. No policy in Canada is more generally accepted than that commitments of any kind, involving possible participation in war, must have prior and specific approval by parliament.

Mackenzie King explained that any attempt to reach a decision on these matters in advance would precipitate a controversy that might destroy Canadian unity. He ended:

> I shall not attempt to forecast what the decision would be in the event of other parts of the Commonwealth actually being at war. Much would depend on the circumstances of the hour, both abroad and at home – upon the measure of conviction as to the unavoidability of the struggle and the seriousness of the outlook, and upon the measure of unity that had been attained in Canada. That is not the least of the reasons why we consider peace so vital, for the preservation of peace is as vital for the unity of the Commonwealth as for the unity of Canada.[16]

When the Australian prime minister, J. A. Lyons, suggested to the Imperial Conference that it should at once issue a statement of Commonwealth support for the British government's efforts to 'secure world appeasement and peace', it was Mackenzie King who was worried that such a resolution could become the subject for debate in dominion Parliaments and impair any united front. Chamberlain drafted something suitable for publication, but even then Skelton minuted: 'Don't like this – it covers all foreign policy really.'[17] Indeed the secretary of state for India, Lord Zetland, observed:

> Most of the meetings are now taken up with reservations by Mr. Mackenzie King in connection with any statement of the Conference which can possibly suggest that members of the Commonwealth have undertaken to co-operate in any matter whatsoever! You will have yourselves observed indications . . . of fissiparous tendencies on the part of liberal party in Canada, and the Canadian prime minister is suffering from a bad attack of cold feet in consequence.[18]

When Sir Thomas Inskip suggested to the conference that the dominions should consider developing their internal capacity for the production of munitions and war materials, Mackenzie King even objected to a possible scheme of defence centralization. His policy was to keep Canada united. Canadian public opinion would not support larger defence appropriations and was opposed to extraneous commitments.[19]

Perhaps Malcolm MacDonald, the secretary of state for the dominions, was rather optimistic when he reported to the Cabinet on 17 June that the policies of members of the Commonwealth were closer than they had been before the conference:

> Mr. Mackenzie King was about to visit Germany where he would see Herr Hitler. After expressing sympathy with Hitler's constructive work

and telling him of the sympathy which was felt with Germany in England, he intended to add that if Germany should ever turn her mind from constructive to destructive efforts against the United Kingdom all the dominions would come to Britain's aid and that there would be great numbers of Canadians anxious to swim the Atlantic! No doubt we should have our difficulties with the Dominions in the future, but the Conference had been a great stride forward in the direction of unity. He thought much of the success was due to the skilful and attractive Chairmanship of the Prime Minister.[20]

In Canada a slight drift away from isolationism was discernible after the Imperial Conference. Canadian press reaction tended to be relief that no definite action had been taken.[21] The change in Mackenzie King's attitude was the important result. He was more sympathetically inclined to the possibility of Canada going to Britain's aid if Britain were the victim of aggression. His favourable impression of Chamberlain seems to have been responsible for this.[22]

After the Imperial Conference Mackenzie King visited France, Belgium and Germany. Reuter reported him as saying at the Paris exhibition that 'any threat to England would immediately bring Canada to her side'. The Canadian press account, which Mackenzie King said was the correct interpretation, was more qualified: it suggested that if liberty and freedom were imperilled the British Empire would be brought 'together again in preservation of it'.[23] Mackenzie King had spoken to MacDonald on 21 June about his European trip: the Canadian had stressed how strong the isolationist movement was in Canada, and said that he was going to Germany as he was anxious to allay the suspicion that the British were always anxious to meet the French and avoid meeting the Germans.[24] Hitler saw Mackenzie King on 29 June and seemingly mesmerized the Canadian visitor. After reading Mackenzie King's report, O. G. Sargent of the Foreign Office minuted with Vansittart's concurrence: 'It is curious how easily impressed and reassured Hitler's visitors are when Hitler tells them that Germany needs to expand at somebody else's expense but of course does not want war!' According to Mackenzie King's account, Hitler was told:

> If the time ever came where any part of the Empire felt that the freedom which we all enjoyed was being impaired through any act of aggression on the part of a foreign country it would soon be seen that all would join

together to protect the freedom which we were determined should not be imperiled.

He also let Hitler know how impressed the dominion prime ministers had been with Chamberlain: they had expected to find a man with rigid views but had been delighted to discover his liberal and broadminded outlook. When Mackenzie King saw Hermann Goering, he apparently went further in indicating the unity of the Commonwealth in the event of German aggression. Goering enquired whether Canada would aid Britain if that country tried to prevent a union of Austria and Germany. The general was told that Canadian action would be determined by 'fair play and justice'.[25]

When the Canadian prime minister finally sailed for home he carried with him a lasting impression of the two men who he thought could preserve the peace of Europe: Chamberlain and Hitler. Writing to Chamberlain on 6 July, Mackenzie King expressed his confidence:

> I continue to have you and your great problems much in my thoughts. It will require immense patience and forbearance to save some appalling situations but I am returning to Canada with the feeling that you and your colleagues are wholly aware of the fact, and will be equal to the situation.

Chamberlain replied reassuringly: 'You may in any event be assured that we shall continue with patience and persistence, our present endeavour to bring peace and order into a disturbed Europe.' After Mackenzie King landed in Canada he saw the British high commissioner, Sir Francis Floud. Floud reported that Mackenzie King had been 'completely hypnotised' by his reception in Germany, and he doubted even whether Hitler had been warned along the lines suggested by the Canadian prime minister.[26]

Following the Imperial Conference the Canadian view of the European situation continued to be influenced by the assessments made by the British Foreign Office. Loring C. Christie wrote to his superior in external affairs, O. D. Skelton, after reading the Foreign Office prints on Prague, that the apprehensions he had formed during a visit to Germany and Czechoslovakia in 1924 had been confirmed:

> [Eduard] Benes [president of Czechoslovakia] is a clever intriguer and blackmailer, incessantly at it and missing few tricks. The net result seems to be that his country is not on really good terms with a single one of her

five neighbours and is on definitely bad terms with three of them . . . A big question mark is how far, through his democratic window dressing, through his being such a white haired boy at Geneva and his cleverness at stacking the cards there, his architecture of the Soviet alliance network with its interlocking across the channel through France, has succeeded in outwangling and compromising the U.K.[27]

Following the march of Nazi troops into Austria on 12 March 1938, Chamberlain told the Cabinet that he felt that the *Anschluss* 'had to come', and the question to be considered was how to prevent 'an occurrence of similar events in Czecho-Slovakia'.[28] At the meeting of the Cabinet committee on foreign policy on 18 March it emerged that there were two principal objections to a guarantee to Czechoslovakia: it might mean the end of the Commonwealth; and, in any case, it would be logistically impossible to save Czechoslovakia. MacDonald warned the Cabinet that Britain could find itself engaged in a European war to prevent Germans living in the Sudeten districts of Czechoslovakia from being united with Germany, and that on this issue the British Commonwealth might well break in pieces:

> Australia and New Zealand would almost certainly follow our lead. Eire would no doubt take the same line partly because she would feel that on an issue of this kind she could not take a line different from our own, but South Africa and Canada would see no reason whatever why they should join in a war to prevent certain Germans from rejoining their fatherland.[29]

This dominion attitude was an important factor in the British decision outlined by Chamberlain in a speech to the House of Commons on 24 March 1938 that there could be no automatic promise to assist France if it were called upon to help Czechoslovakia under the terms of the Franco-Czech treaty of 1925, as Britain had no vital interests in that area.[30]

During the Czech crisis in May, Canada was not represented at the high commissioners' meetings in London.[31] Mackenzie King emphasized that his government had been informed of, but not consulted on, Chamberlain's statement of 24 March. The Conservatives demanded a definite statement of Canadian foreign policy, while a CCF member clamoured for the assurance that Canada would never participate in a foreign war without the consent of the people and not just the consent of Parliament.[32] But Canadian opinion was such that Lord Tweedsmuir, the governor-general of Canada, wrote to Chamberlain:

I am delighted to see that you have British opinion solidly behind you. You certainly have Canada's. At first the Press and people were inclined to be critical, but now the feeling on your side is unanimous + cordial. You have no warmer admirer than my Prime Minister.[33]

When on 24 May Mackenzie King gave a carefully reasoned but cautious statement on foreign policy, there was nothing that could be detected as a significant departure from the Canadian policy pursued over the previous few years. Canada was bound by no commitments, either to remain neutral or to engage in war. It would be for the Canadian Parliament to decide on the merits of the situation.[34] From March to September all major Canadian political groups were opposed to any Canadian commitment to Europe. Canadian orientation was more towards the geographical situation of the country as part of the North American continent than as a member of the Commonwealth. It anything, this view was reinforced when Roosevelt made in public those assurances he had given earlier to Mackenzie King: on 18 August 1938, speaking at Kingston, Canada, the American president said:

> The Dominion of Canada is part of the sisterhood of the British Empire. I give to you assurance that the people of the United States will not stand idly by if domination of Canadian soil is threatened by any other empire.[35]

The need to placate the French element was a significant factor. It does not follow that Canada was pledged to a policy of neutrality: it was rather one of no commitment.

Following the *Anschluss* the British Cabinet considered defence matters, and the question of supplies from Canada was raised. A mission went to both the United States and Canada to investigate the war potential in those countries, and in June the Cabinet considered the creation of a war potential for aircraft production in Canada. There were fears that Mackenzie King, already antagonistic towards training establishments in Canada, might turn against the proposal. Chamberlain, in presenting the case to the Cabinet, used arguments put by Vincent Massey, the Canadian high commissioner in London, that the scheme would get the Canadian government to take a more active interest in other proposals for co-operation in imperial defence, such as the arrangements for the recruiting and training of pilots and other Canadian air personnel. The prime minister said:

If Canada could become interested in the provision of aircraft to this country the aloofness of that Dominion from Imperial defence and its dissociation from the problems of the United Kingdom might be reduced. It was not inconceivable that the whole attitude of Canada towards the defence of the Empire might be changed.

The Cabinet agreed to examine what sort of aircraft should be manufactured in Canada.[36]

As the situation in Czechoslovakia deteriorated a meeting of ministers on 30 August learnt again that if Britain were to threaten to go to war, she should consult the dominions in advance as that threat would in practice commit not only Britain but at least some of the dominions. MacDonald argued that consultation with the dominions would mean that Britain would not be in a position to utter the threat. If Britain did so, it would 'put a great strain on the loyalty of the Dominions and might break up the Commonwealth'.[37] When the Cabinet met on 12 September to discuss the Czechoslovakian crisis it was pointed out that the attitude of the dominions had been as forecast at the meeting of ministers on 30 August. The foreign secretary, Lord Halifax, had been warned by Vincent Massey, the Canadian high commissioner, that the majority of Canadians would be against any forward action, in the hope that Britain would not be involved in war.[38] From 12 September to 1 October care was taken to keep the dominions informed of British policy. MacDonald even said that the dominions had more information at their disposal than members of the Cabinet. One hundred and forty telegrams were sent to dominion governments and fourteen meetings were held with dominion representatives. The high commissioner for Canada was given special authority by his government to attend the meetings of dominion high commissioners held in London.[39] On 13 September, against the background of reports of German troop movements and fighting in Czechoslovakia, Chamberlain, in consultation with a group of ministers, decided to put Plan Z into operation: during the last days of August the prime minister had thought of an offer to go to Germany to see Hitler. Before flying to Berchtesgaden Chamberlain saw a report from the chiefs of staff which reaffirmed their view that no pressure that Britain or France could bring to bear could prevent Germany defeating Czechoslovakia. The war would be an unlimited war with Britain receiving between 500–600 tons of bombs a day for two months while able only to deliver 100 tons, and together with France 200 tons.[40]

The Canadian government, led by an enthusiastic Mackenzie King, approved of Chamberlain's plan. On 13 September the Canadian Cabinet refused to indicate an attitude. That day Massey, for the first time since his posting in 1935, telephoned Ottawa, to say how seriously the British government regarded the Sudeten disturbances. Mackenzie King not only sent a personal message to Chamberlain expressing his 'admiration for the vision and courage shown in your decision to have a personal interview with Hitler' and his Cabinet's 'deep satisfaction' with this move, but also took the unprecedented step of publicizing his views. This was, however, support for the appeasement of Europe. On 8 September Loring Christie, second only to Skelton in the Canadian Department of External Affairs, had written a memorandum suggesting only a 'qualified' Canadian participation in a war over the Sudetenland. The Canadian government should 'give no lead to take the people into Europe'.[41] Robert Barrington-Ward of *The Times*, lunching with Massey on 16 September, found the high commissioner opposed to a world war fought to keep dissident minorities under Czech rule. The next day Massey spoke of the 'timid and isolationist Canadian Government' and the 'inert Mackenzie King'.[42] The acting high commissioner in Canada, however, did report on 16 September that there were no signs that the Canadian government was trying to shelter behind Roosevelt's Kingston declaration, and to press for a policy of neutrality and isolation from European affairs in collaboration with the United States.[43]

Mackenzie King also contacted the German foreign minister, Joachim von Ribbentrop, in the hope that he would let Hitler know that the Canadian prime minister believed that the efforts of the Führer would 'serve to preserve and further the peace of the world'. The British ambassador, Nevile Henderson, delivered the message, and reported to Mackenzie King that it had been 'most useful and timely'.[44]

The Canadian government approved of the plan to cede the Sudetenland to Germany. It trusted Chamberlain's methods and motives: 'They are regarded as designed to promote world peace and merit support, even though the terms may be considered very high.'[45] When Chamberlain flew to Godesberg on 22 September he anticipated a cession of the Sudetenland in line with the agreed formula. But Hitler conceded only that German troops could be withdrawn from the mixed areas in Czechoslovakia, after a plebiscite in those areas.

As this news reached London, the role of the dominion high commissioners assumed a new importance: they tried to determine British policy. On the night of 22 September Massey was woken with the news that a telegram had been circulated to the dominion capitals that Hitler's attitude had been unsatisfactory. MacDonald explained this to the dominion high commissioners the next day: Hitler's insistence upon the occupation of the Sudetenland by German troops was 'a challenge to the whole principle of peaceful negotiations'. This aroused speculation that the Führer was a man of wider and more dangerous ambitions than he had admitted to Chamberlain at Berchtesgaden. Massey supported the stand of the South African high commissioner, Charles te Water, that the occupation of the Sudeten areas by German troops should not be regarded as a question of principle and that there should be a compromise on methods. Chamberlain took special note of this view.[46] Hitler did make minor concessions to Chamberlain on 23 September: the supervisory commission was to be international, and the date-line advanced to 1 October. Massey found this vaguely encouraging.[47] On 24 September at 5.30 p.m. Chamberlain told the Cabinet that he was sure that Hitler was anxious to secure the friendship of Britain and was not aiming for the domination of Europe, but only racial unity. The prime minister saw no chance of getting a peaceful solution on any lines other than those proposed.

> That morning he had flown up the river over London. He had imagined a German bomber flying the same course. He had asked himself what degree of protection we could afford to the thousands of homes which he had seen stretched out below him, and he had felt that we were in no position to justify waging a war today in order to prevent a war hereafter.[48]

The dominion high commissioners were told at 8.30 p.m. of Chamberlain's report to the Cabinet. The official minutes suggest that the high commissioners were personally in favour of the proposals being accepted, and that Massey did not foresee any difficulties in Canada over this. Massey's diary suggests that the high commissioners took a rather different view from MacDonald:

> We are all prepared to pay a higher price for peace than he [MacDonald]. The difference is because the Dominions are removed further away from Europe not because our sense of honour is less acute. Bruce [the Australian High Commissioner], whose government uses him (unlike mine in relation to their H.C.) feels very strongly that the German proposals *can't* be allowed to be a *casus belli* and says so on behalf of his Govt.

Te Water and [Walter] Dulanty [the Irish High Commissioner] speak with great vehemence as well. I take the same line but of course as an individual.[49]

The next morning MacDonald told the Cabinet that Britain should declare that if the German army crossed the frontier it would go to war with Germany. MacDonald did report that three of the high commissioners felt that Britain had accepted the principle of a transfer a week previously. It was Sir Samuel Hoare, the home secretary, who said that he had information that there was a possibility that if Britain entered the war to help Czechoslovakia, Mackenzie King would hold a referendum. Canada was likely to reject any proposal for joining a war. If war broke out 'it might not be in the interests not merely of ourselves but of our allies, that we should delay joining in.' Chamberlain argued:

It was clear that a position had arisen in which we might before long be involved in war. If that happened, it was essential that we should enter war united, both as a country and as an Empire. It was of the utmost importance, therefore, that whatever steps we took, we should try to bring the whole country and Empire along with us, and should allow public opinion to realise that all possible steps had been taken to avoid a conflict.

At a meeting of the Cabinet later that evening Chamberlain announced that he planned to send Sir Horace Wilson to see Hitler with the proposal for an international commission to put into effect proposals already accepted by the Czechoslovak government. If Hitler did not respond suitably Wilson would be authorized to say that it seemed certain that Britain would be drawn into war alongside France. Chamberlain felt that this move might help to rally the dominions to Britain's side.[50]

That day Massey, 'greatly perturbed' by the firm stand demanded by the British press, was horrified that there might be war over the method of transfer of the Sudeten territory which was already ceded. Through Geoffrey Dawson of *The Times* he organized the high commissioners, and on 26 September reported that all emphasized that failure to improve on the terms of the German memorandum should not involve the Commonwealth in war. When Chamberlain saw the high commissioners on the evening of 26 September he gave them, according to Massey, the impression that he was 'as anxious as any of us not to allow a matter of method to be the cause of a world war but he had an inflexible sense of principle and a principle he feels is now at stake'. This worried the high commissioners. They were further perturbed by a telegram from Nevile Henderson in Berlin that unless Britain advised Czechoslovakia to make peace with Berlin 'we should be exposing Czechoslovakia to the fate of Abyssinia'. Stanley Bruce, the Australian high commissioner, spoke to the inner Cabinet at 4.30 p.m. on 27 September and said that the attitude of the high commissioners would be that 'the terms of the German memorandum were not a sufficient cause for a world war'. That evening at 9.30 p.m. the Cabinet learnt from Chamberlain that there were reports that the Czechoslovaks would offer a feeble resistance, but that 'more disturbing than this was the fact that the Dominions were far from happy about the situation'.[51] MacDonald saw the high commissioners immediately afterwards and learnt from Massey that 'the minority of Canadians who were not favourably disposed towards the British connexion would, long after the war was over, continue to use the fact that Canada had become involved in it to reinforce their view'.[52]

It seems that Mackenzie King was prepared to recommend that Canada fight. Massey did not know of this decision. Mackenzie King was in touch with his chief lieutenant in the Cabinet, Ernest Lapointe, who was in Geneva. On 24 September Lapointe sent a telegram to Mackenzie King advising him that the immediate cause of a war would be minority problems in central Europe, a matter which was not likely to enthuse Canadians. Lapointe urged that the declared policy of leaving the Canadian Parliament to decide should be maintained, and no statement made before the outbreak of war. Following Lapointe's advice Mackenzie King decided against any definite Canadian declaration of support, but he planned, in the event of war, to summon Parliament within two weeks, and to submit to it a policy of Canadian participation. Five years later Mackenzie King wrote:

> I had . . . made up my mind to advocate Canada's immediate participation, but I know I should have had at that time, instead of a unanimous parliament at my back, a House of Commons and a Senate each of which would have been wholly divided.[53]

London did not know what Mackenzie King was prepared to do. Massey was the most active of the high commissioners in the campaign against a forceful policy.

Judging from reports of the press, and of observers, English-speaking Canada was prepared, if necessary, to go to war behind the mother country.[54]

Chamberlain's speech on 27 September made 'the deepest impression' in Canada. He said: 'How horrible, fantastic, incredible it is that we should be digging trenches and trying on gas-masks here because of a quarrel in a far-away country between people of whom we know nothing.' Canadian opinion was likely to be in agreement with these views, but the following statement was contentious: 'However much we may sympathise with a small nation confronted by a big and powerful neighbour we cannot in all circumstances undertake to involve the whole British Empire in war simply on her account.' It was generally felt in Canada that Britain had no right to involve the dominions in any war, and as Stephen L. Holmes, the acting high commissioner, wrote: 'It is to the credit of the strict academic constitutionalists that they do not yet seem to have commented on this.'[55] What French Canada thought is difficult to assess: its newspapers denounced Germany but did not say much about foreign entanglements for Canada. Holmes reported on 26 September that there was evidence that French Canadian opinion was showing signs of abandoning its isolationist tendency. Provided there was no conscription it was felt that French Canada would not oppose a policy of active support of Britain.[56]

On 27 September the Canadian Cabinet issued a statement that the government was ready for the immediate summoning of Parliament should efforts to preserve the peace fail.[57]

On balance it does seem that Canada, though possibly divided, would have gone to war. But at the time of Munich the British government did not know this. Massey implied that Canada would participate, but with consequences that would mean a break in the Commonwealth. The news that Chamberlain was to meet Hitler at Munich was, according to the acting high commissioner in Canada, received with 'considerable relief amounting perhaps to undue optimism'. Mackenzie King was relieved by the Munich settlement and sent a congratulatory cable to Chamberlain. The Canadian Conservative leader as well as the Canadian press also welcomed the agreement. A dissentient voice, however, came from J. W. Dafoe, who in an editorial on 3 October in the *Winnipeg Free Press* enquired 'What's the Cheering for?'[58]

After Munich Chamberlain told the Cabinet: 'In our foreign policy we were doing our best to drive two horses abreast: conciliation and rearmament.'[59] Increased production capacity was necessary, and it was hoped that some of the dominions, including Canada, would assist. On 19 October the British Cabinet considered the report of the air mission to Canada and decided to place an 'educational' order for eighty Hampden aircraft. This was to be done without any attempt to get from the Canadian government an assurance that the production capacity would be available to Britain in time of war. Orders were also placed for a maximum of forty fighters and twenty general reconnaissance aircraft. An Air Ministry expert was to be sent to explore the possibility of a group scheme for producing aeroplane engines in Canada. Kingsley Wood, in his memorandum on the air mission, warned of the seriousness of the political issue in Canada: Mackenzie King had only agreed to a communiqué on the mission after an amendment had been inserted which emphasized that the Canadian government was in no way involved in the arrangements which were to be concluded directly between the British government and Canadian industry. The Canadian prime minister feared that a reference to the delivery of big bombers across the Atlantic would suggest a restriction on the Canadian Parliament's freedom to choose what stand to take in the event of war. The Canadian government was also embarrassed by the mission which was discussing the training of pilots in Canada for the Royal Air Force.[60] Roosevelt, anxious to provide Britain with the means to build an extra 20,000–30,000 planes to give superiority over Germany and Italy in the air, in October through a close personal friend who was British, Colonel Arthur Murray, passed a suggestion via Lord Tweedsmuir, the governor-general in Canada, to Mackenzie King for the appointment of liaison officers between Canada and the United States so that information on aspects of aircraft design, engines and manufacture could pass confidentially between the Canadian, American and British governments. Roosevelt was opposed to using existing official channels.[61]

Canada also played an important role in the Anglo-American trade treaty, mooted in 1937, but finally only signed between the United States, Britain and Canada on 17 November 1938, a move seen as being in the direction of consolidating Anglo-American co-operation. Mackenzie King wanted an Anglo-American agreement, but he faced divisions in his Cabinet. Canada, for political reasons, had to be compensated for its losses by concessions in the American market.

On 30 September 1938 Mackenzie King urged Chamberlain to conclude the trade negotiations in the interest of world peace and economic appeasement. The Canadian government had agreed to modify all margins of preference enjoyed by Canada in Britain necessary to facilitate an agreement between Britain and the United States. Mackenzie King even urged Chamberlain to travel to the United States to sign the trade agreement. The press in Britain and the United States welcomed the agreement as strengthening the ties of friendship between the two countries. The co-operation of the dominions, especially of Canada, in matching the British concessions to the United States was also seen as proof of Commonwealth solidarity, and the desire of the member states for closer friendship with the United States. Mackenzie King stated that he hoped that the arrangements would strengthen 'the friendly relations between the two countries with whose futures those of Canada are so closely associated'.[62]

There were conversations between Canada and the United States on defence in November 1938, but these were private and held on condition that Canada did not disclose their nature to Britain. The British high commissioner was assured that these conversations had been 'of a relatively trivial nature'.[63] Some in Canada still had faith in the appeasement of Europe. Opinion was seen to be divided between those who were isolationist and those who were imperialist. On 12 January 1939 Mackenzie King quoted approvingly a statement made by Sir Wilfrid Laurier in 1910:

> If England is at war, we are at war and liable to attack. I do not say that we will always be attacked; neither do I say that we should take part in all the wars of England. This is a matter that must be guided by circumstances upon which the Canadian parliament will have to pronounce, and will have to decide in its own best judgement.

The isolationists in the Liberal Party objected. Conservatives agitated for recognition that there was co-operation with Britain on defence. But the government denied any such co-operation. The bickerings in Parliament over the possibility of Bren guns being manufactured in Canada, and the hesitations over the training of pilots for the Royal Air Force, were indicative of the government's difficult position.[64]

When Hitler occupied Prague in March 1939, and Chamberlain in guaranteeing Poland abandoned the appeasement of Europe and moved to a policy of attempting to deter Germany, Mackenzie King on 20 March told the Canadian House of Commons that Chamberlain had repeatedly spoken of the need for consultation amongst the powers before any commitments were made, and that Canada approved of this. Quebec was uneasy. The St Jean Baptiste Society organized a meeting in Montreal. Delegates unanimously warned that French Canada was opposed to Canadian participation in foreign wars. The mayor of Montreal promised to head any anti-conscription movement. In Ontario the premier, Mr Mitchell Hepburn, moved a resolution pledging the co-operation of the government and the people of Ontario with Britain, and urged the federal government to introduce legislation enabling the manpower and natural resources of Canada to be mobilized immediately in case of war. In the debate most members spoke of their ardent loyalty to Britain, and the resolution was carried without a hostile vote. Mackenzie King insisted that the attendance of Massey at the meetings of the dominion high commissioners in London should 'not be regarded or represented as constituting consultation of Canada'. The British high commissioner in Canada wrote on 25 March about Mackenzie King:

> It is abundantly clear that he hopes to be able to maintain until the last possible moment a position of detachment from Europe and indeed the rest of the Empire and that he is if anything less disposed to co-operate with other countries in the defence of democracy than are the Government of the United States.

Mackenzie King was worried that Canada was going to be invited to join some form of military alliance between Britain and other European countries. This would cause him 'grave embarrassment'. An alliance between Britain and Russia would be especially regrettable: 'From the Canadian point of view particularly that of French Canadians and other Roman Catholic communities that association would still be regarded as very unfortunate.'[65]

With moves towards negotiations with Russia, Britain asked the prime ministers of the dominions to make a statement of 'general appreciation and support' for the policy that the British government was pursuing. On 27 April Mackenzie King explained to the high commissioner in Canada that he could not 'conscientiously' make such a statement: there was considerable opposition in Canada to the manner in which Britain appeared to be becoming entangled with the Balkan and east European countries, and above all with

Russia.[66] As war seemed more likely the British government prepared for the contingency that some dominions might remain neutral. It was thought on the basis of dispatches from the high commissioner that Canada would participate in any circumstances then likely. But the Canadian Parliament would have to be consulted; this might cause a week's delay.[67]

This was what happened. On 23 August Mackenzie King told the British high commissioner that he thought Chamberlain's reaffirmation of the guarantee to Poland 'clear and fair'. By 25 August Mackenzie King had decided Canada's course. The British high commissioner learnt that Mackenzie King, with the consent of his colleagues, was drafting a telegram to Hitler and Mussolini reminding them that the only way to secure justice was through peaceful negotiation. He would then summon the German and Italian representatives to tell them that his Cabinet was unanimous in its decision to 'fight whole-heartedly' should war break out. The high commissioner was further authorized to tell the British government that, while the Cabinet was unanimous in its decision to fight, this could not be put into effect until the country had agreed through Parliament. This decision was to be kept secret: 'Canada must be allowed to make her own choice as a nation . . . it will cause harmful impression if anything is said suggesting that she should come in automatically as though she were a Colonial possession.' In the Foreign Office R. H. Hadow minuted: 'Canada is all right.' The high commissioner in Canada reported unprecedented activity on the part of the government in organizing measures of preparedness, and a remarkable desire to co-operate with Britain. The Defence Department was given practically a free hand with money for their preparations, and a governor-general's warrant was signed for this without parliamentary sanction.[68] All this was particularly important as Roosevelt had told the British ambassador in Washington on 26 August that if war came he would delay the signature of the neutrality proclamation for probably five days during which time 'it would be open to the British authorities to crowd on any ship or transport into Canada all possible arms and ammunition on manufacture that could be expected'.[69] As Gerald Campbell, the high commissioner in Canada, wrote: 'co-operation with this office and with United Kingdom policy generally which . . . had in the past been at the best carefully pondered and at the worst flatly refused, now became the order of the day.'

Campbell cited the instance of the crossing into Canada of aircraft ordered by Britain from the Lockheed factory in California.[70]

When Mackenzie King broadcast to Canada on 3 September he explained that 'no stone had been left unturned, no road unexplored in the patient search for peace'. He spoke in terms of the forces of good and evil. He explained that he would seek authority from Parliament for effective co-operation by Canada at the side of Britain, and had no doubt that this authority would be given. This co-operation was voluntary. Mackenzie King repeated this theme of 'the conflict between the forces of good and evil' when he addressed Parliament. This debate settled controversy: the minister of justice, the leading representative of French Canada, declared that it was impossible to stay out of war; Senator Arthur Meighen denounced those who thought Canada should and would take refuge under the wing of the United States. French Canada remained opposed to conscription, and the government promised not to introduce this measure, but apart from a few irreconcilables, there was little opposition from French Canadians, who were resigned to participation in the war. Campbell wrote that they had 'a clear conviction that the forces which have brought on the present struggle are raising issues to which no democratic people . . . can remain indifferent'. The other minorities in Canada had no hesitation in deciding that Canada should participate in full strength. Canada declared war on 10 September. In effect Canada was at war as soon as Britain, as all war measures were in full operation.[71]

It seems strange that Canada did fight on this issue, particularly in the light of views frequently expressed about the dangers of becoming involved in British quarrels in Europe, and the possible internal repercussions within Canada. There was no strategic reason for Canada's fighting: Roosevelt had guaranteed Canada's security in his Kingston speech in September 1938. The economic arguments are not convincing and were not raised. Perhaps when it came to the choice, imperial solidarity still counted in Canada. The British element was strong, and patriotic fervour was not lacking. The royal visit in May 1939 possibly played its part in consolidating public opinion. At the end of August a crowd of 20,000 in Toronto spontaneously sang 'Land of Hope and Glory' at the end of the royal tour film. By May Quebec was reportedly not unfavourably inclined towards fighting. But there were people like the Canadian minister in Washington, Herbert Marler, a Montrealer of Swiss extraction

whose family had been in Quebec for generations. He was a nationalist and an isolationist, and advised the Canadian government that
whatever Roosevelt might say, the United States had no intention of
becoming involved in European troubles. In September 1938 it had
been forecast that Canada would be divided if the Cabinet recommended that it fight. A year later this danger was not so real. Perhaps
Chamberlain's repeated efforts to find a peaceful solution helped to
convince Canada of the justice of the British cause. Canada did not
fight for a vague concept of collective security, but for the values of
the Commonwealth. As Campbell wrote,

> While it would be untrue to suggest that Canada guards her independ-
> ence one whit less jealously today than she did a year ago the visit of
> Their Majesties earlier this year and the ordeal which now faces the
> democracies of the world have served to show, if the lesson were needed
> as I think it was, in some quarters here, that equality of status is not
> incompatible with co-operation in common aims, loyalty to a common
> allegiance, and the defence of common principles.[72]

Notes

[1] Bruce Hutchison, *Mackenzie King: The Incredible Canadian* (London,
    1953), p.2.
[2] Ritchie Ovendale, *'Appeasement' and the English Speaking World: Britain,
    the United States, the Dominions and the Policy of 'Appeasement', 1937–
    1939* (Cardiff, 1975), p.22.
[3] E. M. Andrews, *The Writing on the Wall: The British Commonwealth
    and Aggression in the East 1931–1935* (Sydney, 1987), pp.4–5, 19–21;
    Ritchie Ovendale, 'Britain, the Dominions and the Coming of the Second
    World War, 1933–9', in Wolfgang J. Mommsen and Lothar Kettenacker
    (eds.), *The Fascist Challenge and the Policy of Appeasement* (London,
    1983), pp.323–38 at p.323
[4] Claude Bissell, *The Imperial Canadian: Vincent Massey in Office* (Toronto,
    1986), pp.72–106; Vincent Massey, *What's Past is Prologue* (London,
    1963), p.242.
[5] See James Eayrs, *In Defence of Canada: Appeasement and Rearmament*
    (Toronto, 1965), pp.16–29 for an account of the 'Riddell incident'; Public
    Record Office, London, DO 114/66, fols.42–5, 6109/A322/1, Meeting
    with Dominion High Commissioners, 5 December 1935.
[6] See Eayrs, pp.3–33 for an account of Canada and the Abyssinian crisis.
    The documents are published in *Documents on Canadian External Rela-
    tions*, v: *1931–1935* (Ottawa, 1973), pp.378–430.
[7] Eayrs, op. cit., pp.48–52.

200   Ritchie Ovendale

[8] Scottish Record Office, Edinburgh, Lothian Papers, 327, pp.218–22, Loring C. Christie to Lothian, 20 October 1936.

[9] F. H. Soward, *Canada in World Affairs: The Pre-war Years* (Oxford, 1941), p.70.

[10] Anonymous, 'The Dominions and Imperial Defence', *Round Table*, xxvii (1936–7), 547–8; *Canadian Parliamentary Debates House of Commons* 1937 (1), cols.237–54, 25 January 1937; cols.551, 836, 4 February 1937; col.937, 16 February 1937; cols.994, 1006–7, 1023–4, 18 February 1937; col.1055, 19 February 1937.

[11] Cordell Hull, *The Memoirs of Cordell Hull*, I (New York, 1948), pp.528–9; Eayrs, op. cit., pp.41–3.

[12] Hull, op. cit., I, pp.520–5.

[13] *Foreign Relations of the United States* (hereafter cited as *FRUS*) 1937 (2), Department of State to British embassy, 17 January 1937; pp.8–10, British embassy to Department of State, 27 January 1937.

[14] Ibid., pp.11–13, Hull to Atherton, telegram no.45, 12 February 1937.

[15] Public Record Office, London, FO 371/20670, A2082/2082/45, Lindsay to Vansittart, 8 March 1937; Minute by Vansittart, 31 March 1937.

[16] Public Record Office, London, CAB 32/128, E(PD)37 3rd Mtg, Lock and Key, 21 May 1937.

[17] Quoted by Eayrs, op. cit., p.58.

[18] India Office Library, London, Zetland Papers, 8, fol.105, no.24, Zetland to Linlithgow; Private, 13 June 1937. See also Kenneth McNaught, 'Canadian Foreign Policy and the Whig Interpretation: 1936–1939', *Report of the Canadian Historical Association* (1957), 43–54, for a discussion of the significance of 'unity' in Canada and Mackenzie King's philosophy on this.

[19] CAB 32/128, fols.4–17, E(PD)37 5th Mtg, Secret Lock and Key, 24 May 1937.

[20] CAB 23/88, fols.278–80, Cab24(37)5, Secret, 17 June 1937.

[21] Toronto *Globe and Mail* (Independent Liberal), Montreal *Gazette* (Conservative), Ottawa *Journal* (Conservative), and Ottawa *Citizen* (Liberal). Quoted by *The Times*, 18 June 1937.

[22] See Ovendale, *'Appeasement' and the English Speaking World*, pp.53–4.

[23] Gwendolen Carter, *The British Commonwealth and International Security* (Toronto, 1947), p.278.

[24] Public Record Office, London, FO 371/20750, C6349/5187/18, Pitblado to Caccia, Secret, 2 September 1937; Enclosing copy of note by MacDonald of Interview with Mackenzie King, 21 June 1937.

[25] Ibid., Mackenzie King to Eden, Personal and Confidential, 6 July 1937 (copy); Minute by O. G. Sargent, 25 July 1937; Minute by Vansittart, 26 July 1937; Memorandum by Mackenzie King of Interview with Hitler, 29 June 1937.

[26] Ibid., Mackenzie King to Chamberlain, Personal and Confidential, 6 July 1937 (copy); Chamberlain to Mackenzie King, Personal and Confidential, 29 July 1937 (copy); C6349/5187/18, Pitblado to Caccia,

Secret, 2 September 1937; Enclosing Sir Francis Floud to Sir Henry Batterbee, 9 August 1937 (copy).
27 *Documents on Canadian External Relations*, vol.VI: *1936–1939*, p.1080, no. 881, Memorandum from Christie to Skelton, Secret, 30 November 1937.
28 CAB 23/92, fols.5–6, Cab12(38)1, Secret, 12 March 1938.
29 CAB 27/623 Pt.2, fols.1–27, FP(36) 26th Mtg, 18 March 1938, Lock and Key; Appendix 1, Memorandum by Halifax, 18 March 1938.
30 Iain Macleod, *Neville Chamberlain* (London, 1961), pp.224–5.
31 Public Record Office, London, DO 114/92, pp.17–21, Appendix 1, no.5, F82/69, Note of Meeting with dominion representatives on 25 May 1938.
32 *Canadian Parliamentary Debates House of Commons*, 1938(2), pp.1935–6, 1 April 1938; 1938(3), p.2878, 13 May 1938.
33 Cambridge University Library, Templewood Papers, XIX(C) 11, Chamberlain to Hilda Chamberlain, 6 April 1938 (copy).
34 *Canadian Parliamentary Debates House of Commons*, 1938(3), pp.3177–89, 24 May 1938.
35 Hull, op. cit., I, p.587.
36 CAB 23/94, fols.5–8, Cab30(38)5, Secret, 30 June 1938; CAB 24/277, CP143(38), Memorandum by Wood on Creation of a War Potential for Aircraft Production in Canada, Secret, 16 June 1938; see PREM 1/239, for Mackenzie King's Protests about the Publicity over the Air School in Canada; CAB 24/277, fols.1–16, CP148(38), Conference of Ministers on Air Mission to United States and Canada, Secret, 24 June 1938. See *Documents on Canadian External Relations*, vol.vi: *1936–9*, pp.204–36 for an account of the training of pilots in Canada.
37 CAB 23/94, fols.1–33, Notes of a Meeting of Ministers, Secret, 30 August 1938.
38 CAB 23/95, fols.9–35, Cab37(38), Secret, 12 September 1938.
39 DO 114/94, pp.3–4, Memoranda General.
40 Zetland papers, 10, fol.56, Zetland to Brabourne, Private, 16–20 October 1938; Churchill College, Cambridge, Inskip Papers, 1, fol.11, Diary, 14 September 1938 (copy).
41 *The Times*, 15 September 1938; Vincent Massey, *What's Past is Prologue* (London, 1963), p.258; DO 114/94, p.46, Appendix III, no.8, F82/130, Mackenzie King to Chamberlain, telegram no.43, 14 September 1938; Christie Papers, Notes on the Canadian Position in the Event of a German–Czech Conflict involving Great Britain, 8 September 1938, quoted by Eayrs, op. cit., p.72.
42 Anonymous, *The History of the Times: The 150th Anniversary and Beyond 1919–1948*, 4 Pt.2 (London, 1952), p.759.
43 FO 371/21778, fols.362–6, C11285/5302/18, F82/218, Dominions Office to Foreign Office, 28 September 1938, transmitting Mason to Devonshire, 16 September 1938.
44 Eayrs, op. cit., p.65.

[45] *Daily Telegraph,* 22–3 September 1938; *News Chronicle,* 22 September 1938.

[46] Massey, op. cit., p.259; DO114/94, pp.30–1, Appendix I, no.16, F82/208, Note of a Discussion between MacDonald and dominion representatives, Most Secret, 23 September 1938; PREM 1/242, fol.47, Meeting of MacDonald and dominion high commissioners, 23 September 1939; the relevant paragraph is marked.

[47] Keith Robbins, *Munich 1938* (London, 1968), pp.286–7; DO 114/94, pp.31–2, Appendix I, no.17, F82/220, Note of a Discussion between MacDonald and dominion representatives, Most Secret, 24 September 1938.

[48] CAB 23/95, fols.179–84, Cab42(38), 24 September 1938.

[49] DO 114/94, pp.32–3, Appendix I, no.18, F82/220, Note of a Discussion between MacDonald and dominion representatives, Most Secret, 24 September 1938; Massey, op. cit., pp.259–61.

[50] CAB 23/95, fols.240–5, Cab44(38), Secret, 25 September 1938.

[51] CAB 23/95, fols.261–76, Cab46(38)1, Secret, 27 September 1938; Ovendale, *'Appeasement' and the English Speaking World,* pp.167–9.

[52] DO 114/94, pp.36–7, Appendix I, no.22, Note by the Duke of Devonshire of a Talk between MacDonald and the dominion high commissioners on 27 September 1938, 28 September 1938.

[53] Mackenzie King Papers, Lapointe to Mackenzie King, 24 September 1938; Mackenzie King to Greenwood, 1 November 1943. Quoted by Eayrs, op. cit., p.71.

[54] Anonymous, 'Overseas Reactions to the Crisis: Canada', *Round Table,* xxix (1938–9), 42–3; Soward, op. cit., p.115; *Sunday Times,* 25 September 1938; *Observer,* 25 September 1938; *Daily Telegraph,* 28 September 1938.

[55] Neville Chamberlain, *The Struggle for Peace* (London, 1939), pp.274–6; FO 371/21777, fols.46–53, C12253/5302/18, Dominions Office to Hadow, 11 October 1938 transmitting F82/320, 734/154, Holmes to Harding, Secret, 29 September 1938.

[56] *Daily Telegraph,* 27 September 1938; DO 114/94, pp.51–4, Appendix II, no.15, F82/228, acting high commissioner in Canada to MacDonald, telegram no.213, Most Secret, 26 September 1938.

[57] Ibid., p.53, no.17, F82/254, acting high commissioner in Canada to MacDonald, telegram no.216, 27 September 1938.

[58] See Ovendale, *'Appeasement' and the English Speaking World,* pp.177–9.

[59] CAB 23/95, fol.164, Cab53(38)2, Secret, 7 November 1938.

[60] CAB23/95, fols.31–2, Cab49(38)12, Secret, 19 October 1938; CAB 24/270, fols.175–6, CP224(38), Memorandum by Wood on Creation of a War Production Potential for Aircraft Production in Canada, Secret, 13 October 1938.

[61] National Library of Scotland, Edinburgh, Elibank Papers, 8809, fols.109–10, Note of Conversation between Roosevelt and Murray at Hyde Park,

Confidential, 23 October 1938; Murray to Roosevelt, 30 October 1938 (copy).

62 Richard N. Kottman, *Reciprocity and the North Atlantic Triangle, 1932–1938* (Ithaca, 1968), pp.265–6; FO 371/21506, fols.86–9, A7627/1/45, Hankinson to Caccia, 4 October 1938, transmitting T766/449, Chamberlain to Mackenzie King, telegram no.56, Immediate Confidential, 4 October 1938; *The Times*, 19 November 1938; *New York Times*, 19 November 1938; *Canadian Parliamentary Debates House of Commons* 1939(1), p.59, 16 January 1939.

63 FO 371/22821, fols.1–5, D185/41, S. Holmes to N. Archer, 9 December 1938 (extract).

64 Eayrs, op. cit., pp.91–7, 119–22; Anonymous, 'Canada and the War Danger', *Round Table*, xxix (1938–9), 570–83.

65 DO 114/98, p.9, no.10, F706/117, high commissioner in Canada to Dominions Office, telegram no.79, Secret, 24 March 1939; no.11, F706/118, high commissioner in Canada to Dominions Office, telegram no.80, Secret, 24 March 1939.

66 Ibid., p.16, no.21, F706/155, high commissioner in Canada to Dominions Office, telegram no.148, Secret, 26 April 1939.

67 CAB 16/183A, DPP(P)54, Enclosure, Memorandum by Inskip on the Position of the dominions in the Event of War, Lock and Key, 5 May 1939.

68 DO 114/98, pp.29–30, no.44, F706/219, high commissioner in Canada to Dominions Office, telegram no.264, Secret, 23 August 1939; p.31, no.49, F706/225, high commissioner in Canada to Dominions Office, telegram no.275, Most Secret, 25 August 1939; FO 371/23966, fols.172–3, W12646/10478/68, high commissioner in Canada to Dominions Office, telegram no.276, Immediate Most Secret, 25 August 1939, Minute by R. H. Hadow, 28 August 1939; DO 114/98, p.33, no.52, F706/263, high commissioner in Canada to Dominions Office, telegram no.278, Secret, 25 August 1939.

69 *Documents on British Foreign Policy*, vol.VII, p.262, no.317, A5801/98/45, telegram no.375, Lindsay to Halifax, 26 August 1939.

70 DO 114/98, p.39, no.65, WG3/1/2, high commissioner in Canada to Dominions Office, no.283, Very Confidential, 29 September 1939.

71 DO 114/98, pp.39–43, no.65, WG3/1/2, high commissioner in Canada to Dominions Office, no.283, Very Confidential, 20 September 1939.

72 *Daily Telegraph*, 29 August 1939; Lothian Papers, 389, fols.145–6, Grant Dexter to Lothian, 13 May 1939; DO 114/98, p.43, no.65, WG3/1/2, high commissioner in Canada to Dominions Office, no.283, Very Confidential, 20 September 1939.

10

Ernest Bevin, George C. Marshall and Lester B. Pearson, January 1947 to January 1949: A North Atlantic Triangle?

M. THORNTON

The notion of a North Atlantic Triangle is in essence a very Canadian concept; the preferred British and American description would largely be of a special relationship or relationships. John Bartlet Brebner, in the preface of the original edition of his 1945 book *North Atlantic Triangle: The Interplay of Canada, the United States and Great Britain*, put forward as his main aim to explain: 'the interplay between the United States and Canada – the Siamese twins of North America who cannot separate and live'.[1] However, he had further to concede that the relationship could not be explained in purely North American terms: 'Most notably of all, the United States and Canada could not eliminate Great Britain from their course of action, whether in the realm of ideas, like democracy or of institutions, or of economic and political processes.'[2] Brebner also felt that he had to give more attention to Canada in this triangle than it would normally warrant, an issue that more than one generation of historians has had to consider.

John Holmes has pointed out that Canada was really the product of a different triangle, a *ménage à trois*: 'with two mother countries and an over-weaning uncle'.[3] The North Atlantic Triangle was reordered in the opinion of Holmes by 'manifest destiny', a train of events Canada could not essentially control. Holmes also illuminates how Brebner's description was appealing and necessary in the post-war world, and that 'Anglo-American goodwill and co-operation were the best guarantee of Canada and of peace in general'.[4]

Ernest Bevin, as British foreign secretary, spoke before the Overseas Empire Correspondents' Association in the Waldorf Hotel, London, 13 May 1948. In the company of a number of Canadian journalists Bevin made an impressionistic point similar to that made by John Holmes on 'manifest destiny': 'it isn't difficult to organize the West from the Mediterranean probably not only to Ireland but to Canada and the United States. We think alike. Our law and traditions are the same. There will be an almost inevitable coming-together.'[5] By the time of Bevin's comments in the Waldorf Hotel, diplomatic developments had already taken place for Bevin to suggest that Canada and the United States would be organized into an alliance with Europe. The historical legacy of similar laws and traditions that were seen as being at the heart of a North Atlantic Triangle were a gross simplification of the relationship between the United States, Canada and Britain. Bevin's presentation that determinism was at work, was to ignore his own orchestration of a number of international policies that depended on negotiation, bargaining and the will of personalities.

Ernest Bevin, George C. Marshall and Lester B. Pearson did not form a direct or indirect political triumvirate, nor did they constitute a triangle reflecting very close personal relationships. More significantly, as senior foreign-policy representatives of their respective nations, they developed policies that produced close and special relationships between Britain, the United States and Canada. For a triangle to have existed between Bevin, Marshall and Pearson, a continuity of ideas and assumptions would have had to exist among the partners; one dissenting voice created a disharmony and discontinuity in the relationship.

All three are notable for their individual contributions to international affairs in the early Cold War years following the Second World War. The role of Ernest Bevin, British foreign secretary (July 1945 to March 1951), in the origins of the Cold War has been elevated to a pivotal role. Bevin was particularly significant with regard to encouraging the United States to take over Britain's burdens in the Near East in 1947, and in the formulation of new international structures for Western security in 1948. General George C. Marshall, as secretary of state for the United States (January 1947 to January 1949), had his name attached to a plan for European economic reconstruction which has been seen as the economic arm of United States foreign policy whose primary political goal was the containment of Communism. Lester Pearson, as Canadian undersecretary of state for external affairs (September 1946 to September 1948) and secretary of state for external affairs (September 1948 to June 1957), is associated with increasing Canada's role in international organizations. Ultimately, Lester Pearson gave his name to a particular

form of Canadian diplomacy known as Pearsonian internationalism. Pearson forms an interesting North Atlantic Triangle all to
himself, since he had diplomatic postings in Washington and London,
as well as at home in Ottawa.[6]

The time frame of this chapter covers the entire period when Marshall was secretary of state, a portion of the tenure of Bevin as
foreign secretary and incorporates the transition period of Pearson
from under-secretary to secretary of state for external affairs. The
similarities of title in themselves did not provide a uniformity of
political responsibilities, and in fact constitutional requirements,
conventions, party affiliations and personal characteristics led to
differences in power and authority in the context of their own political system, irrespective of the foreign-policy issue concerned. Political and constitutional divisions in Britain and Canada provide for
some shared values, but the historical development and cultural divisions counterbalance any similarities that might superficially appear
to exist. The presidential system in the United States produces a
dramatic contrast with Britain and Canada with regard to the
secretary of state and his constitutional role and importance in foreign-
policy formulation. Marshall is also interesting for negating any
major comparative generalizations by attempting a non-partisan
political approach in the State Department.

In general terms and not unexpectedly all three individuals could
be associated with a liberal-pluralist-Western-democratic approach
to politics. A career trade unionist, a career military man and a
career diplomat, Bevin, Marshall and Pearson respectively, came to
share some similar conclusions about international affairs by very
different roads. All three made difficult but very conscious decisions
to undertake governmental foreign-policy responsibilities at an
extremely high level.

George Marshall had a very good working relationship with Bevin,
a position acknowledged by President Truman.[7] Robert Ferrell claims
that this was until the London meetings of the Council of Foreign
Ministers (November–December 1947). He cites Dean Acheson as
supporting the view that Bevin's imprecision and confusion at London
(although over minor matters) were considered by Marshall to be
deliberate and thus unacceptable to his organized mind.[8] In
comparison with Truman's views on Bevin, Marshall could be seen
as a great supporter. Truman, although a renowned plain speaker,

found Bevin uncouth, and to reinforce the point referred to him as both 'a son of a bitch' and a 'boor'.[9]

Lester Pearson recalls meeting Bevin at a Commonwealth meeting in 1949, but not really getting to know him until the conference of Commonwealth foreign ministers in Ceylon in January 1950. In his memoirs Pearson refers to Bevin as: 'a very great man, representative not only of a new Commonwealth but a new Britain'.[10]

In looking at 1947 and 1948, an extensive catalogue of Cold War international events could be analysed. To incorporate a theme of the North Atlantic Triangle reduces the catalogue considerably. Canada, for example, was not involved in the deliberations of the Council of Foreign Ministers, much to the chagrin of Lester Pearson.[11] Canada was not involved in the Allied Control Council governing Germany or a participant in the Berlin airlift beginning in 1948. Nevertheless, in this period Canada is a significant actor at the United Nations; an important 'neutral' authority over the problem of Palestine, which brings Canada into direct contact with Britain and the United States; and Canada is an important player in the development of a Western security pact alongside Britain and the United States. In terms of looking at the importance of a North Atlantic Triangle, two contrasting areas elevate themselves for analysis: the Palestine problem and the magnified Cold War problem of Western security. Emphasizing the roles of three leading public officials and dissimilar personalities provides a narrowing manageability. Looking at Canada, Britain and the United States in this period is significant for emphasizing the multilateral nature of the Cold War, and one step onwards from the Anglo-American perspectives that have proliferated in the 1980s.[12]

Palestine or 'Squaring the Circle'

Avi Shlaim has used the ambiguous description of having to 'square the circle' to describe Cold War problems as they related to the partition of Germany in the early post-Second World War years.[13] It is even more appropriate to the problem of Palestine and partition as addressed by Britain, the United States and Canada in 1947 and 1948, and eloquently contrasts any fallacious image that a North Atlantic Triangle might provide. As Ritchie Ovendale (in *Britain, The United States and The End of The Palestine Mandate, 1942–*

1948) has concluded from copious research, although the Anglo-American special relationship was not sacrificed because of Palestine, 'Palestine was just an unhappy tangle'; 'squaring the circle' seems an important alternative to a North Atlantic Triangle.[14] Since Ovendale has concentrated in great detail on Anglo-American problems in his 1989 study, it is appropriate that I should look at the added feature of Canada and the multidimensional relationship generated by considering a North Atlantic Triangle.

The Canadian secretary to the Cabinet, Arnold Heeney, registered a rift in British and American approaches to Palestine as early as October 1945.[15] Britain was being pressed by the United States to allow increased Jewish immigration into Palestine, and in turn the British wanted the United States government to share responsibility for Palestine. This shared responsibility failed to materialize, leaving Britain with the problem of Palestine and voicing criticism of the United States.

Britain's position on Palestine was immensely difficult, covering political, strategic, economic, moral and religious issues. Bevin's position was not confused; he was in fact clearly aware of the necessity of withdrawing from Palestine and the principle of withdrawal had his clear support. Where he became confused and indecisive in his policy was over the implementation of withdrawal. The predominant financial imperatives necessitated a policy, and the least offensive policy became the acceptance to refer the Palestine policy to the United Nations; a policy accepted by the British Cabinet in February 1947.

The British Embassy in Washington on 11 February 1947 provided confidential information for the Canadian Embassy, transmitted to the Department of External Affairs, as to why partition would not work in Palestine.[16] In good British Foreign Office style, four advantages of partition were outlined first. In summary these were: the prospect of 'finality'; it provided an area Jews could not control, particularly for immigration purposes; independence was provided to 'half' the Arabs of Palestine; and in principle partition had the support of the Jewish Agency.[17] However, disadvantages prevailed in British thinking, and eight problems were felt to outweigh the advantages. In summarized form these were that: the Arab governments were worried about Jewish penetration into Arab countries of the Middle East; their people were also supporting this view in concert with Arabs of Palestine; a very large Arab minority would be left in the Jewish state; the 'best' land in Palestine would accrue to the Jewish state because of the disposition of the Jewish settlements; it was difficult to exclude the largest Arab town, Jaffa, from the Jewish state; under partition an Arab state would be unable to support itself; it was further believed that incorporating an Arab state within Transjordan was unacceptable to Arabs from Palestine; and finally the Arab states would inevitably make representation to the United Nations.[18] Canada and the United States were expected to concur with the analysis.

As Alan Bullock clearly concludes, Attlee, Bevin and the British chiefs of staff were opposed to partition.[19] Bevin was not so concerned about the concept as yet again about the paradox of implementation. Whatever initial solutions partition provided, the long-term problem of annexation by Jews would remain. Bevin, to his regret, had also failed to elicit the support of America in a solution, which is a strange failure, given that Marshall appears to have been offended at the lack of notice America was given on Britain's withdrawal from Palestine.[20]

Palestine as an issue can be seen to divide British–American relations in 1947 and 1948, but did not necessarily drive a decisive wedge between Bevin and Marshall, particularly with Marshall coming into office at the start of 1947 when Greece appeared a more pressing problem, and the United States has been described as having no firm policy on Palestine at this time.[21] As far as Truman was concerned, Palestine became a threat to Anglo-American relations. Taking the issue to the United Nations internationalized the problem (incidentally involving Canada in a significant way), and Marshall and Bevin had arguably more pressing problems with regard to Germany and the considerable issue of European economic recovery. Marshall was himself at times critical of his own president, something Ernest Bevin could applaud.[22]

Interestingly, Pearson disagreed with his prime minister, Mackenzie King, over Palestine, but the differences were not the same as the minor Marshall–Truman differences. Mackenzie King also differed considerably in his views on Palestine from those held by Truman. Mackenzie King saw Palestine as a far-away problem concerning the British that should be avoided by Canada. Pearson's internationalist instincts and fondness for the United Nations made it a Canadian concern. He also believed very strongly in the partition idea, and his views prevailed against opposition even within the Canadian delegation to the United Nations.

Lester Pearson became very directly involved with the Palestine issue through the United Nations. A special session of the United Nations met in April 1947 to consider the problem of Palestine. Pearson was elected to the chairmanship of the Political Committee for the General Assembly which established a Special Committee on Palestine (UNSCOP). Canada was chosen as a neutral state to be on UNSCOP and formally represented by Mr Justice Rand of the Supreme Court of Canada, and assisted by Mr L. Maynard of the Department of External Affairs.[23] The committee of inquiry after visiting Palestine, although boycotted by Arab groups, made a majority recommendation (including Canada) for the partition of Palestine.

As Lester Pearson's recent biographer, John English, has pointed out:

by November 1947 Mike [Pearson] had asserted full control of Canadian policy. The *New York Times* lauded his efforts as 'tireless' on the Palestine issue. His dedication to the internationalization of issues was obvious, as was his fear of the growing chasm between American and British views on the subject.[24]

Whether Pearson had 'asserted full control' is debatable, but both English and John Holmes characterize Pearson's role and performance at the United Nations over Palestine as the early establishment of Canada's international image as a 'moderate mediating middle power'.[25]

Mackenzie King was critical of the younger Pearson for wanting Canada to figure significantly in international affairs, claiming that Pearson should have spent more time in Ottawa.[26] He bemoaned Pearson's involvement in international problems, particularly the difficulties and potential obligations in Palestine and Korea. Mackenzie King's own record states:

I feel a good deal of concern with the part Pearson takes in New York [the United Nations]. I think he is much too active in the name of Canada. His own report shows that he does not hesitate to advise both the United Kingdom and the United States as to what it is wisest for them to do.[27]

The situation worsened when Pearson wanted to support an American resolution supporting the use of force by the United Nations to partition Palestine. Britain's attitudes towards the Middle East and Britain taking the problem to the United Nations forced the United

States to develop a specific policy on Palestine.[28] After the UNSCOP report in favour of partition, Marshall 'explained that the United States would have to be ready to send troops to Palestine . . . on 17th September'. Marshall gave implied support to the majority report.[29] As King noted, this might cause problems with Great Britain.

> As I said to Pearson we would raise a very serious question in Canada if it came to be seen that what we were doing was requiring war in Palestine in order to support the United States in an attitude which was being wholly and strongly opposed by Britain. In this case, I thought we should do as Britain proposed to do, namely abstain from voting altogether. I stressed the point that if, in addition to it being alleged that we were being dominated by the United States on economic matters, we were being dominated as well on military matters, we would have a hard battle to face in our own country. I have really become increasingly alarmed at what may grow out of the Department of External Affairs.[30]

Mackenzie King was very much in favour of the British position on Palestine, but Louis St Laurent and his under-secretary, Pearson, were not. On 17 February 1948 Louis St Laurent provided the Cabinet with a three-and-a-half-page memorandum on Palestine.[31] This was prompted by the Security Council having to consider partitioning Palestine with 'military protection and support'. He went on:

> Obviously the United Kingdom is not in sympathy with the plan actually proposed by the Assembly, and its consequent refusal to take part in implementing the plan for partition with economic union has seriously aggravated the crisis with which we are now faced.[32]

St Laurent perceived the greatest element of danger to lie in the breakdown of communication between the American and British governments.

> As far as we can tell, the two Governments have not discussed the matter with one another on any responsible level. An acrimonious public debate may break out between them at any minute. There is ample material for recriminations on both sides, and much ill feeling.[33]

It was further believed that Canada would suffer from this, but the nature of the suffering was unspecified. The prime minister felt smugly satisfied when George Marshall on 20 March 1948 showed a preference for a temporary trusteeship rather than a forcible partition:

> now that the Americans themselves had confessed through the Secretary of State that they were wrong in the policy they had proposed of partitioning Palestine, implying thereby that the British were right in not

countenancing force to that end, we should not be led to supporting the American position again . . .

I thought the only honest thing for Canada to do was to say that she did not know enough about the situation to side with either the United States or the United Kingdom and that she would therefore abstain from voting [at the UN] on a question that involved siding with one side or the other.[34]

Truman and Marshall did show agreement in their attempting to work out a plan for the enforcement of the mandate of the United Nations in February 1948. In a letter to Mrs Eleanor Roosevelt (the late President's wife), a strong pro-Zionist, Truman showed his dissatisfaction with British policy: 'Britain's role in the Near East and Britain's policy with regard to Russia has not changed in a hundred years. Disraeli might just as well be Prime Minister these days.'[35] Eleanor Roosevelt was unhappy with reversals in United States policy towards Palestine at the United Nations. As Ritchie Ovendale has pointed out, she had accepted the necessity to use troops in Palestine to uphold the United Nations' decisions and was 'unhappy' with the March reversals.[36]

Marshall and Pearson were close in their views on partition at this time, although both were aware of the difficulties of putting partition into practice. Pearson was heavily constrained by his prime minister, and Marshall could be seen to be a comparatively moderating influence against the many pro-Zionists pressurizing President Truman to be active. As Jewish and Arab fighting took place in Palestine, the difficulties between Washington and London persisted.

Eban A. Ayers (assistant press secretary) recalls Truman's curt remarks in his diary for 17 February 1948:

The British, of course, are planning to withdraw from their mandate, and he [Truman] said efforts are being made to induce them to continue longer than the time limit set. He said he had gone pretty far toward threatening Ernest Bevin as to what we might do in the Mediterranean if the British draw out of Palestine.[37]

Marshall did not show quite the same opposition to the British position.

On 16 May 1948 a request was received by the government of Canada from Moshe Shertok 'who described himself as the Foreign Secretary of the Provisional Government of the State of Israel' that Canada recognize the new state.[38] The United States government granted *de facto* recognition on 14 May even though Marshall had pressed Truman to delay recognition.[39] Against this advice Truman went ahead, but the United Kingdom awaited assurances that the government requesting recognition had control over a known and defined area and could fulfil international obligations.[40]

Lester Pearson showed his own 'impatience' (his word) with both Britain and the United States in a telegram to Norman Robertson, the Canadian high commissioner in London. He recorded this in his memoirs:

> The legal argument of the United Kingdom that there is no difference between Arabs invading Palestine and Jews who may be attempting to set up a state within a United Nations resolution, does not impress me very favourably, though no doubt it is explained by strategy and oil. On the other hand the United States' revolving-door policy, each push determined to a large extent by domestic political considerations and culminating in the sorry recognition episode of last Saturday, inspires no confidence and warrants little support.[41]

He went on to acknowledge that once partition failed there was little Canada could do: 'except privately to help remove difficulties and differences between Washington and London and these occurred frequently'.[42] Mackenzie King's warnings, if not apparitions, had materialized, proving that his longevity in political office was justified.

By November 1948 the Canadian government had agreed that a *de facto* recognition of Israel was required. Canadian and French abstentions in the United Nations delayed admission of Israel to the United Nations. It was not until May 1949 that Israel was admitted, obtaining sufficient support in the Security Council and a vote in the General Assembly of thirty-five to eleven.[43]

Palestine had been a divisive issue for the North Atlantic Triangle in 1947 and 1948, and had other pressing issues of Germany, Greece, Turkey, economic reconstruction and Western security not required co-operation between Britain and the United States, then Palestine might be remembered as an even more inglorious episode in relations between Britain, the United States and Canada. Bevin, Marshall and Pearson were hampered in pursuing clearly individualistic foreign policies towards Palestine by their own domestic critics; Bevin was particularly impeded in his foreign-policy decision-making by financial constraints.

Palestine, for all its strategic importance in the Middle East, does not provide a very good example of a Cold War problem that had the power to unite Western allies. The Soviet Union both accepted partition and recognized Israel, and although ulterior motives might be attributed to these decisions, the real disharmony lay between Canada, America and Great Britain.

Western Security: The 'ABC' Triangle

In contrast to the issue of Palestine, the problem of Western security against a growing Soviet threat united Bevin, Marshall and Pearson in a spiritual union and, in more concrete form, paved the way for the North Atlantic Treaty Organization. Ernest Bevin, in a Cabinet paper entitled 'The First Aims of British Foreign Policy' on 4 January 1948, put formally before the British Cabinet his idea of Western union.[44] This was essentially the strange idea of consolidating together the 'ethical and spiritual' forces of a Western democratic system comprising the Americas and the dominions, but where possible 'Scandinavia, the Low Countries, France, Portugal and Greece', and inevitably Spain and Germany.[45] Bevin concluded his brief paper with the news that he had 'already broached the conception of what I called a spiritual union of the West tentatively to Mr. Marshall and Mr. Bidault, both of whom seemed to react favourably without of course committing themselves'.[46] Although not expressed as succinctly as in this paper, the same idea was presented to the House of Commons in a rambling address on 22 January.

Mackenzie King was informed formally of British views on Western security in a communication from Ernest Bevin via the British high commissioner in Ottawa, Alex Clutterbuck. Clement Attlee's views, as expressed in this communication of 10 March 1948, were presented as in favour of three potential systems for military alliance; the United Kingdom, France and Benelux countries as a system with United States backing; an Atlantic security system with the United States very closely concerned; and thirdly, a Mediterranean security system.[47] The Canadian response was immediate; Lester Pearson was designated as the Canadian representative to join officials of the United Kingdom and United States governments in exploratory talks.

Lester Pearson, as under-secretary of state, was fully informed of both British problems in Europe as well as responses of the United States to European security problems. Ambassador Hume Wrong, in Washington, on 11 March 1948 wrote to Pearson expressing his view that Marshall would respond with his 'soldier's judgement' and a 'course of boldness' to capture the initiative from the Soviet Union.[48] Marshall was, however, a little slow formally to approve Canadian participation in exploratory security talks in Washington because of a short absence from Washington, but by 16 March official invitations were issued. The British decided to send Mr Gladwyn Jebb of the Foreign Office and General Hobbs of the Ministry of Defence. Bevin gave the British delegation only general advice, asking them to seek out United States views on important questions of principle.[49]

Much of Pearson's advice came from a subordinate, the acting under-secretary, Escott Reid, but Pearson also operated within the requirement of consulting with his minister and prime minister, a fact of which he was formally reminded.[50] Escott Reid was never slow to present his own views and included these with a draft of a suggested treaty.[51] Five days later Reid (while still in Ottawa) acknowledged in a letter to the Canadian high commissioner in the United Kingdom, Norman Robertson, that discussions in Washington: 'aroused my apocalyptic fervour and my passion for drafting international agreements'.[52]

Reid saw the proposed pact of mutual assistance as a development of policies both from Marshall and Bevin:

> The purpose of the Marshall Plan embodied in the European Reconstruction Programme and the Bevin Plan for Western Union is to build up first in Western Europe and then in the whole non-Soviet world a dynamic counter-force to totalitarian aggression.[53]

With Pearson's contribution to Western security becoming important, a Marshall–Bevin–Pearson triangle had chronologically come into place (Marshall Plan–Western union–Pentagon negotiations).

The March discussions at the Pentagon were considered so top secret that cover stories were invented for the participants, including a report that Jebb was in the United States to advise Sir Alexander Cadogan on Security Council matters relating to Kashmir, Palestine and Czechoslovakia, while Pearson informed colleagues that he was leaving for Lake Success (United Nations) for a few days to help General McNaughton who was supposedly 'under the weather'.[54]

Reid helped to prepare Pearson for discussions with long memoranda, including his own views of membership of the new security organization. He believed Australia, New Zealand and South Africa should be invited to join, a view not shared by Pearson.[55]

Reid also questioned the assumption that the immediate Soviet threat was to Norway, and warned of the threat to Italy.[56]

The issue of Western union was kept alive in communications between Marshall and Bevin in March, with Bevin receiving the following message from Marshall:

> We share the concern you expressed to Ambassador Douglas over the extension of Communist dictatorship in Europe and agree on the need for determining the best course to be adopted to prevent its further extension.
>
> The present Anglo-French-Benelux negotiations at Brussels will, I hope, result in comprehensive arrangements for the common defense of the participating nations. Such a result would appear to be an essential prerequisite to any wide arrangement in which other countries including the United States might play a part.[57]

The first meeting of the representatives of America, Britain and Canada was on 23 March 1948: Canada was represented by Pearson, Foulkes, Stone and Wright; the British representation included Lord Inverchapel, Gladwyn Jebb, General Hobbs and 'two members of the staff of the British Embassy'; and the American delegation comprised Mr Lewis Douglas, Mr Hickerson, General Gunther, and 'two other officials of the State Department'.[58] Pearson found it necessary to seek instructions from Ottawa after this first meeting, since the question was raised of Canada's accession to the Brussels Treaty. His view was that: 'there is neither more nor less reason than for accession by say Brazil or Australia'.[59] The reply from Louis St Laurent and Mackenzie King was:

> They feel that the essential thing is for the U.K. and the U.S. to underwrite the security of the signatories of the Brussels Treaty and the Scandinavian countries. They would therefore accept anything which the U.K. and the U.S. jointly agree is required to defend our common interests. They would be prepared to recommend to Parliament if need be, accession by Canada to a Pact of which the U.K., the U.S. and France were members if no other Atlantic nations were signatories. They would, however, prefer an Atlantic Pact which would include other Atlantic nations as well as the signatories of the Brussels Treaty.[60]

The Canadians were reducing themselves to humble participants with this attitude, but in the next few days the Canadians found their *cause célèbre* in desiring a sentence or an article on economic co-operation. What becomes article 2 of the North Atlantic Treaty and is sometimes referred to as the 'Canadian Article' has a well-documented history, not to be covered here.[61] The proceedings in the Pentagon themselves were temporarily confused by each country producing drafts of a treaty, but by 31 March (with Pearson having returned earlier to Ottawa) the State Department had circulated a rough draft treaty (after unofficial congressional soundings), incorporating the Canadian suggestion on economic co-operation.[62] Further, the hoped-for effects of obtaining a pledge from the United States to support Western European democracies, embodied in a treaty, were beginning to materialize.

A significant product of the Pentagon talks is that they provided a direction beam for America, Britain and Canada in the following Washington Security Talks. The most reasonant image is that provided by Sir Nicholas Henderson, who described the final Pentagon talks paper as: 'some new navigational device to keep the negotiations on a steady course throughout the many months ahead'.[63] These months, of course, included July to September when the full Washington Security Talks took place between America, Canada and the Brussels Treaty countries.

It was not an easy route for the new Western security pact. Ambiguous advice emanated from the State Department for Marshall to digest; the American Congress had to be wooed; if things were left too long, Truman would have to win an election to see the pact through to its conclusion; and the Brussels Treaty members, notably France, had to perceive its additional value. All of these issues were satisfied or resolved, some partly because the Berlin blockade from 24 June 1948 concentrated European and North American minds on security issues, and partly because Bevin could convince Marshall that the psychological effects of an Atlantic pact were of immeasurable value.[64]

Not to be forgotten, the Palestine problem was there in the background, and some Americans wanted it in the foreground. John Baylis cites Dean Acheson as pressing upon Canada the point that: 'an understanding over Palestine was necessary if the security pact was to be concluded'.[65] The further problems and frustration of creating a final North Atlantic Treaty have been told elsewhere,[66] but at least here the considerable debt owed to Bevin, Marshall and Pearson for their work on Palestine and Western security in 1947 and 1948 is hopefully apparent. Bevin's 'Atlantic Vision', to steal a phrase from Lester Pearson's *Memoirs*, helps to justify Denis Healey's accolade that Bevin was 'incontestably Britain's greatest foreign secretary this century'.[67] Marshall is remembered for an Economic Recovery Programme that was largely the work of the policy planning staff, but his no-nonsense approach was of value both over Palestine and in his opposition to the Soviet Union that justified a Western security pact. Lester Pearson had a 'trial by fire' in his dealings with Britain and the United States over Palestine and an easier journey with regard to Western security.

Conclusion

A characterization of these three statesmen from January 1947 to January 1949 could be that of 'patience, firmness and prudence'.[68] Marshall used these words to describe his policy towards the Soviet Union in May 1948, but they might reasonably be employed to describe Bevin, Marshall and Pearson. In the years of the late 1940s under consideration, British policy under Bevin exhibited signs of patience, American foreign policy was one of firmness under Marshall's direction, and Pearson's mark on Canadian foreign policy was to make it more prudential. The North Atlantic Triangle itself could be described as a triumph of patience, firmness and prudence.

Having started with John Brebner, perhaps it is apposite to conclude with his prophetic thoughts from 1945. Brebner suggested:

> No such group of nations is more experienced or more capable of contributing to collective security than Great Britain, the United States and Canada . . . Their largest and most difficult task is the discovery of the positive principles by which to govern their post-war co-operation with their other great allies, with the smaller nations and with their present enemies. Yet they also still have a good deal to learn about the most immediate problem of getting along together.[69]

Notes

[1] J. B. Brebner, *North Atlantic Triangle: The Interplay of Canada, the United States and Great Britain* (Toronto, 1966, reprinted from 1945), p.xxv. In his introduction to Brebner's book, Donald Creighton provides an interesting analysis of the same point.

[2] Ibid.

[3] J. W. Holmes, *The Shaping of Peace: Canada and the Search for World Order, 1943–1957*, I (Toronto, 1979), p.138.

[4]   Ibid.

[5]   Note taken by Leslie Bishop of the *Winnipeg Free Press*, sent by Norman Robertson (high commissioner for Canada in the UK) to L. B. Pearson (under-secretary of state). Department of External Affairs File, RG 25, ACC 89/90/029, Box 45, File 125(S) National Archives of Canada (hereinafter NAC).

[6]   J. English, *Shadow of Heaven: The Life of Lester Pearson*, I: *1897–1948* (Toronto, 1989). English makes this point not only about Pearson, but also about Norman Robertson and Hume Wrong, who 'had lived within the North Atlantic triangle' (p.319).

[7]   E. A. Ayers's account in R. H. Ferrell (ed.), *Truman in the White House: The Diary of Eban A. Ayers* (Columbia, Mo., 1991), p.299.

[8]   R. H. Ferrell, *The American Secretaries of State and Their Diplomacy, XV: George C. Marshall* (New York, 1966), p.140. Ferrell in end-notes suggests that the published accounts of Dean Acheson, Lucius Clay and James S. Forrestal support this view (p.284).

[9]   E. A. Ayers, op. cit., pp.291 and 300.

[10] L. B. Pearson, *Memoirs*, II: *1948–1957: The International Years* (London, 1974), p.107.

[11] Report of the Secretary of State for External Affairs for the year ending December 1947, March 1948 (Microfiche, Brotherton Library, University of Leeds).

[12] Anglo-American perspectives include: R. A. Best, *Co-operation with Like-Minded Peoples: British Influences on American Security Policy* (New York, 1986); R. Ovendale, *Britain, the United States and the End of the Palestine Mandate, 1942–1948.* (Woodbridge, 1989); N. Peterson, 'Who Pulled Whom and How Much? Britain, the United States and the Making of the North Atlantic Treaty', *Millennium: Journal of International Studies*, 11, 2 (1982); D. Reynolds, 'A Special Relationship? America, Britain and the International Order since the Second World War', *International Affairs*, 62, 1 (Winter 1985/6); N. J. Wheller, 'British Nuclear Weapons and Anglo-American Relations, 1945–54', *International Affairs*, 62, 1 (Winter 1985/6), 71–86. P. G. Boyle, 'The British Foreign Office and American Foreign Policy, 1947–48', *The Journal of American Studies*, 16 (1982), 373–89.

[13] '. . . the search for a solution to the problem of Germany which would safeguard the security of Europe and satisfy the basic security needs of both superpowers, represented an attempt to square the circle' (Avi Shlaim, 'The Partition of Germany and the Origins of the Cold War', *Review of International Studies*, 11, 2 (April 1985), 123).

[14] Ovendale, op. cit., pp.306–7.

[15] A. D. P. Heeney (secretary to the Cabinet) to Air Marshal Robert Leckie, chairman, Chief of Staff Committee, 5 October 1945, Privy Council Office, RG 2, vol.94, p-70, NAC.

[16] Department of External Affairs File RG 25, vol.2152, NAC (wrongly dated 1946 – receiving stamp 12 February 1947).

17 Ibid.
18 Ibid.
19 A. Bullock, *Ernest Bevin, Foreign Secretary* (Oxford, 1985), pp.359–63.
20 Ibid., p.370.
21 Ovendale, op. cit., p.197.
22 Bevin did in fact send congratulations to Marshall (via the British ambassador, Oliver Franks) on a speech Marshall made in Portland, Oregon, in 1948. Ernest Bevin, Private Office Papers, FO 800/515, 1948, United States (Microfilm, Brotherton Library, University of Leeds).
23 See Report of the Secretary of State for External Affairs for the year ending March 31, 1948 (Microfiche, Brotherton Library, University of Leeds), p.11. Lester Pearson as under-secretary contributed to the report.
24 English, op. cit., p.325.
25 Ibid., also J. Holmes, *The Shaping of Peace: Canada and the Search for World Order 1943–1957*, II (Toronto, 1982), p.63.
26 J. W. Pickersgill and D. F. Forster, *The Mackenzie King Record*, vol.IV: *1947–1948* (Toronto, 1970), p.135.
27 Ibid., p.161.
28 Ovendale, op. cit., p.222.
29 Ibid., p.224.
30 Pickersgill and Forster, op. cit., p.163.
31 St Laurent, 17 February 1948, RG 2, vol.94, p-70.
32 Ibid.
33 Ibid.
34 Pickersgill and Forster, op. cit., p.179.
35 M. Truman, *Harry S. Truman* (Norwalk, Conn., 1972), p.385.
36 Ovendale, op. cit., p.292.
37 E. A. Ayers, op. cit., p.246.
38 L. St Laurent, secretary of state for external affairs, Memorandum to Cabinet, 25 May 1948, RG 2, vol.94, p-70, op. cit.
39 Ovendale, op. cit., p.302.
40 RG 2, vol.94, p-70, op. cit.
41 Pearson, op. cit., p.216.
42 Ibid., p.217.
43 F. C. Pogue, *George C. Marshall: Statesman* (New York, 1987), p.378.
44 CAB 129/23, Public Record Office, London.
45 Ibid.
46 Ibid.
47 RG 25, File 283(S) Mutual Assistance Pact UK–USA, 1948 (Microfiche, Brotherton Library, University of Leeds).
48 Ibid.
49 Pearson to Mackenzie King and St Laurent on 22 March 1948, explaining the position of the British delegation (ibid.).
50 Reid to Pearson (Ottawa to Washington), 23 March 1948: 'I gave the Minister your telephone message about your discussions ... He

emphasized that, before you agreed to anything, it would be necessary for you to seek instructions' (ibid.).

[51] Ibid., 18 March 1948.

[52] Ibid., 22 March 1948.

[53] A lengthy paper by E. Reid, 14 March 1948 (ibid.).

[54] Pearson to Wrong, 18 March 1948 (ibid.).

[55] Reid to Pearson, 18 March 1948 (ibid.).

[56] Ibid.

[57] Recorded in a written communication between Attlee and Mackenzie King, 20 March 1948 (ibid.).

[58] Pearson to Reid, 23 March 1948 (ibid.).

[59] Ibid.

[60] Reid to Pearson, 23 March 1948 (ibid.).

[61] See Pearson, op. cit., E. Reid, *Time of Fear and Hope* (Toronto, 1977) and *Radical Mandarin* (Toronto, 1989).

[62] Wrong to Pearson, 31 March 1948, RG 25.

[63] J. Baylis, *The Diplomacy of Pragmatism: Britain and the Formation of NATO, 1942–1949* (London, 1993), p.97.

[64] Ibid., pp.100–1.

[65] Ibid., p.104.

[66] See, for example: Baylis, op. cit.; J. Smith (ed.), *The Origins of NATO* (Exeter, 1990); Peterson, op. cit.; M. H. Folly, 'Breaking the Vision Circle: Britain, the United States and the Genesis of the North Atlantic Treaty', *Diplomatic History*, 12 (1988); C. Wiebes and B. Zeeman, 'The Pentagon Negotiations March 1948: The Launching of the North Atlantic Treaty', *International Affairs* (1983), 351–64.

[67] *The Independent Magazine*, 7 October 1989.

[68] RG 25, File 283(S), op. cit.

[69] Brebner, op. cit., p.336.

Index

Index of Historians and Economists Cited in the Text